T0004531

PETER

RITCHIE
CHARACTER
STUDY
SERIES

PETER

J. DENNISON

RITCHIE

John Ritchie Publishing

40 Beansburn, Kilmarnock, Scotland

ISBN-13: 978 1 914273 41 4

Copyright © 2023 by John Ritchie Ltd.
40 Beansburn, Kilmarnock, Scotland
www.ritchiechristianmedia.co.uk

All rights reserved. No part of this publication may be reproduced, stored in a retrievable system, or transmitted in any form or by any other means – electronic, mechanical, photocopy, recording or otherwise – without the prior permission of the copyright owner.

Typeset by John Ritchie Ltd., Kilmarnock
Printed by Bell & Bain Ltd., Glasgow.

ABOUT THE AUTHOR

In 1974, John was awakened and trusted Christ after seeing a friend die. As a teenager, he helped in children's work and gospel series and eventually became a school teacher. Then, in 1991, the assembly in Livonia, Michigan commended him to full-time gospel service. Later, in 1997-1998, he and his wife Michelle studied Spanish and have since been privileged to see the Lord save souls and plant assemblies in Mexico and in Phoenix, Arizona. John is responsible for a Spanish publishing work, is an associate editor for Truth and Tidings Magazine, and has authored a book for teens called "Choices."

Contents

Foreword

Of the over 3,200 characters in the Bible, Simon Peter surely ranks as one of the most relatable. Perhaps he is most famous for his personality defects and his frequent failures – a true Elijah-like man "subject to like passions as we are" (James 5:17). And yet, the more we read his Biblical biography, the more we want to be like him. Wouldn't you be thrilled to have his love for Scripture, his passion for the gospel, his consistency in prayer, his Christlikeness in character, and even his balanced handling of failure?

Consider Peter's Excellence

- Except for the Lord Jesus, Peter is mentioned more often in the New Testament than any other man.

- Peter is present or involved in 1/3 of the verses of the New Testament.

- Seven New Testament books give us 66 accounts of scenes where Peter is specifically mentioned.

- Peter converses with the Lord Jesus more than any other person in the New Testament.

- Peter is mentioned first in all lists of disciples.

- Peter is the only man other than the Lord Jesus to have ever walked on water.

- Peter is the first person in the New Testament to call Jesus – the Christ.

- To Peter alone, the Lord gave the "keys to the kingdom".

- Scripture records more of Peter's failures than those of all the other apostles combined.

- After His resurrection, the Lord Jesus appeared individually more times to Peter than to anyone else. Of "the 12", the Saviour had a private, post-resurrection meeting only with Peter (1 Cor 15:5), and only gave *him* a personal commission (John 21).

- In the Acts of the Apostles, Peter preached five sermons, saw more souls saved after preaching one sermon than anyone else, was uniquely privileged to be present when Jews, Samaritans and Gentiles first received the Holy Spirit, and spoke first at the conference in Jerusalem in Acts 15.

- Through the vision of the sheet of animals let down from heaven, the Lord exclusively revealed to Peter His plan for the gospel to be shared with Gentiles.

- In his two inspired epistles, Peter uses 116 Greek words that no one else uses including priesthood (*hierateuma)*, love as brethren (*philadelphos*), and Creator (*ktistēs*).

- Peter is the only believer who knew he would die before the Rapture.

Without question, the New Testament Christians held Peter in high esteem because they had witnessed in real time the Lord transforming him into a solid believer and a significant leader. The Apostle Paul gave his evaluation when he spoke of "James, Cephas, and John, who seemed to be pillars" (Gal 2:9). Even the carnal Corinthians respected him so much that one splinter group named themselves after him by saying, "We are of Cephas" (as in 1 Cor 1:12). Undoubtedly, as you follow his story, you too will come to appreciate how Peter excelled in his knowledge of Scripture, his leadership, his preaching, his miracles, his boldness, and his love for Christ.

Consider Peter's Example

Simon Peter truly is a five-star supporting character in the New

Testament story. Of course, the main character is singular and sublime, the One whom Peter uniquely calls: "Our Lord and Saviour Jesus Christ" (2 Peter 1:11; 3:18). The role of a supporting character is to appear, act and speak so as to highlight the best in the main character. Peter is not a perfect man, but he constantly directs our attention to the One who is. His character is noble, rich, and complex. Thus, this volume only scratches the surface of the Biblical biography of one of the Lord's most useful servants. But as great a man as he was, Peter frequently steps onto the stage, enters the spotlight, and then just as quickly steps aside. He functions like a contrasting hue in a beautiful weaving that helps emphasize the main colour. It is fascinating to observe how Peter's actions, decisions, words and writings serve the Holy Spirit's grand goal in the New Testament: "that God in all things may be glorified through Jesus Christ" (1 Peter 4:11).

In this book, I have set out to review Peter's life thematically with three main objectives. First, I wanted to cover the main events in his life and as many details as possible. I also wanted to learn practical lessons from Peter's actions, words, character, and accomplishments. Finally, I hoped to appreciate something of Peter's Lord and Saviour whom he loved profoundly. On the one hand, I owe Peter an apology for not having presented him as well as he deserves. At the same time, in preparing this sampler of his life, I have repeatedly thanked God for him.

Perhaps the words of the Psalmist provide the best summary of the life and times of Simon Peter: "The steps of a good man are ordered by the Lord: and he delighteth in his way. Though he fall, he shall not be utterly cast down: for the Lord upholdeth him with his hand" (Ps 37:23-24).

So, as you read through this volume I hope it will help you to share in the Lord's delight in the life of Simon Peter. May it also fill you with hope and awe to ponder what God did both in him and through him in a short span of 35 years. Above all, may you respond to the call of the New Testament as you reflect on this great servant of God: "Whose faith follow" (Heb 13:7).

CHAPTER 1

Peter the Convert

"To get a man soundly saved...you must in some way or other graft upon the man's nature a new nature, which has in it the element of the Divine."

William Booth

When Peter was converted as described in John chapter one, he had no idea how boundless and amazing the package of blessings was that he had received. He also could not have imagined how salvation would change both his life on earth as well his eternal destiny. Yes, he had obtained everlasting life "Being born again, not of corruptible seed, but of incorruptible, by the word of God, which liveth and abideth for ever" (1 Peter 1:23). Yet it will take eternity for Peter to unpack all he received at the moment of conversion, as God, by "his divine power hath given unto us all things that pertain unto life and godliness" (2 Peter 1:3). But, how did that unforgettable moment of conversion come about for Simon Peter and how did it impact him?

Mr. James Smith courteously but abruptly ended our visit with a man who desperately wanted to be saved. As we drove away down a country road, he detected my shock and confusion over leaving a troubled soul in tears. Eventually, he turned and said, "John, evangelists are like spiritual obstetricians. You must remember that, naturally and spiritually, God brings babies into our world through a process in which He does not need human help. However, just like in the physical birth of babies, sometimes souls get stuck, and the Lord wants you to help them by showing them a verse or clarifying a gospel truth. Otherwise, just stay out of the way. If you try and bring a soul to birth too quickly, he might live (be born again), but you might damage him for the rest of his spiritual life."

Andrew was a true soul winner! The three times he appears alone in the gospels, he is bringing someone to the Christ. For example, in his initial evangelistic endeavor, "He first findeth his own brother Simon" (John 1:41). Andrew's wisdom in the handling of his brother is noteworthy, and it appears to have positively impacted Simon Peter for the rest of his life. Consider the following:

a. Andrew first pursued soul-winning by sharing the good news with someone close to him. The Lord Jesus confirmed this pattern with the wild man of Gadara. When the Saviour freed him from demonic possession, He told him, "Go home to thy friends, and tell them how great things the Lord hath done for thee, and hath had compassion on thee" (Mark 5:19). Peter followed Andrew's example and opened his house, so Jesus could preach the gospel to Peter's family and neighbours in Capernaum. One of them, a paralytic brought to Jesus by four friends, was saved in what is widely believed to be Simon Peter's house. Thus, it would not have been any surprise to Peter when the Saviour commissioned his 11 Jewish disciples by saying, "Repentance and remission of sins should be preached in his name among all nations, beginning at Jerusalem" (Luke 24:47). Peter would first lead these same men in the evangelisation of his fellow Jews (Acts 1:14), beginning on the Day of Pentecost. May God give us a burden for our families and communities as we seek to live out this divine principle as seen in both the conversion of Peter and in his evangelism of others afterwards.

b. Andrew shared his personal experience with Peter by saying, "We have found the Messias!" (John 1:41). Paul likewise relates his testimony in both Acts 22 and Acts 26, and alludes to his conversion frequently in his writings (e.g., 1 Tim 1:15; Gal 2:20). When Paul wrote to the Corinthians about the gospel he had preached, he said, "I delivered unto you first of all that which I also received" (1 Cor 15:3). Peter also demonstrated this mindset as he often included himself in his teaching providing implicit references to his own experience of salvation. For example, he wrote about "our sins" (1 Peter 2:24) and that "Christ suffered for us" (1 Peter 2:21; 4:1). Having a clear personal testimony and learning how to share it effectively is Biblical and has can have significant impact in reaching out to the lost.

Andrew was patient. First, he had to find Peter, which implies a diligent pursuit. Then, he had to bring him to Christ. The Greek word "brought" (*ago*) is often used to describe the action of leading away a prisoner. The implication is that the soul-winner will experience resistance to the gospel much like when a criminal resists officers sent to arrest him. Peter was strong-willed and likely a challenging personality to budge. While Peter was probably a spiritual "tough nut to crack," with humility and patience, Andrew demonstrated that persistence is necessary to overcome resistance.

c. While not explicitly stated, Andrew appears to have focused on the issue of sin. Undoubtedly, he would have related to his brother the powerful sermons of John the Baptist, who preached "the baptism of repentance for the remission of sins" (Mark 1:4). As a Jew, Peter knew the law, and "by the law is the knowledge of sin" (Rom 3:20). Without question, the day he met Christ, he repented of his sins. Repentance was so indelibly impressed on him that Peter mentions repentance in every sermon he preaches in the book of the Acts, and later wrote about the desire of the Lord that "all should come to repentance" (2 Peter 3:9).

Part of what brought him to repentance was that "Jesus beheld him" (John 1:42). Beheld (*emblepo*) refers to "earnest looking" (Vine) or "to look straight at" (Louw-Nida). In the words of the writer to the Hebrews, Peter must have sensed that "all things are naked and opened unto the eyes of him with whom we have to do" (Heb 4:13). Although they had never met, Peter was standing in front of the omniscient, all-seeing God who knew his name, his family background (son of Jonah, or John), and his character. Peter must have felt like the Samaritan woman who said Jesus was a man "who told me all things that ever I did" (John 4:29).

Several years after his conversion, Peter denied the Lord Jesus. His restoration for that sin came about by his coming to repentance and confessing, "Lord, thou knowest all things" (John 21:17). Divine omniscience had an immense impact on his Christian life, so that when he and the disciples prayed over a replacement for Judas, the prayer began, "Thou, Lord, which knowest the hearts of all men..." (Acts 1:24). Even at the famous conference at Jerusalem years later, Peter reminded everyone, "God...knoweth the hearts" (Acts 15:8). An understanding and appreciation for the all-seeing and always-seeing eye of God upon a sinner or saint will more quickly lead to an awareness of sin and genuine repentance.

a. While facing sin was indispensable, Andrew was "Christ-focused" in his evangelism. This later characterizes Peter's ministry as he went "preaching peace by Jesus Christ" (Acts 10:36). At home and perhaps in synagogue school, Peter would have learned certain traits of the coming Messiah (Hebrew) or Christ (Greek). Having then heard that John the Baptist had identified Jesus as the "Lamb of God which taketh away the sin of the world" (John 1:29), Peter trusted Christ personally. He later wrote that the Lord Jesus is the one "Who his own self bare our sins in his own body on the tree" (1 Peter 2:24). At conversion, Peter clearly appreciated the substitutionary work of Christ on his behalf, and Christ was always the centre of his preaching thereafter.

b. The character of the soul-winner reproduces itself in the convert. Andrew was humble and selfless. He was not looking for "likes" on his Facebook page or "followers" on his Instagram account. He simply wanted his brother in the flesh to become a believer in the Lord. John the Baptist saw Andrew saved, and John's mindset about Christ was that "He must increase, and I must decrease" (John 3:30). Andrew demonstrated that same conviction when, after bringing Peter to Christ, he drops into the background in the New Testament. He was happy to have Christ as the focus instead of himself and equally delighted if the Lord were to use his convert in a greater and more public way than he himself had been used. Thus, he never complained that Peter was selected to be one of the unique three friends of Christ, that Peter was mentioned first in all the lists of the disciples, that the Lord gave Peter the keys of the kingdom, that Peter was chosen to proclaim the famous sermon on the Day of Pentecost, or that the Lord revealed to Peter first that the gospel was also for the Gentiles (Acts 10). To the contrary, to see Peter prosper and God using him would have filled him with joy and made him worship the Lord.

The chain of evangelism from John the Baptist to Andrew and from Andrew to Peter and from Peter to thousands of souls demonstrates the potential when one believer shares the gospel. May it motivate you, the reader, to think of who the Lord may add next to your spiritual family tree. Perhaps your next convert will be another D.L. Moody, George Whitfield, Corrie ten Boom, Charles Spurgeon, or Fanny Crosby? With God, all things are possible!

Peter seemed to appreciate that his conversion was solely due to the grace of God. We know he was originally from the fishing village of Bethsaida, located on the northeastern shore of the Sea of Galilee, the town the Scripture calls "the city of Andrew and Peter" (John 1:44). At some point, it appears that Peter, his wife, and his family moved to Capernaum, another fishing village on the northwest corner of the Galilean sea. They took up residence there because Scripture tells us that in Capernaum Jesus "entered into the house of Simon and Andrew" (Mark 1:29). In both Bethsaida (house of hunting) and Capernaum (village of Nahum, or comfort), the people seemed to be hardened and set against the gospel. Jesus reminded both Bethsaida and Capernaum of "the mighty works, which were done in you" (Matt 11:21). In Bethsaida, Christ healed a blind man (Mark 8:22-26) and "cured those who had need of healing" (Luke 9:11). In Capernaum, he healed a demon-possessed man (Mark 1:21-28), Peter's mother-in-law (Mark 1:29-31), a leper (Mark 1:40-45), a paralytic (Luke 5:17-26), a man with a withered hand (Mark 3:1-5), the servant of a centurion (Luke 7:1-10), two blind men (Matt 9:27-31), a mute man (Matt 9:32-33), and a woman with a hemorrhage (Luke 8:43-48). While in Capernaum, He also raised Jairus' daughter from the dead (Luke 8:41-42, 49-56) and performed the miracle when Peter found a coin in a fish's mouth to pay the temple tax (Matt 17:24-27). They were very privileged cities, but of Bethsaida, Jesus said, "It shall be more tolerable for Tyre and Sidon at the day of judgment, than for you." (Matt 11:21-22). To Capernaum, He said, "…it shall be more tolerable for the land of Sodom in the day of judgment, than for thee" (Matt 11:23-24).

As Peter witnessed the apathy and unbelief in these two villages, he must have felt like Ruth when she asked Boaz, "Why have I found grace in thine eyes?" (Ruth 2:10). Peter indeed seemed to appreciate God's unmerited favour towards him. At the conference in Jerusalem over the issue of the salvation of Gentiles, it was Peter who stood up and said, "But we believe that through the grace of the Lord Jesus Christ we shall be saved, even as they" (Acts 15:11). Later in life, he referred to the Lord as "the God of all grace, who hath called us unto his eternal glory by Christ Jesus" (1 Peter 5:10).

Tombstones can convey an ocean of information in a teaspoon of truth. For example, there is a monument in Uniontown, Pennsylvania, which reads, "Here lies Jonathon Blake; he hit the gas instead of the brake". The tombstones of some of the great men and women of the Christian faith also convey great truth in few words. For example, in the West Norwood Cemetery in London, England, a tombstone reads, "Here lies Charles Spurgeon waiting for the appearing of his Lord and Saviour Jesus Christ". Peter, the Apostle, is one of the great heroes of the faith. Perhaps his headstone could have been inscribed with the words: "From ordinary to extraordinary – by Jesus Christ".

When Simon Peter trusted Christ, the Lord told him that his name would be called Cephas, which means a large stone. Christ did not call Peter a brick, as bricks are identical and are all formed from the same mold. Rocks, though, are unique, and Peter certainly stands out as a one-of-a-kind saint. In Scripture, he was not unusual in terms of his name as there are nine men with the name of Simon and four with the name of Simeon (see chart below).

Simon: Simon (75 times in the New Testament of which 50 refer to Simon Peter)

Simon (brother of Andrew)	Matthew 4:18	A man who was determined
Simon the Zealot/Canaanite	Matthew 10:4	A man who was divided
Simon, the half-brother of Jesus	Matthew 13:55	A man who was disinterested

Simon the Pharisee	Luke 7:40	A man who was disdainful
Simon the leper	Matthew 26:6	A man who was diseased
Simon of Cyrene	Matthew 27:32	A man who was drafted
Simon Iscariot (father of Judas)	John 6:71	A man who was disgraced
Simon the Magician	Acts 8:9	A man who was deceitful
Simon the tanner (in Joppa)	Acts 9:43	A man who was disloyal
Simeon: Simon (brother of Andrew)	Acts 15:14; 2 Peter 1:1 [margin]	A man who was determined
Simeon in the temple	Luke 2:25	A man who was devoted
Simeon, called Niger	Acts 13:1	A man who was different
Simeon, the second son of Jacob	Revelation 7:7	A man who was destructive

Fifty times he is called Simon and on two occasions when the audience is Jewish, he is referred to as Simeon (Acts 15:14; 2 Peter 1:1 [margin]). At his conversion, the Lord promised that Simon would become known as Cephas - and he was. He was known to the Corinthians as Cephas (1 Cor 1:12, 3:22; 9:5), and Paul called him Cephas when he wrote to the Galatian believers (Gal 2:9). As always, the Lord kept His promise.

Cephas is the Aramaic word *kephas*, which, according to the gospel writer, "is by interpretation, A stone (*Petros*)" (John 1:42). John may have just been giving the Greek translation of his new nickname (i.e., *Cephas* is translated as *Peter* in Greek). Thus, some versions such as the NASB give the text as saying, "Which is translated, Peter". Six times he is identified as "Simon...called Peter", (Matt 4:18; 10:2; or as "Simon, whose surname is Peter" (Acts 10:5,18,32; 11:13).

However, it could also be that the Lord was focusing on the meaning of the name (stone) to describe what Simon would become: a unique and stable servant called Petros (Peter). Usually, though, stones are rough and require the skill of a stonemason to give them form and function. Jesus, who gave him the promise of a changed character, had worked for over a decade as a carpenter. In a small village like Nazareth, a carpenter would work with wood and he also would likely work with stone. As the master carpenter and mason, Jesus promised that He would apply similar skills to Peter's life to shape him into a godly man. At the moment of Simon's salvation, the Lord did not focus on abilities, activities, or accolades for Peter. His emphasis was on a profound process – "Thou art...thou shalt be" (John 1:42). The Lord was committed to the transformation of his character.

First, he would change completely his position before God so that Peter would always be able to say, "I once was...but now I am...". Peter shared that perspective with other Jewish Christians when he wrote, "Which in time past [you] were not a people, but are now the people of God: which had not obtained mercy, but now have obtained mercy" (1 Peter 2:10). Paul wrote similarly to the Ephesians, "...ye being in time past Gentiles...[and]...at that time ye were without Christ, being aliens from the commonwealth of Israel, and strangers from the covenants of promise, having no hope, and without God in the world: But now in Christ Jesus ye who sometimes were far off are made nigh by the blood of Christ" (Eph 2:11-13). Thus, Peter went from death to life, darkness to light, guilt to forgiveness, sickness to health, filth to cleansing, slavery to freedom, and from being hell-bound to heaven-bound. As Paul wrote, "Therefore if any man be in Christ, he is a new creature: old things are passed away; behold, all things are become new" (2 Cor 5:17). Thank God, the Lord, who radically changed Peter's position before God in an unforgettable moment, has completely altered ours as well.

That day, the Lord began a work of art with flawed raw material; Peter, at best, was just a normal man. The Jewish leaders once described him and John as "unlearned and ignorant men" (Acts 4:13). To our modern ears, it sounds like they were rough, uncouth fishermen. However, J.N. Darby translates the words as "unlettered and uninstructed men". Other versions translate these two adjectives as "uneducated and untrained men" (NKJV, HSCB, NASB, LEB) or "uneducated, common men" (ESV, RSV). While the first word, *agrammatos*, can mean "illiterate", Peter clearly could read as he had memorized large sections of the Old Testament and some of the writings of Paul (2 Peter 3:15-16). He also wrote two letters that form part of the New Testament canon. According to Thayer, the first word, *agrammatos*, more likely means here, "unversed in the learning of Jewish Schools". Louw-Nida defines it as "having a lack of formal Rabbinic training". Peter had clearly been to synagogue services and likely attended synagogue school as a boy. However, he was a fisherman and had never studied formally with a rabbi like Paul who had spent time at the feet of Gamaliel (Acts 22:3).

The second word, *idiotes*, does not have the meaning it sounds like when transliterated to English. Instead of meaning a lack of intelligence, Liddle and Scott's *An Intermediate Greek-English Lexicon* provides the definition: "one in a private station, opposite to one taking part in a public affair". Mr. Vine confirms the distinction between the words by saying, "While *agrammatoi* ("unlearned") may refer to their being unacquainted with rabbinical learning, *idiotai* would signify "laymen" in contrast with the religious officials".

As Christians, we should appreciate that secular education can provide training of the mind which God can then sanctify and use as He did in the cases of Moses, Daniel, Luke, and Paul. At the same time, no one has to take an IQ test for salvation or service. God does not give new believers a placement exam to determine their abilities and where they could best fit in His plans. Instead, He provides individuals with the gift of salvation, and He calls them into service. In so doing, He equips them with the needed skill sets and grace to accomplish His will.

Like Peter, we should appreciate that, no matter what our educational experience or financial success has been, God can still use us. Looking back on his life as a simple, Galilean fisherman whom the Lord used, Peter could relate to Paul's words: "Not many wise men after the flesh, not many mighty, not many noble, are called: But God hath chosen the foolish things of the world to confound the wise; and God hath chosen the weak things of the world to confound the things which are mighty" (1 Cor 1:26-27). Peter recognized that any ability a believer has is because of God's favour and kindness. Thus he wrote, "As every man hath received the gift, even so minister the same one to another, as good stewards of the manifold grace of God" (1 Peter 4:10).

But, the divine development-project in Peter, aimed far higher than just making him useful. The Bible does not photo-shop the biography of Simon Peter or even "touch up" his defects and failures. Peter had rough edges such as impetuousness, making promises he couldn't keep, misjudging situations, and pursuing self-preservation rather than declaring the truth. Thank God, though, the flaws and failures of converted souls are no limitation to divine plans and power. The Lord would transform a fisher into a fisher of men. He would take a man who would cringe and tell a lie when challenged by a servant girl and make him into a man who would courageously tell the truth to the unbelieving leaders of the Jews in Jerusalem (Acts 3-4). He would take a man who could not detect a false disciple like Judas and give him the ability to identify false believers like Simon Magus in Samaria (Acts 8:20-23), and give warnings about "false prophets" and "false teachers" in his written ministry (2 Peter 2:1).

Peter appreciated both what the Lord did for him at conversion and what the Lord was continuing to do in him day by day. He later wrote to believers and said, "You yourselves like living stones are being built up as a spiritual house, to be a holy priesthood, to offer spiritual sacrifices acceptable to God through Jesus Christ" (1 Peter 2:5). But what kind of living stones? Peter also wrote of Christ Himself as "a living stone rejected by men but in the sight of God chosen and precious" (1 Peter 2:4). In making Simon a Peter (*Petros* – stone), the Lord would make him more like Christ.

On the day of Peter's conversion, and for some time afterward, others likely saw problems, but the Lord saw potential. The Lord knew what He could do both *with* Peter and *in* Peter. "Thou shalt be called" is a future passive indicative use of *kaleō* - it was a "word of the Lord" guarantee which He assuredly would fulfill. In total, he is referred to as Peter 156 times in the New Testament as the Lord honoured His promise to change Simon's name. More importantly, Paul would have said that the Lord had clearly transformed Simon's character. Paul wrote to the Galatians of "James, Cephas, and John, who seemed to be pillars" (Gal 2:9). Through all Simon's trials, activities, experiences, and failures, the Lord reworked Peter's character so that he lived up to his new name. In the end, he was reliable, stable, and precious, just like a temple stone. And the Lord, who completed His plan to transform Peter, is desiring to do the same great work in every believer today. Paul explained about God that "For whom he did foreknow, he also did predestinate to be conformed to the image of his Son, that he might be the firstborn among many brethren" (Rom 8:29). There is an unseen and incremental transformation going on in believers right now inching us more towards the character of our Lord. Ultimately, heaven's objective will be achieved as "we know that, when he shall appear, we shall be like him; for we shall see him as he is" (1 John 3:2). As we anticipate the great, final and complete transformation that awaits us, may we sing the words of that hymn written by Jim Hill: "What a day, glorious day that will be!"

CHAPTER 2

Peter the Galilean

Considering the different regions of Israel, we learn more in the New Testament about the cities and villages of Galilee than about any other section of Israel. The New Testament speaks about "Nazareth of Galilee" (Matt 21:11), "Cana of Galilee" (John 2:1); "Bethsaida of Galilee" (John 12:21); "Capernaum, a city of Galilee (Luke 4:31), and "every town of Galilee" (Luke 5:17). Other locations in Galilee mentioned in the Gospels include Chorazin (Luke 10:13); Magdala (Matt 15:39); Caesarea-Philippi (Matt 16:13); and Tiberius (John 6:23).

We must remember, though, that there is only one way to Jerusalem – up! Jesus lived in Galilee, the most northern region of Israel, and, along with Joseph and Mary, "when he was twelve years old, they went up to Jerusalem" (Luke 2:42). Hiram, King of Tyre, planned to float wood down to Joppa from Lebanon. From Joppa, which is to the west of Jerusalem, he told Solomon, "Thou shalt carry it up to Jerusalem" (2 Chron 2:16). The Israelites were taken captive to Babylon which is to the east of Israel. From there, King Cyrus wrote that anyone who wanted, "...let him go up to Jerusalem" (Ezra 1:3). Hazael, King of Syria was in Gath, in the south of Israel and he "set his face to go up to Jerusalem" (2 Kings 12:17). From all four directions, Jerusalem is viewed as being the high point.

In one sense, the Judeans in Jerusalem would look down physically on others in all directions. In the first century, the Jews of the beloved city also looked down on others morally and spiritually. The woman of Samaria, a region north of Judea, was keenly aware of this reality as she told the Lord Jesus, "...the Jews have no dealings with the Samaritans" (John 4:9). Further north beyond Samaria lay Galilee, the most northerly region of Israel. The Judean mindset towards that region at the time of the first century seems to have been one of similar prejudice as they looked down also on the Galileans.

The Characteristic of Galileans

Peter slipped through the door of the palace of the high priest to watch the events unfold during the Jewish trials of Jesus. Soon, "he was sitting with the officers and warming himself in the light of the fire" (Mark 14:54, Darby). He looked and acted like everyone else to keep his identity as a disciple of Jesus Christ hidden. But then, as "Peter sat outside in the courtyard...a servant girl came to him, saying, 'You also were with Jesus of Galilee'" (Matt 26:69). Shortly thereafter, others came and said to Peter, "Surely you also are one of them, for your speech betrays you." (Matt 26:73, NKJV). Peter's identity was quickly determined by his vocabulary, tonal pattern, and accent, as the Galileans had developed a unique way of speaking Aramaic. "Their speech distinguished them from Jews in Jerusalem and Judah, particularly their difficulty in distinguishing the sounds of the gutturals which are important in Hebrew and Aramaic" (Watson's Biblical and Theological Dictionary, 1856).

This only magnifies the miracle on the day of Pentecost when Peter gave his great sermon. As a sign to authenticate the descent of the Holy Spirit and the message Peter preached, "they were all filled with the Holy Ghost, and began to speak with other tongues (*glōssa*), as the Spirit gave them utterance" (Acts 2:4). Not only were Peter and the apostles preaching the gospel in languages they had never studied before, "every man heard them speak in his own language (*dialektos*)" (Acts 2:6). The people "were all amazed and marvelled, saying one to another, Behold, are not all these which speak Galileans?" (Acts 2:7). A Jewish fisherman like Peter at best might speak Greek, Aramaic, and Hebrew. Therefore, instantly being able to preach in Egyptian without having studied the language would require a miracle by God. Peter not only spoke in other languages such as Egyptian and Arabic, but he spoke without a Galilean accent. Suddenly, he was able to master the gutturals and speak in the specific regional dialects of the audience present in Jerusalem for the Day of Pentecost.

The Culture of Galileans

The development of new accents and dialects is an interesting phenomenon that occurs mostly due to the influence of foreign languages being spoken in a region. The native language spoken in an area can assimilate vocabulary and sounds from the imported language and blend the two together. This is how pidgin languages (1st generation), and creole languages develop. Currently, in the southwest of the USA, this process is taking place where English and Spanish are spoken, and it is often humorously referred to as "Spanglish". According to the International Standard Bible Encyclopaedia, "The population of Galilee was composed of strangely mingled elements - Aramaean, Iturean, Phoenician and Greek. Their mixed origin explains the differences in speech which distinguished them from their brethren in the South". In addition, "the Via Maris trade route passed through Galilee, exposing them to many different peoples and cultures as traders and travellers would stop in the region and some would remain and permanently reside in the area".

In the days of Joshua, parts of Galilee were assigned to the tribes of Zebulon, Naphtali, Issachar, and Asher. However, when Israel split into the Northern and Southern Kingdoms, little time passed before the Northern Kingdom descended into idolatry. As a discipline from God, "In the days of Pekah king of Israel came Tiglath-pileser king of Assyria, and took...Kedesh, and Hazor, and Gilead, and Galilee, all the land of Naphtali, and carried them captive to Assyria" (2 Kings 15:29). Within a decade, during the reign of his successor Shalmaneser, most of the Jewish population was relocated to other areas of the Assyrian empire (2 Kings 15-17). At the same time, Shalmaneser introduced people from other areas into Samaria which had been part of the northern kingdom.

God's eye, though, remained on the land of Israel and specifically the northern region. About 700 years before Christ, Isaiah prophesied, "When at the first he [God] lightly afflicted the land of Zebulun and the land of Naphtali, and afterward did more grievously afflict her by the way of the sea, beyond Jordan, in Galilee of the nations" (Isa

9:1). Just as God promised, "The invading Assyrian soldiers took that route when they invaded the Northern Kingdom" (Bible Knowledge Commentary). And if that came true, what followed in Isaiah's prophecy would also come to pass. Thus, Isaiah continued and in the next verse he described the arrival of Christ the Messiah by saying, "The people that walked in darkness have seen a great light: those who dwelt in a land of deep darkness, on them has light shone" (Isa 9:2 margin). This description of the northern kingdom including the region of Galilee was accurate because, in their idolatry, they "walked in darkness" and then were exiled to a "land of deep darkness" as part of God's loving discipline for their disobedience. This resulted in a pagan king controlling the land that they had once claimed as their own. Thus, Isaiah, seeing the influence and impact of non-Hebrew people with their religion and culture in the northern part of Israel, referred to that area as "Galilee of the Gentiles". The promise was that the idolatrous, disobedient, and dispersed people of Northern Israel would eventually see the great light of the coming Messiah who would live most of his life in their region.

Eventually, the southern kingdom was also exiled, and it looked as though the devil had successfully dispersed Israel like dying embers from a fire; the light of God's testimony appeared to be near extinction. However, God had promised Abraham the land, a people, and a Saviour and He would honour His Word.

In the end, "Idumea (the most southerly region) was populated by immigrants from Arabia to the southeast, Judea contained descendants of Jews who had returned from Babylonian exile in the fifth and sixth centuries B. C. while Samaria was populated by the descendants of people whom the Assyrian Empire forcibly moved" (Religion-today.blogspot.com). While the history of the Jewish repopulation of the north is somewhat vague, "The archaeological evidence reveals a sudden change about the start of the first century B.C. Over a period of a couple decades, dozens of new villages appear. This indicates that a new, rather large, population comes into Galilee. The trend continues for the next half century or so, with many new settlements appearing and then growing larger" (https://www.

oneplace.com/devotionals/israel-insights/who-were-the-galileans-in-the-days-of-jesus-11649794.html). According to "Josephus and archaeological evidence...the Galileans – at least the vast majority of them – were descendants of people who relocated to Galilee from Judea". Therefore, they were Jewish by race, although they had adopted into their culture and language non-Hebrew influences. The purist Judeans were quick to notice the Galilean accent and what they considered less than pure Jewish culture and religion.

Also, Galileans may not have ascribed to the finest details of the sect of the Pharisees or been known for their adeptness to debate orthodoxy and theology either. In fact, "Their ignorance in law and disinterest in study was an almost never ending source of fuel for Judean snobbery" (http://www.oneplace.com/devotionals/israel-insights/who-were-the-galileans-in-the-days-of-jesus-11649794.html). While no great schools appear to have existed for the meticulous study of the Mosaic Law and the traditions of the elders in the north of Israel, "the Galileans were also the most religious Jews in the world during Jesus' time. They revered and knew the Scriptures well. They were passionately committed to living out their faith and passing their faith, knowledge, and lifestyle to their children. This led to the establishment of vibrant religious communities; a strong commitment to families and country; and active participation in the local synagogues the community centres of that day". (https://www.thattheworldmayknow.com/the-amazing-galileans). Thus, Matthew records that "Jesus went about all Galilee, teaching in their synagogues" (Matt 4:23). Peter and John's adept references and quotes from all parts and genres of Scripture throughout the New Testament clearly support the idea of their having been taught the Word of God at home as well as through regular attendance and education at their local synagogue.

The Criticism of Galileans

Politically, Galilee and Judea had generally been under distinct governments since the tenth century B.C. and that was still true at the time of the Lord Jesus. Luke wrote, "Now in the fifteenth year of the reign of Tiberius Caesar, Pontius Pilate being governor of Judea, and Herod being tetrarch of Galilee..." (Luke 3:1).

Herod Antipas, the son of Herod the Great, was responsible for the administration of Galilee, while Pilate, a Roman procurator, was governor of the province of Judea. Separate governmental administrations in the different regions undoubtedly moulded the cultures and customs of its respective citizens which only amplified the differences between them. Additionally, the Galileans had become more tolerant of Greek influence upon their lifestyles giving cause for Jewish humour about their country cousins to the north who lacked true Jewish sophistication.

The prevailing mindset in Israel at that time was that financial prosperity was a sign of divine approval and blessing. Thus, it appears that resentment may have fuelled the fires of Judean criticism of the Galileans. "Galilee offered better agricultural and fishing resources than the more mountainous territory of Judea, making the wealth of some Galileans the envy of their southern neighbours" (R. T. France, The Gospel According to Matthew — The New International Commentary on the New Testament).

But beyond envy, the Judean perspective was that Galileans were morally and religiously lax in comparison with their Judean brothers. The four gospels tell us that Jesus "went about all Galilee, teaching in their synagogues" (Matt 4:23), so there were likely some communities such as Nazareth and Capernaum who were faithful in holding synagogue services. At the same time, Galilee was the most distant point in Israel from Jerusalem so perhaps Judeans took note that some from the north did not appear for all the annual feasts in Jerusalem. Also, Banias (Caesarea-Philippi) in the very north of Galilee was considered a historical and significant centre of pagan worship.

John tells us that Jesus went to Jerusalem for the Feast of Tabernacles and He preached to a crowd at the temple. The question immediately arose as to whether Jesus was the Messiah. Some asked, "Shall Christ come out of Galilee? Hath not the scripture said, That Christ cometh of the seed of David, and out of the town of Bethlehem?" (John 7:41-43).

It was hard for Judean Jews to imagine anything of God coming out of Galilee, much less their Messiah. Later, the leaders of the Pharisees gathered to arrest Jesus. Nicodemus pleaded for a just interrogation for Him, but they refused. Their statement is indicative of their attitudes toward the northern region when they stated, "Out of Galilee ariseth no prophet" (John 7:52).

Thus, when Christ was teaching, "There were present at that season some that told him of the Galileans, whose blood Pilate had mingled with their sacrifices. And Jesus answering said unto them, 'Suppose ye that these Galileans were sinners above all the Galileans, because they suffered such things?'" (Luke 13:1-2). The Lord asked the question to prompt His present audience to face their sins and repent. At the same time, perhaps Jesus was reflecting upon the Judean mindset that all Galileans were sinners in the sense of lacking moral uprightness and strict religious adherence according to the revered traditions in Jerusalem.

The Judean criticism included a political component. A right-wing politically activist group had developed known as "The Galileans". The group was headed by a man called Judas the Galilean who strongly and violently opposed the Roman government and the taxes they levied on the people. Gamaliel, the great Jewish Rabbi, referred to an event when there "rose up Judas of Galilee in the days of the taxing, and drew away much people after him" (Acts 5:37). It is likely that some of those Galileans who had followed this Judas were the ones Pilate's undercover soldiers slew while they were making sacrifices to God. In one rebellion, this Judas "also perished; and all, even as many as obeyed him, were dispersed". Despite his death, many of his followers continued to propagate his teachings which were adopted by the Zealots who shared an equal passion in opposing Roman taxation and regulation.

"As our Saviour and his apostles were of Galilee, they were suspected to be of the sect of the Galileans" (Charles Buck Dictionary). Perhaps that very issue of taxation was behind the challenge to Peter in Capernaum when they asked, "Doth not your master pay tribute?" (Matt 17:24-25). It was likely that they were testing his political stance on taxation to see if he aligned with the Zealots and "the Galileans".

The negative view of Galileans continued through the centuries that followed. By the fourth century, Flavius Claudius Julianus Augustus, a proliferate writer and philosopher, came to be the Roman emperor. From his palace he wrote essays in which he derisively referred to Christians as Galileans. Thus, his nickname - Julian the Apostate. His hatred eventually became so public that he enacted "a law that no one should ever call the Christians by any other name" (The Ultimate Bible Dictionary, Matthew George Easton).

Therefore, Galileans like Peter were very aware of the Judean criticism of their linguistic and historical backgrounds as well as their moral and religious practices. Additionally, Peter and the disciples would be conscious of the Roman suspicion of Galileans. That very suspicion became evident when the Jewish leaders said to Pilate about Christ: "He stirreth up the people, teaching throughout all Jewry, beginning from Galilee to this place" (Luke 23:5).

The Commencement with Galileans

After 400 years of intertestamental silence, God began to deal with His people and prepare the way for His Son. Peter recalled the gospel that was proclaimed: "That word, I say, ye know, which was published throughout all Judaea, and began from Galilee, after the baptism which John preached" (Acts 10:37). John the Baptist primarily focused his ministry on the northern part of Israel as is evidenced by two of his converts, Andrew and John, who were from Bethsaida in Galilee.

When it was time to announce the incarnation and virgin birth of the Saviour, "the angel Gabriel was sent from God unto a city of Galilee, named Nazareth" (Luke 1:26). While born in Bethlehem of Judea, the Lord Jesus was brought up and lived in Nazareth for roughly 30 years. Galilee also became the primary focus of His ministry and miracles during the years of His public ministry. According to Matthew, Jesus was the "great light" of Isaiah's prophecy who had come to the dark region of Galilee to illuminate minds and hearts (Matt 4:16; Isa 9:2).

Even after He rose from the dead, Jesus continued to focus on that region of Israel. He had promised his disciples, "After I am risen again, I will go before you into Galilee" (Matt 26:32). So, upon His resurrection, "Then the eleven disciples went away into Galilee, into a mountain where Jesus had appointed them" (Matt 28:16). It was from that mountain in Galilee, that Jesus gave them their great commission to spread the gospel around the world. The Lord was not done with that despised region either. About four or five years later, we read, "Then had the churches rest throughout all Judaea and Galilee and Samaria, and were edified" (Acts 9:31). The Lord had established assemblies in Galilee gathered to His blessed name!

All his life, Peter would be known by the region of his birth, and it was likely in a despising tone that a man in Caiaphas' house the night Jesus was arrested said to him, "thou art a Galilean" (Mark 14:70). That same night, a servant girl also referred to "Jesus theGalilean" (Matt 26:69). Upon reflection, what an honour for Peter to be identified like Christ! In confirmation and reminder of that link, when Jesus ascended to heaven leaving Peter and the other 10 disciples below on the Mount of Olives, "two men stood by them in white robes,and said, "Men of Galilee, why do you stand looking into heaven?'" (Acts 1:11). Even the angels appreciated that the men who had come from the region of our Saviour as all his disciples except for Judas (of Kerioth) were Galileans. What an affront to Judean pride that the Messiah would focus on Galilee, but also employ lowly, uncultured, and despised Galileans to be his messengers. Clearly, as Paul wrote, "God hath chosen the foolish things of the world to confound the wise; and God hath chosen the weak things of the world to confound the things which are mighty; And base things of the world, and things which are despised, hath God chosen, yea, and things which are not, to bring to nought things that are: That no flesh should glory in his presence" (1 Cor 1:27-29). The Lord delights in using believers of lowly backgrounds in His service and to accomplish His will. He did with Peter and 10 other disciples from Galilee, and He still does today.

CHAPTER 3

Peter the Family-Man

Winston Churchill once said, "There is no doubt that it is around the family and the home that all the greatest virtues, the most dominating virtues of humans, are created, strengthened and maintained". The Apostle Peter would have agreed as we learn more in Scripture about Peter's family relationships, than those of any other Apostle. Consider that:...

He Was a Son

Jesus did not Google Peter's name nor do a Facebook search yet, when He met him for the first time, Jesus said to him, "Thou art Simon the son of Jona" (John 1:42). Jona is the common Greek name, *Iōannēs*, (John) which, according to Thayer's "A Greek-English Lexicon of the New Testament", means "to whom Jehovah is gracious". God had been kind to Peter's father, and He was about to save Peter's soul.

Scientists estimate that there are approximately 1,000,000,000, 000,000,000,000,000 stars in the universe, and yet the Psalmist penned about the Lord: "He counts the number of the stars; He calls them all by name" (Ps 147:4, NKJV). Likewise, He knew Peter's name, his personality traits, and his family background. May it also comfort us to know that the same Lord had full knowledge of our sins, our genetic makeup, our families, our talents, our character flaws and the traumas we have experienced. Despite all that, He saved us anyway!.

At the end of John's Gospel, Jesus called him "Simon, son of Jonas" (John 21:15,16,17). Specifically, the word "son" is not included in the Greek text, so it literally reads: "Simon of Jona". In those days, it was common to identify a child by his father. For example, in the genealogy of Christ in Luke 3:23-38, seventy-one father-son relationships are provided, and the word "son" is not found in the text even once. Each family relationship is described with the expression: _____ of _____. In Peter's case though, the Holy Spirit inspires the authors of Scripture to refer to him on certain occasions by his name before it was changed (Simon) or his relationship to his father at birth (Simon, son of Jonas). Referring to him by his birthname and family connection underlines the natural or fleshly way Peter is thinking, speaking, or acting. For example, after Peter denied the Saviour, the Lord refers to him three times as "Simon of Jonas" (John 21:15-17). Peter still had the same sinful nature within him that he had received from his father at birth. As Peter would learn, the divine works of salvation and restoration are incredible, but they do not remove or reform the sinful nature within.

Peter gave his famous confession in Caesarea Philippi having observed the flawless character and unparalleled power of the Lord Jesus. On that occasion, he correctly identified the Saviour as "the Son of the living God" (Matt 16:16). At that point, the Lord Jesus then identified Peter as Simon Bar-jonah. In Hebrew, son is the word "*ben*" (e.g. Ben-jamin means "son of my right hand"). In Aramaic, "*bar*" means "son" just as "*huios*" means "son" (e.g. "sons" of Zebedee) in Greek. Thus, *Bariōnas* or *bar-jonah* means son of Jonah.

Many translations give the idea that his father's name was Jonah, although that would seemingly contradict the Lord Jesus calling Peter's father John in John 1:42 and John 21:15-17. Perhaps, though, this is the shortened version by which his father was often identified or, according to some commentators, it could have been the family surname. In Greek, *Iōannēs* is John and *Iōnas* is Jonah which means "dove". When Hezekiah thought he was going to die due to infection from a boil, he said, "I did mourn as a dove" (Isa 38:14). Perhaps each time the Saviour mentions Peter's father, it is because he is calling Peter to mourn his sins and his sinful nature. The Lord refers to him as Simon of Jonah at his conversion in John 1:42, when Peter faced his sins against God. In Matthew 16:17, the Lord used the name Simon because Peter had rebuked the Lord for speaking about the coming cross. In John 21:15-17, Peter has to face three questions about his love and devotion after having denied the Lord three times. The Lord often permits circumstances in our lives as believers that grant us windows into the sinfulness and selfishness of our flesh. For Peter and for us, these are both saddening and humbling experiences. Repentance for salvation and restoration is painful, but absolutely essential. The beauty is that in the dark and painful moment when we face our guilt and danger, we can turn and appreciate the grace of God to us.

He Was a Sibling

It is commonly noted that when Aquilla and Priscilla are mentioned in the Bible they are always found together, highlighting both closeness and co-operation in their relationship. Similarly, the frequent mentions of Peter and Andrew together as brothers and workers together indicate their close friendship and team spirit. Of the 13 times Andrew is mentioned by name in the New Testament, 11 times Peter is mentioned with him. Six times he is identified as Peter's brother (Matt 4:18; 10:2; Mk 1:16; Luke 6:14; John 1:40; 6:8). Clearly, they were more than blood relatives sharing 50% of their genes; they were also spiritual brothers sharing 100% of the same Saviour. What a blessing it is to have family with whom we can share the things of God! Not everyone is given that privilege as it is not earned or deserved by anyone. It is simply a gracious gift from the Sovereign Lord. Christ never enjoyed that kind of fellowship with His unsaved, half-brothers and sisters in their home in Nazareth. He denied Himself that privilege, but He often gives it out to others just as He did to Peter.

It is no surprise, then, that Peter uses the bond, friendship, and closeness of physical brothers as a standard for interpersonal relationships among believers. He wrote in his first epistle of our *philadelphia* - our "love of the brethren" (1 Peter 1:22). Also, in his second letter he commands that a believer should improve his character by choosing to add "to godliness brotherly kindness" (2 Peter 1:7). Also, Peter is the only New Testament writer to speak of the brotherhood (*adelphotēs*) when he wrote of "your brotherhood in the world" (1 Peter

5:9, NKJV), and to "Love the brotherhood" (1 Peter 2:17). He is also the only New Testament writer to use the word *philadelphos* (adjective form) indicating that we should "love as brothers" (1 Peter 3:8, NKJV). Therefore, if we do not learn the proper, Biblical, and sincere way to love our siblings in a physical family, we will be lacking in our treatment of our spiritual brothers and sisters in the family of God.

Andrew saw Peter saved (John 1:42), but he was never competitive with his brother. Peter seems to have been a natural leader. In the fishing business it was Peter's boat (Luke 5:3), and it is with Peter that the Lord has dealings on the beach, even though there were six other disciples fishing with him (John 21). In the four lists of the apostles in the New Testament, Peter is always mentioned first. On three occasions, only three of the 12 were selected to witness the special activities of the Saviour (the healing of Jairus' daughter, the Mount of Transfiguration, and the Garden of Gethsemane). Peter is mentioned first, and Andrew is not included. Even when there was a discussion with the Lord on the Mount of Olives about future events, Peter is mentioned first, Andrew, who is also present, is mentioned last. It is beautiful to appreciate that true brothers, both physical and spiritual, will be supportive and thankful for any privileges that the other receives. Likewise, true brothers would not gloat or look down on a sibling for not having been granted a privilege by the Lord. Peter and Andrew seem to have had a nice balance of being able to work together with mutual respect and yet never suffering from envy or competitiveness.

Family life and work life are parallel in that they are two of God's great training instruments for spiritual life. Even before they were called to spiritual relationships and work, God had been moulding their character by developing their relationship at home and teaching them how to work together in a family fishing business. Matthew and Mark tell us "they were fishers" (Matt 4:18; Mark 1:16). When the Lord arrived on the shore to call them, Matthew says Peter and Andrew were "casting a net into the sea" (Matt 4:18), and Luke reports that they "were washing their nets" (Luke 5:2). Their training and experience in secular life would serve them well for the spiritual work that the Lord had for them.

Therefore, time as a child or teenager in the home, at school, and at a job might seem to have little to do with spiritual and assembly life. However, the Lord uses that critical period in life to establish character, develop a work ethic, and cultivate an ability to work with others. Paul agreed as he pointed to family relationships as the standard for treatment among believers. To Timothy he said, "Rebuke not an elder, but intreat him as a father; and the younger men as brethren; The elder women as mothers; the younger as sisters, with all purity" (1 Tim 5:1-2). Therefore, we should cherish family life and time interacting with parents, children, and siblings. Proper relationships can be learned in the home so that we will know how to treat properly others in the assembly.

He Was a Spouse

To the Corinthians, Paul said, "Have we not a right to take round a sister as wife, as also the other apostles, and the brethren of the Lord, and Cephas?" (1 Cor 9:5, Darby). Therefore, it appears that when Paul sent the letter to Corinth, a number of the apostles were married, and he specifically mentions Peter. During the life and ministry of the Lord Jesus, we know that Jesus went to Capernaum where he healed "Simon's mother-in-law" (Luke 4:38, Darby). While we never read of Peter's wife or his children in the gospels or in the book of Acts, he was definitely a married man.

Mothers-in-law have a stereotypical negative reputation, but it was David's father-in-law, Saul, who tried to kill him multiple times. It is interesting that in the Bible, Abraham's servant treated Isaac's future mother-in-law with great respect and kindness. Besides giving gifts to Rebekah "he gave also to her brother and to her mother precious things" (Gen 24:53). Ruth also treated her former mother-in-law Naomi with kindness in bringing her grain and with respect as she took advice from her. Peter equally treated his mother-in-law graciously as Mark tells us that "Simon's wife's mother lay sick with a fever, and they [Peter and Andrew] told him about her. And he [Jesus] came and took her by the hand, and lifted her up; and immediately the fever left her" (Mark 1:30-31). She was living where Peter lived, and he sought the best for her by bringing Christ into the home for her healing and blessing.

In truth, we know nothing about Peter's wife. However, was he appreciating her when he penned his instruction for married couples in 1 Peter 3? Peter's point is that the greatest impact a woman can have on a marriage is not through her appearance, culinary skills, domestic abilities, earning potential, or vocational training. Her greatest impact is through her character. Even in the extremely difficult situation where believing women have unsaved husbands, "they, without a word may be won by the conduct of the wives, when they observe your chaste conduct accompanied by fear" (1 Peter 3:1-2).

Peter is the only apostle about which we can be sure he was married when Christ called him to follow. Thus, he is the disciple that provides valuable instruction for Christian husbands. Paul in his writing to the Ephesians commands men: "Husbands, love your wives, even as Christ also loved the church and gave himself for it" (Eph 5:25). Likewise, Peter gives instruction to men as to the means by which they can contribute to the good of their marriage. He said (1 Peter 3.7):

A - "dwell with them according to knowledge".

The most obvious and basic meaning is to spend time together. How interesting that Peter is only recorded once to have been outside a three-day walk from his home in Capernaum. He seems to have primarily focused his work in such a way that he could also give priority to his wife and family. And when he did move about, his wife went with him (1 Cor 9:5).

Louw-Nida gives the definition of "dwell" as "to conduct oneself in relation to a person with whom one lives". Peter is not simply saying that spouses should live under the same roof. That is a given. Beyond that, a husband should strive to get to know his wife and adjust his behaviour accordingly. Instead of "knowledge", other versions render the word *gnosis* as "understanding" or "an understanding way" (NKJV, NASB, ESV, HCSB). Peter is calling each Christian husband to study, learn, and appreciate the way his wife thinks, how she makes choices, what she feels, the potential she has for God, etc.

B - "giving honour unto the wife, as unto the weaker vessel".

There is no allowance in Scripture for any husband to be a despotic power-monger. A wife is biologically different and generally not as physically strong as her husband. Imagine the difference between a tough, Galilean fisherman and his Jewish wife who looked after the domestic affairs in their home. The implication is that just as there are biological and physical differences between a husband and a wife, there are also other features unique to each gender. While spiritual capacity is the same for both, the genders are different in their emotions and distinct in their perspectives. A Christian husband is to embark on the pursuit of comprehending his wife, not to criticize her but to respect and value her as a woman.

C - "being heirs together of the grace of life; that your prayers be not hindered".

The Lord gave Peter the task of confronting Ananias and Sapphira, a Christian couple who had shared in deceit. From them, Peter would have learned that a couple can be united in selfishness and sin. But Peter also knew Zebedee because he and Zebedee's sons, James and John, worked together as fishermen. He would well remember his fishing partners leaving the business with their father and there is no record of Zebedee even questioning their choice to follow Christ. He would have equally known and appreciated James and John's mother. Matthew tells us that the mother of Zebedee's sons was looking on the cross of Christ. The unity of Zebedee and his wife was noteworthy in their genuine devotion and commitment to the Lord, and their goals and sacrifices for their sons.

Peter was a man who believed in the unity of a married couple. In his brief exposition of marital duties, he uses the word *sunoikeo* (to dwell with) and *sunkleronomos* (to share an inheritance). Notice the prefix, *sun,* which means "with". Clearly, Peter's ideal for marriage is the sharing of everything in life including the same spiritual blessings in Christ. Both should enjoy an authentic relationship with the Lord expressed by regular communication with God as they pray together.

He Was a Steward

The gospel writers describe Peter's home in Capernaum in slightly different ways. Luke calls it "Simon's house" (Luke 4:38), Matthew calls it "Peter's house" (Matt 8:14), and Mark says it was "the house of Simon and Andrew" (Mark 1:29). It may have been a family home or Peter's home with his extended family living there too (his brother Andrew and his in-laws). Either way, Peter's home is marked by hospitality as Jesus made it his default place to stay whenever he was in the area (cf. 2:1; 3:19-20; 9:33; 10:10).

Frequently, Peter observed and experienced the hospitality of others. Luke tells us of the day when the Lord Jesus "sent Peter and John, saying, Go and prepare us the passover, that we may eat. And they said unto him, Where wilt thou that we prepare?' And he said unto them, Behold, when ye are entered into the city, there shall a man meet you, bearing a pitcher of water; follow him into the house where he entereth in'" (Luke 22:8-10). They obeyed and "the goodman of the house" shewed them "a large upper room furnished" (Luke 22:11-12). Undoubtedly they were impressed with the sacrifice of the unnamed homeowner so that the Lord could celebrate the Passover with His disciples and institute the Breaking of Bread.

Peter also enjoyed friendship and fellowship in the house where they were meeting in Acts 1 on the day of Pentecost (Acts 2). Following the descent of the Spirit on that unforgettable day, many of the believers from other provinces and countries stayed in Jerusalem instead of returning to their own places of origin. At that time, the local Jerusalem believers opened their hearts and homes. These new believers were "breaking bread from house to house, [and they] did eat their meat with gladness and singleness of heart" (Acts 2:46). Peter is also recorded as being in Matthew's house (Matt 9:9-10); the house of Simon the Leper (Matt 26:6); Cornelius's house (Acts 10:25); the house where they were having the wake for Dorcas (Acts 9:39); "the house of Mary the mother of John, whose surname was Mark; where many were gathered together praying" (Acts 12:12); and he stayed "many days in Joppa with one Simon a tanner" (Acts 9:43).

Peter also loved to show hospitality to visitors arriving in Capernaum. The first time Jesus came to visit, he healed Peter's mother-in-law who then "ministered unto them" (Mark 1:31). Them? With Jesus, came 12 hungry young men, but in Peter's house, all were welcome, and all were fed.

So, Peter was certainly qualified to write: "Use hospitality one to another without grudging" (1 Peter 4:9). That means to be hospitable without "behind-the-scenes talk" (BDAG). Perhaps as Peter penned that word, his mind went to the time Mary was seated at the feet of the Master listening to His words. Meanwhile, Martha, her sister, was flying around preparing a delicious supper while muttering complaints about the lack of help from Mary. By contrast, he may have appreciated his mother-in-law who, without a grumble or a look of disgust, "ministered unto them" (Mark 1:31).

The Lexham Theological Wordbook says that this word is "descriptive of practical kindness paid especially to strangers, often in the sharing of food and drink, lodging, and provision". It also adds that "This word offers a vivid etymological illustration of the notion of hospitality: *philos* (friend) + *chenos* (stranger)—namely, a stranger treated as a friend". The teaching of the Lord Jesus on this subject included the time when he told a chief Pharisee, "When thou makest a dinner or a supper, call not thy friends, nor thy brethren, neither thy kinsmen, nor thy rich neighbours; lest they also bid thee again, and a recompence be made thee. But when thou makest a feast, call the poor, the maimed, the lame, the blind" (Luke 14:12-13). Peter appears to have entertained guests like the Apostle Paul who wrote: "I went up to Jerusalem to see Peter, and abode with him fifteen days" (Gal 1:18). However, he equally invited those whom he would naturally feel less inclined to have in his home. Imagine Peter having Matthew for a meal! For years, he had likely despised that corrupt publican who swindled him out of money by inflating his tax bill. The grace of Christ not only brought about change in Peter's heart, but it also transformed how he used his home. What would have helped him greatly was to remember the value of hospitality in the eyes of the Lord Jesus. The Saviour once promised, "Whoever gives one of these little ones even a cup of cold water because he is a disciple, truly, I say to you, he will by no means lose his reward" (Matt 10:42). For his hospitality alone, Peter will surely receive appreciation and reward from the nail-pierced hand of Christ.

One of the New Testament requirements for a local church leader is that he be "One that ruleth well his own house, having his children in subjection with all gravity; (For if a man know not how to rule his own house, how shall he take care of the church of God?)" (1 Tim 3:4-5). Peter exhibited leadership in his home before he became a leader in spiritual things. His example as a son, a sibling, and a steward demonstrate that he understood the value of family and the importance of the home. He is a New Testament parallel to Joshua who led God's people into a new phase of their experience as they took possession of the Promised Land. While we admire and celebrate the exploits and leadership of Joshua, we get his true priority towards the end of his story. As he reviewed the choices of the gods of Canaan versus the God of the Bible, he stepped forward and declared, "...but as for me and my house, we will serve the Lord." (Joshua 24:15). Just as his greatness as a leader among the people of God began with his leadership at home, it did for Simon Peter as well. While readers of Peter's Biblical biography can easily focus on his great sermons and the miracles he performed, Simon cherished the fundamental priority of the home. He truly was Peter the Family-man.

CHAPTER 4

Peter the Fisherman

The Lord Jesus was a master at using object lessons. Whether it was when He took a child in His arms to teach about kindness and humility (Mark 9:36), when He took a coin in His hand to give a lesson about taxes and priorities (Luke 20:24), or when He had a temple in His view (John 2:19) to instruct about divine power and resurrection, He was expert at using common items to teach vital spiritual principles. On numerous occasions, Peter had a front row seat as the Saviour used familiar objects to explain unfamiliar truths. In one of his first interactions, upon Jesus climbing aboard Peter's boat, the bell rang, and class started. The Lord was about to teach him how to become useful for God. To achieve his educational objectives that day, the Saviour would employ an illustration that Peter knew well – fishing.

It sounds very philosophical to ask, "What is the meaning of life?" However, at some point, each of us must address the more personal version of that question: "Why am I here on earth?". Many people find their sense of meaning and value in their employment. Thus, we can feel miserable and irritable if we receive an unemployment notice (a P45 in the UK). Matthew writes about Peter and Andrew, "For they were fishers" (Matt 4:18). Probably Peter's whole identity was wrapped up in fishing as he had lived by the sea and been learning the trade from an early age.

Others hope to find meaning in the pursuit of possessions. It is noteworthy, then, that Scripture specifically tells us that Peter had a house (Matt 8:14), nets (Mark 1:18), and a boat (Luke 5:3). Still others find meaning in living for family. How interesting that Peter is the only disciple of whom the Gospels record that he was married, as he could not have had a mother-in-law without having married a wife (Mark 1:30).

One additional source to which many people turn for meaning in life is the pursuit of position and influence. Peter was a born leader and seems to have held a significant role in the family fishing business. Matthew and Luke tell us that Peter and Andrew, his brother, were fishermen. However, Luke says that the boat was Peter's, and that James and John were partners with Peter (Luke 5:10). So, Peter had experienced everything that the world could offer including possessions, family, employment, and a prominent role in the fishing business.

Despite enjoying these blessings, when Jesus came aboard Peter was all ears. No doubt, he had heard Genesis 1-2 read many times in synagogue services. The lesson would be what Paul later expressed to the Colossian believers that "All things were created by him [Christ], and for him" (Col 1:16). Likewise, John once heard the chorus of heaven singing to the Lord, "for thou hast created all things, and for thy will they were, and they have been created" (Rev 4:11, JND). Therefore, man's true purpose is to serve God and fulfil His will. While family, work, possessions, and influence have a necessary and proper place, the extent of a man's true usefulness will be in the measure that he lives for God, works for God, and obeys God. That is why the most fulfilled man to set foot on planet earth was the Lord Jesus. As an obedient Son and a perfect Servant, He had the greatest sense of purpose. He made that clear when He said about His Father, "I do always those things that please him" (John 8:29). Thus, the Lord Jesus wanted to share the principles by which He Himself was living so that Peter and the other disciples could find a true sense of meaning in their lives as well. It appears to have impacted Peter greatly as he once wrote that a true Christian "no longer should live the rest of his time in the flesh to the lusts of men, but to the will of God" (1 Peter 4:2).

Willingness to Appreciate Divine Sovereignty

God often sanctifies pre-conversion experiences and abilities as well as secular training. He alone can use these things to make each believer a unique and useful instrument for Him. On Mount Sinai, the Lord charged Moses with the responsibility of overseeing the construction of the Tabernacle. One might wonder how a man who had been raised as a pampered prince in a palace could ever succeed in construction management. Yet, Stephen declared that "Moses was learned in all the wisdom of the Egyptians" (Acts 7:22). He had completed university studies in a land known for building (the Egyptian pyramids) and for great advancements in engineering and metallurgy. Little did he know that God would one day use that training for His purposes and His glory. Likewise, "Luke, the beloved physician" (Col 4:14), would slog through mind-taxing and bone-wearying training. Wasted years? Definitely not! God would sanctify all of that so he could become the personal medic of the Apostle Paul. Also, his training would give him an analytical mind, meticulous research skills, and an exquisite writing ability so that he could complete thorough interviews, detailed investigations, and write his Gospel and The Acts of the Apostles.

Peter, though, did not attend the University of Babylon like Daniel did, nor was he like Paul who could say, "I am verily a man which am a Jew, born in Tarsus, a city in Cilicia, yet brought up in this city [Jerusalem] at the feet of Gamaliel" (Acts 22:3). Peter was born and raised in Bethsaida, a village the name of which means "house of fish" or "house of hunting". It was a small and simple fishing village located on the northern shore of the Sea of Galilee likely near the Jordon River. According to Josephus, in about AD 30, Philip the Tetrarch decided to enlarge the city and give it the name of Augustus Caesar's daughter, Julias. Over the last century there has been much investigation and debate over the location of this ancient community. Recent archaeological excavations at the site of what is known today as el-Araj have given more credibility to that site being the location of Julias (Bethsaida). In part, evidence uncovered from that area has included lead weights for fishing nets, coins from the Roman period, and other buildings and artefacts.

We might think that a young man with such a limited background would have little knowledge or skills that the Lord could use. Ever feel that way about yourself? Thankfully, God says, "For my thoughts are not your thoughts, neither are your ways my ways" (Isa 55:8).

Spending all his life in a fishing village surrounded 24/7 by men talking about fishing was not a waste or a "limited existence". It was exactly what the Lord would use to prepare Simon Peter and at least four and perhaps as many as seven of the twelve apostles (John 21). Their backgrounds would serve them well as they would spearhead the Lord's world-wide project of fishing for men.

Therefore, the Lord's timing and choices in Peter's life were impeccable and they are in your life too. That not only applies to our lives as believers, but also to our lives before we were saved. So, what could the Lord sanctify and use from your childhood experiences, family life, education, training, and employment history? Like Peter, you might be surprised!

Willingness to Use What You Have

Useful people must be "givers" rather than "getters". Thus, the Lord tested Peter as to what resources he had and to what extent he would make them available for divine service. Moses began the same way as he wondered how to convince the people of Israel that he was God's appointed leader. Maybe his mind thought back to the riches and resources he had seen in the Egyptian Palace that Pharaoh employed to lead his nation. Perhaps he did a quick inventory and concluded that he had nothing that God could use. Maybe the Lord would give him some miraculous power or... Suddenly the Lord interrupted his thinking with the challenge, "What is that in thine hand?" (Ex 4:2). In other words, "Moses, are you willing to let God claim and use what you already have?"

So often we can be dreamers of what we could do for God if only we had more gift, more money, a different job, more time, etc. However, before God can use what we don't have, He wants us to surrender to Him what we already possess. Therefore, before He would give Peter something new and something greater such as the keys to the kingdom, the Lord went item by item in Peter's life testing him on this principle. First, He asked to use his boat. Then He asked Peter to use his nets. Eventually He wanted to use Peter's house in Capernaum (Luke 4:38).

The truth of the matter is that everything we call our own has been given to us by God. When the Son spoke to His Father in John 17, He repeated the expression, "thou gavest me". In His prayer, He spoke of what God had given Him including power over all flesh, the disciples, the work, the words, the name, the glory and "all things whatsoever thou hast given me". His overriding prayer was, "Father ... glorify thy Son, that thy Son also may glorify thee" (John 17:1). This was the way the Lord Jesus always operated. When He came into the world, He was appreciating what God had done for Him. In prayer, He said to His Father, "A body hast thou prepared me" (Heb 10:5). He viewed everything He owned as a gift from God and everything He had received was to be used to glorify His Father.

Perhaps it would be helpful if each of us made a list of everything in our lives that the Lord has given us. We should then take that list and ask, "How can we use each item, ability, opportunity, or relationship for Him? Peter learned this key truth and thus challenged the believers who had been dispersed due to persecution when he said, "As every man hath received the gift, even so minister the same one to another, as good stewards of the manifold grace of God. If any man speak, let him speak as the oracles of God; if any man minister, let him do it as of the ability which God giveth: that God in all things may be glorified through Jesus Christ, to whom be praise and dominion for ever and ever. Amen" (1 Peter 4:10-11).

Willingness to Work

"If you want to get a job done well, get a busy man to do it". This sage advice is really the Biblical principle that God uses believers who are already actively developing and displaying a work ethic. Therefore, secular employment and education provide great opportunities for believers to hone their ability to work hard and to persevere. Moses, David, and Amos were shepherds before they became men who spoke on God's behalf. Ezra was a scribe, Matthew was a tax collector, Elisha was ploughman and Paul was a tentmaker. The Bible even tells us that the Lord Jesus demonstrated His work ethic before He began His spiritual ministry so that the people said, "Is not this the carpenter?" (Mark 6:3). Therefore, education and employment provided by God are far more than opportunities for self-advancement and to support a family. They are training times to strengthen the muscle of our work ethic for use in God's service.

Wise King Solomon gave great advice to his son, when he said, "The soul of the sluggard desireth, and hath nothing: but the soul of the diligent shall be made fat" (Prov 13:4). Solomon clearly condemned laziness by making 20 references to the dangers of being idle, a sluggard or a sloth. As a boy, Peter may have heard that advice read in synagogue services, but then, God gave him the privilege of observing for three years the tireless work ethic of the Servant of Jehovah in His great service for God. Without any question, Peter could not have had a better role model!

Although Peter fished all night and came home with nothing to sell or eat, God notes Peter's work ethic. Matthew and Mark say Jesus, "saw two brethren...casting a net into the sea" (Matt 4:18; Mark 1.16). Luke says that Jesus, "saw two ships standing by the lake: but the fishermen were gone out of them, and were washing their nets" (Luke 5:2). Sure enough, even after the death of Christ, which disciple is the first one willing to go to work and provide for his family? Peter. He was the one with initiative and the one who said to six other disciples, "I go a-fishing" (John 21:3). A believer who knows how to work hard in the material world is prepared to learn lessons about spiritual usefulness as well. So, there on the beach, the master teacher, having observed Peter working physically, had good reason to believe that he could one day lead God's workforce to spread the gospel around the world.

Willingness to Obey His Commands

The Lord knew that Peter was a strong-willed man by nature. Likely his grit and willpower served him well in the rough conditions of the fishing business on the Sea of Galilee. However, all personality traits need to be brought under divine control and not be allowed to inhibit usefulness for the Lord. Moses felt incapable and Timothy may have been timid. However, in each case, the Lord called them to submit to God's word and stand for Him, rather than be limited by fears, personal weaknesses, or character defects. Therefore, the question that day in the boat was, "Would a determined, self-made fisherman take instructions from a Carpenter from Nazareth, or would his personality traits limit his potential for the Lord?

We must recall that the first command the Lord gave him was to navigate the boat out a bit from shore so that the Saviour could speak to the multitude on the beach (Luke 5:3). Then, after teaching the people, He told Peter to "Launch out into the deep, and let down your nets" (v.4). Then, finally, He commanded Peter, "Come ye after me" (Mark 1.17). But why the step-by-step process? Could the Lord Jesus not have given him all the steps at once?

This was not the first time for the Lord to lead through a slowly revealed process. Centuries before, God said to Abraham, "Get thee out of thy country, and from thy kindred, and from thy father's house, unto a land that I will shew thee" (Gen 12:1). Abram (as he was then) had to obey that command before God would give him further direction. Step-by-step instruction is not just a divine training policy for "newbies" in His program either. Later, when Abraham had fifty years of experience as a believer, God called him to perform a great act of faith on a mountain. How would God lead him in that experience? The same way He always leads His people - step by step. On that day, God said to him, "Get thee into the land of Moriah; and offer him (Isaac) there for a burnt offering upon one of the mountains which I will tell thee of" (Gen 22:2). God often communicates to His servants what He wants next with the assurance that, upon completion of His already revealed will, they will receive further guidance. Peter was accustomed to telling others what to do in the fishing business. Now, the Lord wanted Peter to learn humility and patience, and to follow His instruction step by step.

God's perfect mode of operation has not changed over time either. Sometimes, the "control freak" in all of us gets frustrated and we want to know the beginning, the end, and all the steps in between.

God knows that if He told us every detail of His plan and there was the slightest part of discomfort or suffering, we might not obey, and the fear of the future would steal our joy in the present. On the other hand, if there was a good result ahead, we might move forward too quickly or do things for personal pleasure and pride rather than doing them for Him regardless of the results.

Peter got off to a good start when the Lord said to him and Andrew, "Follow me". Matthew tells us that "they straightway left their nets, and followed him" (Matt 4:19-20). Peter had learned that circumstances are never a valid excuse for failing to obey the Lord. He would spend the next three years observing the perfect Servant of Jehovah who said about His God, "He wakeneth morning by morning, he wakeneth mine ear to hear as the learned. The Lord God hath opened mine ear, and I was not rebellious, neither turned away back" (Isa 50:4-5). After seeing his Lord follow God's plan and become "obedient unto death, even the death of the cross" (Phil 2:8), Peter wrote that we should be "As obedient children" (1 Peter 1:14) and be prepared to stick to the plan of our God as He reveals it to us step by step. As Peter himself summarised, "Christ also suffered for us, leaving us an example, that ye should follow his steps" (1 Peter 2:21).

Willingness to Work With Others

Good team players are vital for the success of any project whether material or spiritual. Peter understood. The Spirit tells us that when they had enclosed a great multitude of fishes and their net was breaking, "They beckoned unto their partners, who were in the other ship" (Luke 5:6-7). Upon seeing the boatful of blessing, the Spirit explains that Peter was astonished, "And so also James, and John, the sons of Zebedee, which were partners with Simon" (v.10). The first word for "partners" (*metochos*) is used here by Luke and five other times in the book of Hebrews. Lidell and Scott in their Greek-English Lexicon give the definition for the verbal form as "sharing in or partaking of" and, as a substantive, Louw-Nida defines it as "one who shares with someone else as an associate in an enterprise or undertaking".

According to the Lexham Theological Wordbook, the second word translated "partners" (*koinōnos*) is "related to the quality of *koinōnia* [fellowship] but denotes the person who shares and participates with another". So, the first word puts emphasis on the activity of sharing with others in a specific relationship, and the second points to the people in that relationship.

There are great lessons here that are equally applicable to spiritual fellowships. In this case, two brothers were financial associates and partners with another pair of brothers. It was what we might call a fishing or financial fellowship. The relationship of the four young men was harmonious as each likely had distinct responsibilities in the catching, processing, and selling of fish. John wrote of the glorious family fellowship when he said, "That which we have seen and heard declare we unto you, that ye also may have fellowship with us: and truly our fellowship is with the Father, and with his Son Jesus Christ" (1 John 1:3). And when the first local church was formed in Jerusalem, the believers "devoted themselves to the apostles' teaching and the fellowship, to the breaking of bread and the prayers" (Acts 2:42). While a business fellowship, a family fellowship, and an ecclesiastical fellowship all have common characteristics, it is vital to distinguish between them.

The Lord fully knew that Peter and his companions had learned vital lessons about teamwork in their secular employment. If we are companions and true partners linked in the Master´s business of fishing for men, there is no room for competition or free spirits. No worker in God's service should ever allow himself to operate as an independent agent. From the very beginning, God taught this lesson to Adam. In the work of Creation, "God created" and yet "all things were created by him (the Son)" (Col 1:16). At the same time the "Spirit of God moved upon the face of the waters" (Gen 1:2). Therefore, at the beginning of time, the three persons of the Trinity displayed "teamwork" in the creation of the world.

Likewise, in the incarnation, of the Saviour, His baptism, the cross, and even the resurrection of Christ were works with involvement by the Father, the Son, and the Holy Spirit. For example, about the resurrection of Christ, Peter said, "Him, God raised up the third day" (Acts 10:40). Jesus said, "I lay down my life, that I might take it again" (John 10:17. Paul wrote that He [Jesus] was, "declared to be the Son of God with power, according to the spirit of holiness, by the resurrection from the dead" (Rom 1:4). The Holy Trinity is the perfect model of teamwork that we should strive to imitate.

Peter also appreciated the distinct skills each person brought to the fishing business and that the whole was greater than the sum of the parts. This lesson would serve him well since it is a Biblical principle applicable to service in the things of God. The Apostle Paul was incredibly knowledgeable and gifted by God to accomplish great things. Yet, even he makes mention of fellowlabourers such as Priscilla and Aquila (Rom 16:3); Urbane (Rom 16:9); Timothy (Rom 16:21; 1 Thess 3:2); Titus (2 Cor 8:23); Epaphroditus (Phil 2:25); Clement and others (Phil 4:3); Justus (Col 4:11); Philemon (Philem 1), Marcus, Aristarchus, Demas, and Lucas (Philem 24), and God Himself (1 Cor 3:9). He also references his fellow soldiers (*stratiotes*) such as Epaphroditus (Phil 2:25) and Archippus (Philem 2) and fellow prisoners (*sunaichmalotos)* such as Adronicus and Junia (Rom 16:7), Aristarchus (Col 4:10), and Epaphras (Philem 23). In fact, Paul mentions other workers in every one of the epistles he wrote. If he wrote Hebrews, even in that letter a reference is made to Timothy, the writer's co-labourer (Heb 13:23).

But working with others can be harder and more frustrating than untangling fishing lines and nets. Why did the Lord Jesus select two pairs of brothers as the first members of the apostolic team? Brothers, like Peter and Andrew, and James and John, would have the most experience being and working together. At the same time, as brothers, they would also know the weaknesses, flaws, and failings of each other more than anyone else. So, if Peter and those men had learned to work together and respect each other despite their differences and defects, they were ideal candidates to form part of a spiritual team of fishers of men.

Nearly 2,000 years later, God is still looking for good team players. It should not surprise us that Heaven never praises the virtue of men who cannot work with others. We are social creatures and God made us to be peninsulas rather than islands. He has designed us to connect with others socially, emotionally, and in our spiritual service for God. No wonder Peter wrote, of the "unfeigned love of the brethren" and gave clear exhortation: "see that ye love one another with a pure heart fervently" (1 Peter 1:22). We need to work with others and others need to be able to work with us.

Willingness to Face the Truth About Yourself

The generally accepted practice today is that your *resumé* or *curriculum vitae* must be truthful, and make you look as good as possible. If someone has been fired or had a bad review, they usually try to bury that information in their employment application so as not to draw attention to inexperience or failure. However, it is the exact opposite if you wish to be employed in divine usefulness. Before the Lord would call Peter to follow Him and work for Him, He would first give him a look at his sinful heart hidden underneath the exterior of bravado and enthusiasm.

The first lesson was that Peter was going to have come to grips with his own wicked potential. Moses had been refined by palace living in Egypt, and yet, before the Lord sent him to lead Israel, He first let Moses try doing things his way. Seeing an Egyptian whipping a Hebrew, Moses became enraged, and he killed the Egyptian. The flesh would not gain Moses the respect of God's people. Instead, it would only lead him to loneliness as he fled to the back side of the desert. After that lesson sank in for 40 years, the Lord brought him to stand on holy ground at the burning bush where God, the great "I am", would appear.

Similarly, Saul of Tarsus got to see the blinding radiance of the righteousness of Christ when the light shone around him on the road to Damascus. No wonder he later wrote, "For I know that in me (that is, in my flesh,) dwelleth no good thing" and that "sin...dwelleth in me" (Rom 7:18, 20).

All useful servants of God must come to an appreciation of the high standard of divine holiness and the stark contrast of our wickedness. Peter was convinced that Jesus was the Messiah and undoubtedly, he was ready to plunge into activity for the Lord. But before that could occur, the Lord let Peter exhaust his skills and energy to the point where he would have to report, "Master, we have toiled all the night, and have taken nothing" (Luke 5:5). At that point, Simon Peter was ready to appreciate the character and ability of the Lord. Witnessing the Lord's power as the nets miraculously filled, the contrast sank in, and Peter fell low before the Saviour crying, "Depart from me; for I am a sinful man, O Lord" (Luke 5:8). Not surprisingly, this key principle has not changed. Before we can ever be truly useful for God, we must get a good sense of our own sinfulness and our potential to defile and cause damage.

But why did the Lord use fishing as an object lesson? Would it not have been easier to take Peter out of his comfort zone and, instead of a net, put a sword or a shepherd's crook in his hand? Peter eventually showed how hopeless he was in sword fighting when he missed Malchus' head and lopped off his ear. We never read of him even trying carpentry or shepherding sheep. Peter was a specialist at fishing, the Sea of Galilee was his territory, and the boat was his home. The Lord took him fishing to show that even the best Peter could do under his own power would never produce results. He was going to have to depend on the Lord and not on his own abilities, knowledge, or skills if he wanted to serve God.

The fishing lesson began when the Lord "went into one of the ships which was Simon's" (Luke 5:3). Did Peter not wonder, "Why did he pick my boat?". Have you ever asked why He chose you to teach that Sunday School class, raise those children, have that skill, or share in that assembly activity? Why you? The lesson seemed to stick with Peter all his life. He later wrote about the God of all grace (1 Peter 5:10), and that with every ability we have been given, we should be good "stewards of the manifold grace of God" (1 Peter 4:10). That's it! The only explanation for God using wicked and weak sinners like us is His grace. Just like Peter, we should be deeply grateful for the privilege of following and serving our Master no matter what He has called us to do.

In his first letter, Peter quoted Psalm 34:12 describing the believer as "he that will love life, and see good days" (1 Peter 3:10). It is not just that we will love eternal life and see good days in Heaven, we can have that now if we are willing to surrender to His will and to become involved in His service. That kind of life was fully seen in all its beauty in the most obedient and productive life ever - the life of our Lord Jesus Christ. God wants us to have and enjoy that life both now and forever. In the measure that you pursue that type of life, you too will love life and see good days.

CHAPTER 5

Peter the Creationist

The message was clear - move or die! The first wave of Christians fled Jerusalem and their homeland due to a persecution that began because of the martyrdom of Stephen (Acts 7). Many headed north-west landing in Asia Minor (modern day Turkey). Then, Gentile Christians began to be tracked and tortured. Overnight, many disappeared having to relocate to five provinces in Asia Minor. The Apostle Peter heard of the great dispersion (*diaspora*) and set out to write a letter to comfort and instruct faithful but hurting saints. Peter's written message from God would be copied and circulated from hand to hand and from house to house.

But, what do you say to Christians who have lost their homes, jobs, possessions and perhaps family in one night? How do you convince burdened believers that everything happens for a purpose when nothing makes sense? How do you calm fears when God's people feel uncertain and vulnerable?

The Focus on Nature

The late Mr. Harold Paisley once took me to visit a widow in hospital. She was a very faithful and respected sister who was feeling quite down. I was shocked when Mr. Paisley read her Psalm 19 and spoke with her about some of the wonders of birds. I would have thought it better to speak about heaven or to sing, "Standing on the Promises". However, the dear woman wept with joy and it significantly brightened her spirits. As we left the hospital, Mr. Paisley said to me, "It is always helpful to remind Christians in trials of their Creator and His complete power and control".

I think Mr. Paisley may have learned this approach from the Apostle Peter who wrote to hurting saints. Peter fully understood that stress and suffering turn human beings inwardly and we focus on our pain, our loss, our difficulties and our uncertainties. Perhaps Peter discovered this reality in his personal experience when he sat alone after denying his Lord. It was a different kind of trial, but he could still remember the sudden jolt out of his self-pity. Just as he was wallowing in his own feelings and failure, the Lord Jesus questioned him three times: "Lovest thou ME?". At the same time, Jesus commanded, "Feed MY lambs!", "Tend MY sheep!", and, "Feed MY sheep!"(John 21:15-17). Masterfully, the Saviour shifted Peter's focus from Peter and his failure to the Lord and His sheep. So, Peter, knowing that difficulties and trials incline us towards self-focus, issued to his readers the following challenge: "Wherefore let them that suffer according to the will of God commit the keeping of their souls to him in well doing, as unto a faithful Creator" (1 Peter 4:19).

Peter is the only writer in the New Testament to use that noun, "Creator (*ktistes*)". Why? It seems that no other author in the New Testament is associated more with nature than Simon Peter and no other disciple saw more miracles in nature than the great apostle. Consider what he observed at every level of creation and how he came to know and recommend that suffering saints put their trust in "the faithful Creator".

The Fascination with Nature

Beneath the Galilean sky, Peter and his partners would cast their nets and then wait for the fish to fill them. Like David alone with a few sheep under the open sky, Peter had plenty of time for consideration and reflection. While he may have sat still physically to avoid rocking the boat, mentally he likely ran from one observation of nature to another. He had time to look up and study the sun, moon, and stars, look out on the winds and landforms on the horizon and follow birds that circled the boat hoping for an early breakfast. He would also look down daily to observe the sea and the creatures below. As an experienced fisherman, he likely had already accumulated a vast knowledge about nature, but he was about to take a three-year class that would make him appreciate the Creator like never before.

Peter, look up!

One day, Peter, James and John followed the Lord Jesus to the top of a mountain, where suddenly he was blinded as Jesus' "face did shine as the sun" (Matt 17:2). Surely he had observed what the wise king wrote: "The sun also ariseth, and the sun goeth down, and hasteth to his place where he arose" (Eccl 1:5), and he must have meditated on Psalm 19:1-2: "The heavens declare the glory of God; and the firmament sheweth his handywork". He undoubtedly could appreciate what Paul later wrote, "There is one glory of the sun, and another glory of the moon, and another glory of the stars: for one star differeth from another star in glory" (1 Cor 15:41). He must have often sensed the heat and brilliance of the "greater light" that ruled the day under which he had washed and mended nets for many years. But this was a new experience. This light was brighter still, this was "excellent glory" (2 Peter 1:17). Peter and his two friends must have reported that the brilliant lustre of the glory of Christ exceeded any whiteness known on earth as "His garments became radiant and exceedingly white, as no launderer on earth can whiten them" (Mark 9:3, NASB). The glory of the Saviour's face was out of this world; it was like the sun – yes, the sun that Peter had studied but never been able to look at directly. And yet, the glory of the Son of God was brighter still.

There were also the clouds. Peter had seen thousands of cloud formations. As the Lord Jesus allowed his magnificence, which up to that point had been veiled in a body, to radiate, suddenly "a bright cloud overshadowed them" (Matt 17:5). As a boy, Peter had probably learned the story of the pillar cloud that had guided his ancestors across the Red Sea and through the desert. He likely never dreamed that he would one day look up and miraculously see the same Shekinah glory in the cloud that matched the radiant glory of the face of the Saviour.

This was the mini-millennium experience the Lord Jesus had promised that Peter, James and John would see before they died (Matt 16:28). Could Peter trust the Creator who excels the sun in His glory, a glory equal to that of the Father who spoke from the bright cloud?

Peter, look a little lower!

There are three heavens: the dwelling place of God, space, and the atmosphere. One night, the sky went dark and neither moon nor stars shone through. Peter could only look up at the swirling clouds in the atmosphere and no higher. The gusts were matched by surface winds on the Galilean sea. Wind was part of life for fishermen, so that winds that worried landlubbers didn't make Peter's blood pressure rise one bar. But this wind did.

Mark wasn't there, but he would have heard Peter's testimony that "there arose a great storm of wind, and the waves beat into the ship, so that it was now full" (Mark 4:37). Matthew was there and he called it "a great tempest in the sea" (Matt 8:24). Luke, having the reports of the disciples, concluded that they "were in jeopardy" (Luke 8:23). They would have been doomed if it were not for the fact that the Creator of wind and sea was asleep in their boat. They woke Him and He stood up and called out, "Peace, be still!" Instantly, the wind stopped, and the waves calmed like glass. Could Peter trust a man who controlled the unseen winds in the air?

And a little lower!

Inevitably, as the fishermen hauled in their nets, birds launched from land to hover and hope for at least a few nibbles of fish. As a boy, he likely fed them. As an adult, Peter knew their habits and appreciated their unique features, even if they were at times a nuisance. So far, scientists have identified over 8,000 species of birds. Approximately 400 species are found in the Holy Land and about 40 are mentioned in Scripture. (Baker, Encyclopedia of the Bible). Peter heard the Lord Jesus speak of birds that lodge in branches (Matt 13:32), birds that have nests (Matt 8:20), birds that devour seed (Matt 13:4), sparrows that fall to the ground (Matt 10:29), sparrows sold in a market (Luke 12:6-7), eagles that gather (Matt 24:28), and ravens which God feeds (Luke 12:24).

Peter defiantly said it wouldn't happen, but it did. The Lord had told him, "Truly, I tell you, this very night, before the rooster crows twice, you will deny me three times" (Mark 14:30 ESV). He should have bowed in wonder at the Saviour when he denied the Lord the first time and "the rooster crowed" (Mark 14:68 ESV). Only the Lord of Heaven and earth could know exactly when Peter would deny Him and make that rooster wake up and crow right at that point. Even more amazing was that, after he denied the Lord the third time, "Immediately the rooster crowed a second time" (Mark 14:72 ESV). Knowing when the rooster would wake up and crow is one thing, knowing when the rooster would crow the second time would be even harder to predict. So, mixed with Peter's shame and sorrow would be a wonder at the Saviour's control over the birds of the air. Did he not find comfort remembering the words of the Lord Jesus, "How much more are ye better than the fowls" (Luke 12:24)? Could he not trust the heart of One who cares for the birds and has control over them?

Down a bit more!

Peter could drop his eyes down to the kingdom of plants. Peter was there the day the Lord saw "a fig tree afar off having leaves" (Mark 11:13) and, when He drew near hoping to find figs, He found none. That would be strange for a tree that looked alive and usually had the old fruit on it when the new fruit was growing in the spring. Jesus then solemnly decreed, "No man eat fruit of thee hereafter for ever" (Mark 11:14). The next morning, Jesus and the disciples came down the same path by the same fig tree. The disciples must have been wide-eyed with amazement when "they saw the fig tree dried up from the roots". While all the disciples heard it, it was only Peter with his acute interest and observation of nature who "remembered and said to him, "Rabbi, look! The fig tree that you cursed has withered" (v.21). Peter knew that no tree dies and withers that quickly and, if it did, it would dry from the leaves towards the roots. This was the opposite! Peter knew he was in the presence of the trustworthy ruler of the plant kingdom.

Now, Peter, look out!

Peter had likely read and perhaps memorized Psalm 50:10, in which God says, "For every beast of the forest is mine, and the cattle upon a thousand hills". While his primary focus was fish, Peter was also interested in other animals. In his writings, he references the dog and the pig (2 Peter 2:22) as well as the lion (1 Peter 5:8). He also recalled the experience of Balaam when "a speechless donkey spoke with human voice and restrained the prophet's madness" (2 Peter 2:16, ESV). Unquestionably, it was divine power that controlled Balaam's donkey, and it was the same divine power that Peter witnessed controlling another donkey upon which the Lord rode.

Mark seemed to know more of what happened that day than even Matthew who was actually there. It was the day when the Saviour selected two disciples to go to Bethpage and bring the Master a donkey. "The amount of detail Mark recorded implies an eyewitness report; possibly Peter was one of the two disciples sent on this errand" (Bible Knowledge Commentary). One of Mark's unique details about the Lord Jesus is that "he sat upon him" (Mark 11:7). If Peter was Mark's source of information, this miracle in nature also left an impression on him as he watched the Lord riding on a donkey that had never been tamed. Making it more dangerous was the fact that the little burro had just been separated from its mother. The donkey moved steadily and calmly under the hand of the Creator, the "last Adam". Peter appreciated that Jesus was not some unique donkey-whisperer; He was the Almighty God who can control the uncontrollable, even in the animal kingdom.

Keep looking out!

For three years, Peter had watched the Lord Jesus display divine power in his fellow human beings over and over again. All it took was a word or touch from the Saviour and instantly the blind could see, the lame could walk, the maimed could work, lepers were healed, and the dead came alive. Never once was there a legal case of malpractice against the Saviour or a botched healing that left someone worse off. Every time it was instant, complete, and observable, and no case was too complex, too rare, or too far-gone for the Lord of glory. Peter had a front row seat to witness most of the miracles in men, women, and children. But perhaps one that impacted him more than any other was the time that he, himself, swung a sword at the high priest's servant in the Garden of Gethsemane. He may have intended to protect the Saviour from the unruly mob by taking them out one by one. However, he missed the man's neck and sliced off his ear. Right at the point of Peter's embarrassing flop, the Saviour rebuked him, and then "he touched his [Malchus'] ear, and healed him" (Luke 22:51). It almost seems like Jesus touched the side of his head and created a new ear rather than attaching the old one. Clearly, though, the Saviour performed a miracle to recover what was lost due to a bad, emotional decision by Peter. What a comfort to know our Lord can do wonders, even when we have made wrong decisions! That is a Man in whom we trust in any situation that crosses our paths.

Now, look down towards the ground!

Imagine putting a snake, a sheep, an iguana, a mountain lion, and an eagle in one room. It would not be long until you would see a wild cage match with feathers and fur flying everywhere and one or more creatures hurt or dead. Peter had a vision one day and he saw a group of animals that looked like a passenger list from Noah's ark. He reported that in one large sheet there "were all manner of fourfooted beasts of the earth, and wild beasts, and creeping things, and fowls of the air" (Acts 10:11-12). All were alive, but not a growl, a hiss or a scratch. Peter was about to learn a lesson about preaching the gospel to Gentiles, but it must have impressed this nature-observer to see the control of wild beasts and reptiles under the hand of the Creator.

Now, look further down!

Peter probably could not remember the first time he swam in the Sea of Galilee. From watching waves lap on the shore to bigger waves rocking the boat, he had a life-long fascination with the sea. And yet, he had never seen anything like this! He had already witnessed the Lord display His awesome power over the sea with two words from the boat, "Σιώπα, πεφίμωσο" [Peace be still] (Mark 4:39). Everyone knows that even if a wind were to stop instantly, it would take hours for waves to calm. That is, unless the Lord commanded it!

On that occasion, though, they had left the Master up on a mountain as they rowed away from shore to cross the Sea of Galilee. All was well until they were about half way across and suddenly a wild storm whipped up. They rowed, rocked and bailed feverishly. Then, suddenly it seemed as though a ghost was coming toward them walking on the water. At that moment, Jesus spoke and they realized it was the Lord. Stunned, Peter muttered, "Lord, if it be thou, bid me come unto thee on the water. And he said, 'Come.' And when Peter was come down out of the ship, he walked on the water, to go to Jesus" (Matt 14:28-29). Neither the Lord Jesus nor Peter had taken a running start to slide across the water like a skipping stone. Peter knew that only the Creator could suspend the Law of Gravity so He could walk on water. He could even suspend it so Peter could walk on the waves as well.

Peter, look as deep as you can!

How many times had Peter looked into the water to check on his nets? He knew how long they would take to fill and how fickle and unpredictable fish could be. But, when the King of the sea speaks, things can change quickly. Twice, Jesus told him where to lower the nets and both times the nets were instantly filled like overblown balloons. How did Christ, the Carpenter, know where the fish were? The second time he let down the net just ten feet from where it had been all night. Ten hours of fishing and not one minnow, and now ten feet to the right and there are 153 "great fishes" (John 21:11) in the net.

The Lord Jesus also sent Peter to go fishing with a rod. The tax collectors had approached Peter about paying the Jewish temple tax, the "stater" (Matt 17:24-27). The Lord then sent Peter saying, "go thou to the sea, and cast an hook, and take up the fish that first cometh up; and when thou hast opened his mouth, thou shalt find a piece of money: that take, and give unto them for me and thee" (v. 27). Right. There were 20 to 25 species in the Sea of Galilee and likely millions of fish, so how would this work?

Peter cast out the hook and the first fish was likely a *Chromis simonis*, eventually named after Simon Peter (The New Bible Dictionary, Third Edition). The Lord knows where every fish is and can make them swim into a net or eat a coin that falls into the sea. The fish still had not swallowed the coin or spat it out and it was that fish and not another that took the bait on Peter's hook.

From the heights of the sun and clouds down to the depths of the sea, Peter observed miracles at every level of nature. The Lord clearly has super-natural power to complete His will in creation and no less power over our lives as well. So, no wonder then that in the middle of storms and trials of the dispersed believers Peter wrote to them directing their focus and faith toward the Lord of all creation.

The Formation of Nature

Can you imagine Simon Peter in a debate with Charles Darwin or Richard Dawkins? Peter was completely convinced that, "by the word of God the heavens were of old, and the earth standing out of the water and in the water" (2 Peter 3:5). Based on his observation of nature, he would have agreed with Paul: "Because that which may be known of God is manifest in them; for God hath shewed it unto them. For the invisible things of him from the creation of the world are clearly seen, being understood by the things that are made, even his eternal power and Godhead; so that they are without excuse" (Rom 1:19-20).

The sublime truth of intelligent design by our all-wise Creator seems to have brought great comfort to Peter in times of trial. He had just been arrested for preaching about the Lord Jesus and for healing a man who couldn't walk. Immediately upon being released, Peter attended a prayer meeting with the assembly in Jerusalem. In the face of that challenge and the potential to have to deal with even greater persecution ahead, Peter and the believers "lifted up their voice to God with one accord, and said, 'Lord, thou art God, which hast made heaven, and earth, and the sea, and all that in them is'" (Acts 4:24). The reasoning is obvious - if God was intelligent enough to make "all things", is He not wise enough to plan out our lives even if it does involve trials and suffering?

The Future of Nature

Peter not only looked back with confidence to the origin of everything; he also looked forward to the end of everything. Nature is beautiful, but it is not what it was, and it is not what it will be. On the day of Pentecost, Peter preached that "the times of refreshing shall come from the presence of the Lord" which will also be "times of [the] restitution of all things" (Acts 3:19,21). Peter had seen the millennial glory of the Saviour on the Mount of Transfiguration and he longed, like every true lover of nature, for the Lord of heaven and earth to return to His creation.

Only He will bring about the "new heavens and a new earth" of which Isaiah spoke (65:17) when He comes to reign for 1,000 years. He alone will have power to rectify all the damage done to creation since the fall of Adam and even due to the great destruction of nature during the judgments of the Great Tribulation.

Peter also looked beyond the millennial reign of Christ, to another solemn, but exciting day. As an old man, he wrote of, "the heavens and the earth, which are now, by the same word are kept in store, reserved unto fire against the day of judgment and perdition of ungodly men" (2 Peter 3:7). The Lord will make this universe better in the Millennium and the true Adam will exercise His right as Head of Creation. However, the eternal state will eclipse even the greatness of the millennial kingdom.

Peter went on to explain what will happen: "But the day of the Lord will come as a thief in the night; in the which the heavens shall pass away with a great noise, and the elements shall melt with fervent heat, the earth also and the works that are therein shall be burned up" (2 Peter 3:10); "Looking for and hasting unto the coming of the day of God, wherein the heavens being on fire shall be dissolved, and the elements shall melt with fervent heat" (3:12). Peter appreciated nature, but he was no environmentalist. He knew the Lord would act "according to his promise" (2 Peter 3:9,13) and that, "Heaven and earth shall pass away" (Mark 13:31).

So, with that understanding in mind, why live for something that is not permanent? "Since all these things are to be destroyed in this way, it is clear what sort of people you should be in holy conduct and godliness as you wait for and earnestly desire the coming of the day of God" (2 Peter 3:11-12a, HCSB). Without any question, to live for this physical world and the pleasures it offers is a horribly futile investment.

Peter's instruction is really the principle that my driving instructor drilled into me when I was 15-years old. He said, "The best way to drive a car is to look high and drive low". In other words, see what is ahead and make adjustments accordingly. If there is a car blocking the road, step on the brakes. And if you see this world is headed for fire, don't put your money, time, and effort into something that will certainly go up in smoke.

There is a future, though, beyond the fire. There are the new heaven and the new earth which John also witnessed (Rev 21:1). What will be the difference between this "new earth" and that of the "new earth" of the millennium (Isa 66:22)? The Maker of Heaven and Earth will reside in both, but even during the millennium, there will be evidences of the curse from the fall of man - people will die, and every baby that is born will be a sinner. However, the final and ultimate new heavens and new earth will be completely new and neither sin nor Satan will mar them. Now that is a world worth living for! At least that is what Peter thought. Some of his final words are, "Nevertheless we, according to his promise, look for new heavens and a new earth, wherein dwelleth righteousness. Wherefore, beloved, seeing that ye look for such things, be diligent that ye may be found of him in peace, without spot, and blameless" (2 Peter 3:13-14).

Peter denied the Lord Jesus as he sat near a fire on the patio of the high priest's house. Later, on the beach in John 21, Peter looked again at a fire the Saviour had made to cook breakfast, and it was there that he was brought back into fellowship with the Lord. He knew that the Saviour could do great things, even with fire. No wonder Peter looked forward to the final flames on earth and the fiery destruction of this defiled, cursed, and sinful world. He knew that every atom in this world is under the control of the "Lord our maker" (Ps 95:6) who will one day make the new heavens and earth "wherein dwelleth righteousness". So, in the many fiery trials on earth, may God help all his suffering saints to do as Peter says: "Entrust their souls to a faithful Creator" (1 Peter 4:19, NASB).

CHAPTER 6
Peter the Student

"If you cut him, he would bleed Scripture"

Charles Spurgeon

While Spurgeon spoke these words about John Bunyan, the author of Pilgrim's Progress, they could equally be said about the great Apostle Peter. He was a man who viewed the Bible as a treasure to be valued, spiritual food to be consumed, and an authority to be obeyed. He read it, studied it, learned it, preached it, lived it, and loved it. While perhaps best known for his denial, very few believers have ever enjoyed a truly Bible-centric life like Simon Peter. His respect for Scripture is evident and undoubtedly, he could have proclaimed to the Lord, "My heart standeth in awe of thy word" (Ps 119:161).

Early in his Christian experience, Peter learned that a believer's spirituality can be measured by his level of respect and submission to the Word of God. A seemingly natural leader, Peter was accustomed to running his own fishing business, but then, the Lord appeared on the scene. First, the Saviour "prayed him that he would thrust out a little from the land" (Luke 5:3). Although Peter still likely considered himself the skipper of his own boat, he wisely granted his Maker's petition. The Lord then presented him with two commands: "Launch out into the deep, and let down your nets for a draught" (Luke 5:4)! A "word" of petition was one thing, but a "word" of command was another. Now, instead of Peter telling the Saviour what had been done, the Saviour was telling Peter what must be done. The Carpenter was now directing the fisherman, and quick-thinking Peter realized the magnitude of the decision he had to make. The guest on his ship not only wanted to become the captain of Peter's boat, but He also wanted to become the captain of Peter's life as well.

It did not require a high-tech scale to weigh up the pros and cons. Peter had already observed enough in the Lord to trust Him with his soul for eternity, so why would he not trust Him to direct his life? But was Peter willing to let the Saviour guide him with just His Word? Perhaps every fibre of his fisherman's body was screaming at him not to surrender control, but Peter made the right choice. With exuberance, he exclaimed, "Master, we have toiled all the night, and have taken nothing: nevertheless, at thy word I will let down the net" (Luke 5:5). "At thy word" was sufficient reason to navigate his boat towards deeper waters and to surrender the helm of his life over to Christ. And it still is today!

Peter would often hear his Lord repeat the saying, "He that hath ears to hear, let him hear" (Matt 11:15). That day, Peter heard, and he would make hearing the Word of the Lord a priority for the rest of his life. One day, the Saviour was teaching a multitude in the synagogue in Capernaum. Suddenly He said, "There are some of you that believe not" (John 6:64). Witnessing Jesus miraculously provide food for 5,000 men plus women and children convinced many that He could be a source of blessing. Sadly, though, they had only come to view him as a source of physical blessings. So, when the Lord Jesus pointed out their superficiality and His stringent claim that they must surrender and rely entirely on Christ for salvation, many bolted. At that point, the Saviour turned to the remaining disciples and asked, "Will ye also go away?" (John 6:67). Without hesitation, Simon Peter, stepped forward and said, "Lord, to whom shall we go? thou hast the words of eternal life" (John 6:68). Peter understood that the highest authority as to the source of eternal life is the word of Christ.

Inspiration

One day, the Lord Jesus selected Peter as one of the trio of disciples to join Him on the Mount of Transfiguration. Peter later recalled that on that occasion, "...there came such a voice to him [Christ] from the excellent glory, This is my beloved Son, in whom I am well pleased. And this voice which came from heaven we heard when we were with him in the holy mount" (2 Peter 1:17-18). Peter actually heard the voice of God. But would there be anything just as good as God speaking in an audible voice? As Peter remembered the voice on the mountain, he recalled the equally divine promises from God in the Old Testament that predict the future millennial kingdom when the King of Kings will display His glory just as He did on the Mount of Transfiguration. Peter wrote, "We have also a more sure word of prophecy" (2 Peter 1:19). Peter considered the audible word of God, and the more objective written Word of God, to have equal validity and authority.

Peter also listened to the voice of the Lord Jesus during the three years of the Saviour's public ministry. According to Thomas Newberry, about eight years after the ascension of the Lord Jesus, one day at noon Peter went out on the roof of the house of Simon the Tanner in Joppa (Acts 9:43; 10:9). There, as he bowed in prayer, a sheet with all kinds of animals descended three times, and three times Peter heard a voice saying, "Rise, Peter; kill, and eat" (Acts 10:13). Peter recognized that voice and he replied, "Not so, Lord; for I have never eaten anything that is common or unclean" (Acts 10:14). Later, when Peter related that experience to the apostles and brethren in Judea, he explained: "Then remembered I the word of the Lord, how that he said, John indeed baptized with water; but ye shall be baptized with the Holy Ghost" (Acts 11:15-16). The voice of the Lord Jesus speaking on earth and in heaven had equal authority to the word of the Father which Peter had heard on the Mount of Transfiguration.

For Peter, there was another means by which God had revealed truth. Later in his life, he urged believers, "That you should remember the predictions of the holy prophets and the commandment of the Lord and Saviour through your apostles" (2 Peter 3:2 ESV). The Apostolic writings of the New Testament were equally inspired and on par with the Old Testament writings of the prophets. He specifically mentions, "And count the patience of our Lord as salvation, just as our beloved brother Paul also wrote to you according to the wisdom given him, as he does in all his letters when he speaks in them of these matters" (2 Peter 3:15-16 ESV). For Peter, the New Testament writings by the apostles, including the epistles of Paul, were just as inspired and authoritative as "the other scriptures" (2 Peter 3:16).

Peter understood that the written Holy Scriptures were the "Word of the Lord" just as much as the audible words from the Father and the Son. He believed that that the Old Testament and the New Testament originated with God, not with men. As he explained, "...no prophecy of the scripture is of any private interpretation. For the prophecy came not in old time by the will of man" (2 Peter 1:20-21). The process from the mind and heart of God to the printed page transpired when "holy men of God spake as they were moved by the Holy Ghost" (2 Peter 1:21). Peter showed his consciousness of this when he preached and quoted from the Psalms. He said, "Men and brethren, this scripture must needs have been fulfilled, which the Holy Ghost by the mouth of David spake before concerning Judas" (Acts 1:16).

Peter also appreciated that prophets (plural) and holy men (plural) wrote the Scriptures. By contrast, the revered writings in Islam came from the reported revelation to one man – Mohammed. Likewise, the Mormons claim that one man, Joseph Smith, was the recipient of their sacred books. The Old Testament and the New Testament of the Bible contain writings of 40 different authors from all different backgrounds, living in three different continents, and who employed three different languages over a period of 1,500 years. Now that is unique! Having harmony in the writings of one man by himself can be a challenge. Having no contradictions in a collection of many writers who never knew each other, who lived in different places, settings, and times and who wrote in different genres is evidence that "All Scripture is given by inspiration of God" (2 Tim 3:16).

Peter also noted that the writers of Scripture were holy men. So often in history, founders of religions have been morally and criminally suspect. The writers of the Bible were not perfect men, but they were men who were set apart for God. Peter preached about how "God hath spoken by the mouth of all his holy prophets since the world began" (Acts 3:21). Later, he exhorted the readers of his second epistle, "That ye may be mindful of the words which were spoken before by the holy prophets" (2 Peter 3:2).

Peter believed that each of the writers was unique, and that God carefully selected each human instrument so that his background, life experiences, personality, age, culture, writing ability and voice would shine through in his work. And yet these men were not writing their own ideas and they were not in a trance. They all "spake as they were moved by the Holy Ghost" (2 Peter 1:21). They were moved (*phero*), brought or carried along by the Holy Spirit, thus assuring that the written word is truly the inspired Word of God.

Memorisation

Peter and John were not like Paul, who studied at the "feet of Gamaliel". They "were unlettered and uninstructed men" (Acts 4:13, Darby). But either at home or in synagogue school, Peter had somehow learned substantial quantities of Scripture which he could quote from memory. He did not have the Bible on his iPad or a Bible Reading App on his cell phone; he simply knew the Scriptures. How searching!

It was not a case of Peter having learned a few verses from his favourite book, or that he only learned the classic Bible stories as a boy. Paul wrote, "All Scripture is given by inspiration of God, and is profitable" (2 Tim 3:16). Luke narrates how that when the Lord Jesus was walking with the two on the road to Emmaus, "beginning at Moses and all the prophets, he expounded unto them in all the scriptures the things concerning himself" (Luke 24:27). Likewise, Peter appreciated all the Word of God, and, without a Bible in hand, he quoted from the prophets on the Day of Pentecost (Acts 2:16), the Psalms in Acts 1:20; Acts 2:25 and Acts 4:11, and the Law of Moses in his sermon in Acts 3:22. Also, when he recounted his experience with Cornelius, Peter quoted by memory the teachings of Christ. He said, "Then remembered I the word of the Lord, how that he said, John indeed baptized with water; but ye shall be baptized with the Holy Ghost" (Acts 11:16). His quotation of Scripture reflects his reading and memorisation from every part of the Word of God that was available to him at that time - the 17 historical books, the five poetic books, and the 17 prophetic books of the Old Testament, plus the teachings of the Saviour Himself.

Peter did not recite a few random fragments of Scripture from here and there either. At Pentecost, he quoted five verses from the prophecy of Joel (Acts 2:17-21) and four verses from Psalm 16 (Acts 2:25-28). In the temple, he quoted a section of five verses from Deuteronomy 18 (Acts 3:22-23). Later, before the Jewish leaders, he quoted verses from the second Psalm (Acts 4:25-26). Peter undeniably applied himself to the memorisation of Scripture, and he did it in large sections at a time.

Peter not only memorised Scripture, he also understood it as he often links Scriptures together, quoting from multiple places at the same time. For example, in Acts 1:20, he brings together quotes from Psalm 69:25 and Psalm 109:8. At Pentecost, he brings together Psalm 16:8-11, Psalm 132:11, and Psalm 110:1. In the Jewish temple in Jerusalem, he presents Deuteronomy 18:15-19 and Genesis 12:3. He does the same in his epistles. In 1 Peter 2, he quotes Psalm 118:22, Isaiah 8:14, Exodus 19:5-6, and Hosea 1:9-10. In 1 Peter 3, he cites Psalm 34:12-16 (another complete section), followed by a reference to Isaiah 8:12-13. He also draws on his familiarity with Old Testament passages by making references to Old Testament stories and characters such as Noah (1 Peter 3:20), David (Acts 1:16; 2:25-34; 13:36), Balaam (2 Peter 2:15), and Moses (Acts 3:22).

Peter's intentional memorisation turned out to be critical in his own Christian experience. Upon his sin of denying the Lord, "Peter remembered the word of Jesus, which said unto him, 'Before the rooster crows, you will deny me three times'" (Matt 26:75, NKJV). With that, Peter's restoration process began as the Word of the Lord with all its inherent power flooded his heart. It propelled him to repentance as "he went out, and wept bitterly".

The Psalmist appreciated the preventative value of memorised Scripture when he wrote, "How can a young man cleanse his way? By taking heed according to Your word" (Ps 119:9, NKJV). The Lord Jesus parried attacks of temptation from the enemy by three times saying, "It is written". With each temptation, He quoted an appropriate and applicable Scripture from Deuteronomy. He did not need to run to the synagogue to find something in a scroll of Scripture; He already had it in His mind. The day Peter sinned, he experienced the therapeutic value of the word of the Lord through which God worked to bring about his restoration to sweet fellowship and faithful service. So, some searching questions lie in front of each of us: Have I memorised enough Scripture to preserve me from sin? Have I memorised enough Scripture so that the Lord could restore me if I fell?

Evangelisation

John and Peter held mutual respect and they complemented each other in their ministries and writings. John presents the promise of the Lord Jesus, who said, "Verily, verily, I say unto thee, Except a man be born of water and of the Spirit, he cannot enter into the kingdom of God. That which is born of the flesh is flesh; and that which is born of the Spirit is spirit" (John 3:5-6). That is, much like the bones in the valley that Ezekiel witnessed (Ezek 37:1-14). Unless the Spirit is in operation, no soul will pass from death to life. To put it in a positive way, when the Spirit works, souls will be born of the Spirit and receive spiritual life.

Peter, on the other hand, focuses more on the Word of God than on the Spirit of God. He explained that we receive eternal life, "Being born again, not of corruptible seed, but of incorruptible, by the word of God, which liveth and abideth for ever" (1 Peter 1:23). So, is a person born again by the Spirit of God or the Word of God? The answer is, "YES!" There is a blessed harmony in power and effectiveness between the Spirit and the Word. It is much like Paul describing the control and direction of a believer's life. To the Ephesians, he wrote, "...be filled with the Spirit" (Eph 5:18). In a parallel section in the epistle to the Colossians, he wrote, "Let the Word of Christ dwell in you richly" (Col 3:16). So, should we as believers have the Spirit filling us or the Word dwelling in us? Again, the answer is, "YES!" The Spirit guides us to submit to God's will which He has revealed to us in His Word. Therefore, the two are inseparably linked so that the more we know and obey the Word of God, the more control we give to the Spirit of God. Thus, Peter, writing about the role of the Word of God in salvation, is not contradicting John's emphasis on the role of the Spirit of God. For purposes of evangelism, we equally need to preach the Word and yet we must depend on God to convict and illuminate souls by the Holy Spirit.

On the day of Pentecost, Luke tells us that Peter was filled with the Spirit (Acts 2:4). It is not surprising then that in his famous sermon that day, he quoted multiple passages from the Old Testament as the basis for his message. In half of the 22 verses that comprise his sermon, Peter employs quotations from the Psalms and the Prophets. His other public addresses in Acts, especially those directed to Bible-believing Jews, also contain quotes from Scripture.

While Peter was likely a flamboyant preacher, he knew that the key to successful preaching and to seeing souls saved was the Word of God that he quoted and expounded. He had learned the importance of directing souls to Scripture from the Master Evangelist himself. One day, a Jewish lawyer tempted the Saviour by asking, "Master, what shall I do to inherit eternal life?". Jesus' response was, "What is written in the law? how readest thou?" (Luke 10:25-6). He also heard the Saviour confront the Jews by saying, "Search the scriptures; for in them ye think ye have eternal life: and they are they which testify of me" (John 5:39).

So, when the believers in Jerusalem prayed about the evangelism of Peter and the apostles, they asked God, "that with all boldness they may speak thy word". God answered their prayer, and Peter and the apostles, "spake the word of God with boldness" (Acts 4:29, 31). Peter sums up the evangelism of the first souls saved by reminding them that, "the word of the Lord endureth for ever. And this is the word which by the gospel is preached unto you" (1 Peter 1:25).

It is noteworthy that Peter's exemplary preaching to Jews contained a Biblical basis for the message and Biblical quotes with all their living power. The result? "Many of them which heard the word believed; and the number of the men was about five thousand" (Acts 4:4). Peter did the same with the Samaritans. Luke records that Peter and John "testified and preached the word of the Lord" (Acts 8:25). He also did the same with the first Gentile to whom he preached. Peter told Cornelius, "The word which God sent unto the children of Israel, preaching peace by Jesus Christ: (he is Lord of all:) That word, I say, ye know, which was published throughout all Judaea, and began from Galilee, after the baptism which John preached" (Acts 10:36-37). What was the effect of sharing the gospel supported with Scripture? "And the apostles and brethren that were in Judaea heard that the Gentiles had also received the word of God" (Acts 11:1). Therefore, the secret to successful evangelism, whether with Jews, Samaritans, or Gentiles, is to read, quote, and expound the Holy Scriptures because "faith cometh by hearing, and hearing by the word of God" (Rom 10:17).

Peter's belief in the centrality of Scripture in evangelism is instructive for us as believers today. It is so easy to fall into the trap of thinking that eloquence, creativity, humour, charisma, or a quality visual aid is what is going to interest and win souls. May God help us to realize that whether it is a personal conversation, a Sunday School message or public preaching - the reading, repeating, and exposition of the texts of Scriptures is our most important means of having an impact on souls.

Progression

God does not want believers to be stagnant but rather to be dynamic and growing. Peter grasped the concept and the importance of Christian growth which he used like bookends in his collected writings, First and Second Peter. His first epistle begins with the words: "As newborn babes, desire the sincere milk of the word, that ye may grow thereby" (1 Peter 2:2). He ends his second epistle by expressing his great desire for believers: "But grow in grace, and in the knowledge of our Lord and Saviour Jesus Christ" (2 Peter 3:18). Peter was present to hear his Lord speak of the need for growth and fruit as evidence of salvation. He listened to the Saviour present the Parable of the Seed and the Sowers in which the "good ground" hearer brought forth fruit, "some thirty, and some sixty, and some an hundred" (Mark 4:8). He also heard the Saviour's warnings about the unfruitful fig tree that was in danger of being cut down (Luke 13:6-9) and how that "by their fruits ye shall know them [genuine believers and teachers]" (Matt 7:20).

Peter also knew that spiritual growth depends on a steady and healthy diet of the Word of God. The first time I went to Mexico, I found the explanation as to why the Mexican people can eat and enjoy incredibly hot chili peppers. In a gospel meeting one evening, the baby of a young couple sitting beside me began to fuss. After unsuccessfully trying to calm the child in her arms, the mother took a little tube out of her purse, put a little paste on the tip of her finger, and gave it to the infant. Soon the baby relaxed and went quiet. What was the magic paste? To my shock, the words on the tube were: "pasta de chile" (chili paste). Some say it is genetic, but what I witnessed was a mother developing an appetite in her child that would likely remain with him for life.

Peter's appeal in his first letter illustrates this idea of appetite with the metaphor of milk instead of chili: "As newborn babes, desire the sincere milk of the word, that ye may grow thereby" (1 Peter 2:2). He taught that we should develop an appetite for the reading and understanding of the Scriptures so that we miss it when we are not receiving it. While my good Mexican brothers and sisters might debate it, chili is optional for children, but milk is essential for all. Likewise, regularly assimilating the Scriptures is vital for spiritual health and spiritual growth. We ingest the Scriptures through reading, reflection, study, and application to our lives. Honestly then, how much of an appetite do we have for the Word of God? On a scale of 1-10, how much do we crave it, and how much do we miss it when we cannot read it or hear it being read and taught? How strong is our habit of meditating on Scripture? May God help us to learn from Peter and develop a lifelong love and respect for the Bible, and may we always be ready to say as he did, "Master... at thy word I will" (Luke 5:5).

CHAPTER 7
Peter the Fisher of Men

Before you can take Calculus, you must pass the prerequisites of Algebra and Geometry. The fundamental material in those classes forms the basis upon which you can build your understanding of the more complex subjects of Calculus, Differential Equations, and beyond.

In the boat (Luke 5:1-11), and then on the beach (John 21:1-19), the Lord Jesus called Peter and others to His program in which He would make them fishers of men. They may not have realised it at the moment when Christ summoned them to follow Him, but the Master Teacher had just used the illustration of fishing for fish to fill minds with foundational lessons on how to reach souls (Luke 5:1-11).

Often, when facing a mathematical problem later on in life, we err or we forget how to solve it. Sometimes, it is even necessary to take a review course of material we have previously been taught. Welcome to the life of Peter! Even though the Lord had called Peter from fishing for fish to fishing for men three years earlier, Peter had failed miserably. Now, the master teacher had died, and Peter had a family to feed. While there may be grounds to criticize Peter for lacking patience or for being his old impetuous self, the Lord never condemned him for returning to fishing in John 21:1-14. The Lord seems to appreciate Peter's work ethic and leadership skills as six other disciples followed his example and joined him in the boat. Peter's willingness to work and provide for his own needs was later mirrored by Paul. So as not to become a burden to the believers in Ephesus, Paul said, "Yea, ye yourselves know, that these hands have ministered unto my necessities, and to them that were with me" (Acts 20:34). At the same time, the Lord took advantage of Peter being back in the boat, to reteach him many of the elementary lessons that He had impressed on him on that first occasion when He had commanded Peter to follow Him.

The Call of a Fisher of Men

Look at some of the personnel in this team of men: Peter, with his impetuous and unpredictable habit of doing things without thinking, Andrew, who hardly says anything in Scripture and when he does it is usually just a question, and two steam-rolling preachers known as "The sons of thunder" (Mark 3:17). It would hardly be an A-list group for professional evangelism, but as Paul wrote, "God hath chosen the foolish things of the world to confound the wise; and God hath chosen the weak things of the world to confound the things which are mighty; And base things of the world, and things which are despised, hath God chosen, yea, and things which are not, to bring to nought things that are: That no flesh should glory in his presence" (1 Cor 1:27-29). The Lord surprises us in His choice of instruments as He specialises in using undeserving, incapable, and unexpected believers. That way, no one can brag of his gift, knowledge, or charisma. In reality, most believers are unhappy with themselves due to flaws and failures, and God is not content with the way we are either. He chooses us fully knowing our limitations, so that to be useful in evangelism, we must depend 100% on Him. That way, when we catch a fish, He gets all the credit. At the same time, evangelism (catching fish) is just as much a tool that the Lord uses to transform fishers of men as it is to actually catch fish (i.e. see people saved). The process of relying on the Lord to locate lost souls and to save them is the Lord's plan for all of us, not just "full-time" fishers of men. He knows our strengths and weaknesses, yet He still commands all of us to go out with His gospel in dependence on Him and He will look after the rest.

The Convictions of a Fisher of Men

Why He Wants You to Fish

What makes a believer want to go and fish for men? Peter had only one good reason. Based on all his knowledge and experience, it did not seem like the best time, the best place or the best way to catch fish in the Sea of Galilee that morning in Luke 5. However, Peter understood and proclaimed to the Saviour, "Nevertheless, at thy word, I will let down the net". In his lifetime, perhaps Peter had fished for a number of reasons such as to earn money, have the biggest fish story, expand the business, etc. This time, though, the Lord let him struggle all night and come up empty. It was at that point, He told him to go fishing. Once all other motivations were gone, He gave Peter the one true motivation for evangelism – obedience!

Three years later, the whole group of disciples were put in the same position when the Lord was about to ascend back to heaven. They knew that in themselves they did not have power for miracles, they had no formal seminary training in homiletics, nor did they have personal persuasive abilities to convert souls. The Saviour was leaving, and they could only see the dark prospect of falling back to the way things were before Jesus had called them. Sensing their inability, the Lord had them positioned just where He wanted with no reliance on themselves. Precisely at that point, He gave the commission: "Go!" A desire to submit to His will was the only reason for them to become His witnesses in "Jerusalem, and in all Judaea, and in Samaria, and unto the uttermost part of the earth" (Acts 1:8).

Where He Wants You to Fish

Fishing is like real estate; the key is, "Location, location, location!" Peter and his partners had trolled the shoals knowing all the favourite places to find Galilean fish. That night, the Lord let them use every secret they had learned and every lure in their boxes and still there was not one fish in the boat. Perhaps they tried the hotspots that had produced big catches on previous nights, but this time, they did not produce even a minnow. Then the Saviour said to launch out into the deep. Even a rookie fisherman from Galilee would know you don't catch fish in the deep when the sun is out. In the daylight, fish hide along the shoals for protection. Wisely, though, Peter said, "At thy word...", and he rowed out to the deep.

Sometimes an evangelist can see a place that appears to be ideal for fishing for men. Perhaps there is just enough respect for God, people are asking questions, there has been minimal invasion of other religions in the area, there is a great tent site or a building to rent, or even a coffee shop next door for pre- and post- meeting visits. And yet, the evangelist catches nothing. Contrariwise, sometimes it seems like everything is wrong about the place, and the net fills. It is not just happenstance; it is simply the fact that we need to fish for souls where God wants us to fish. In the review course in John 21, the Saviour tested Peter even more specifically by asking him to let down the net on the right side of the boat. Naturally, it might seem pointless because if fish are not on the left side, isn't it logical to assume they won't be 10 feet away on the right side either? Normally it would be illogical, except that if the Lord tells you to do it, do it anyway!

Philip could have put up a real argument with the Lord in Samaria. He had been preaching faithfully there and the net was filling with many souls being saved. Then, suddenly the Lord sent him to the desert. A desert? Really? Yes, "Arise and go toward the south unto the way that goeth down from Jerusalem unto Gaza, which is desert" (Acts 8:26). Wisely, He immediately set out and, in the middle of nowhere, he found an Ethiopian "trophy fish," a man who would be the first to take the gospel to Africa.

Peter never mentioned it, but he could have reminded the Lord that day in Luke 5 that they had already tried to fish in that location before. That was most likely the case in John 21. Sometimes, the Lord wants us to go back to a place where the fish were not biting and we caught nothing. Sometimes, though, a place where we toiled all night and caught nothing can later produce a catch that bursts the nets. The Lord never criticised the fisherman for using their knowledge, experience, and common sense. He only wanted to remind them that having fish in the net does not depend on location or technique, it depends on Him.

How He Wants You to Fish

Clean nets are not a nice option, but a necessary obligation. The Spirit tells us that when the Lord arrived on the beach, Peter and Andrew were "washing their nets" (Luke 5:2). The Lord found James and John "mending their nets" (Matt 4:21; Mark 1:19). These men understood that the Lord takes note of their attention to detail in how they were fishing for fish. An observer might argue, "Who cares how they do it as long as they catch fish?". The answer is that the Lord cares just as much about how we spread the gospel as He does about souls being saved. The mentality that nothing matters as long as people get saved is not Biblical and not the mind of Christ.

The Bible does give us a certain latitude in evangelism as many words are used to describe this work in the New Testament including: to speak (*laleō*), to state boldly (*parrhēsiazomai*), to reason (*dialogezomai*), to proclaim (*kataggellō*), to announce good news (*ĕuaggĕlizō*), to verbally defend (*apologia*), to testify (*martyreō*), and to herald or publicly proclaim (*kērussō*). So, in our evangelism there is Biblical permission for a street meeting, a children's meeting, a gospel meeting, virtual and social media outreach, and personal conversations about the gospel. However, there is no room for moving outside Biblical guidance for evangelism. We must have clean motives and not be deceitful like some are who are involved in evangelism for personal gain. We must also use correct, Biblical, methods to catch men rather than "broken nets" where it appears as if fish are being caught, but then they swim away (false profession). The evangelical world today provides altars at which people can bow, prayers they can recite, cards they can sign, phrases they can repeat, etc. However, the New Testament never records the Lord Jesus or the apostles calling people to the front of a gathering or inviting them to say a "sinner's prayer. Why? These means and methods often lead people to trust the prayer they have repeated or their "going to the front to dedicate themselves to the Lord", rather than leading them to genuine repentance and faith in Christ. Those who use these kinds of methods may be sincere, but they are unknowingly employing broken nets. While some may point to the reports of large number of conversions when these methods are employed, let us never forget that, with God, the ends never justify the means. Results are never a legitimate justification to do things in ways that do not agree with Scripture.

Peter heard the command of the Lord, "Let down your nets" (Luke 5:4), and, "Cast the net" (John 21:6). In Matthew 17:27, the Lord said to Peter, "...go thou to the sea, and cast an hook, and take up the fish that first cometh up". Peter wisely and humbly obeyed the direction of the Master as to whether it should be a net or a hook. We, as well, still need the Lord's direction on our methods to reach souls today. Very clearly, God's primary method is the preaching of the gospel like a herald in a public forum. This is clear in the Great Commission of Mark 16:15 when the Lord commanded, "Go ye into all the world, and preach (*kerussō*) the gospel to every creature". This is the same word in Luke's accounting of the Great Commission when the Saviour said that, "Repentance and remission of sins should be preached (*kerussō*) in his name among all nations, beginning at Jerusalem" (Luke 24:47). So, while we need to be exercised about personally evangelising individual souls (fishing with a hook), we must continue to practice God's primary method and "preach (*kerussō*) Christ crucified" (1 Cor 1:23) and "Preach (*kerussō*) the word" (2 Tim 4:2).

The Confession while Fishing for Men

Some men like Peter have mastered the art and science of fishing. For the rest of us, as an unknown author once said, "Fishing is the sport of drowning worms". We clearly admit that we have no natural ability, nor have we acquired the skills to fish properly. And when it comes to fishing for men, God equally gives both talent and technique. Therefore, both expert and experienced evangelists and all the rest of us are alike dependent on the Lord to catch fish. Peter had to face that uncomfortable reality for the second time in John 21. The Lord timed the question perfectly, "Children, have ye any meat?". A one-word answer, "No," expressed their complete weakness and the clear necessity to depend 100% on the Lord. The result in fishers of men who come to that understanding is that they are then ready both to take instruction from the Master and give Him all the credit when fish enter the net. This is clear when, minutes after the Lord's inquiry, the nets filled to capacity with 153 fish and John cried out to Peter, "It is the Lord" (v. 7). Our confidence must be in Him!

The Cost of Fishing for Men

A good man will give up almost anything for what he believes is important. And Peter did. The Lord could see in Peter a man who was passionate about fishing, so much so, that he was willing to pay a physical price to fish. Peter said, "We have toiled all the night" (Luke 5:5). Toil (*kopiaō*) means to work to fatigue and exhaustion. Peter was also willing to pay the emotional price, as he would work "all the night". God wants people in His great evangelistic work who are willing to "stick at the stuff". He seeks believers who are committed to persevere until the job is done or time is up. Peter was also willing to pay a financial cost, as he would give up his boats, his nets and his business in order to fish for men. James and John were also tested in a similar way. The Lord would eventually teach, "He that loveth father or mother more than me is not worthy of me" (Matt 10:37). Peter was there to observe when the Lord called James and John. Without a second thought, "they immediately left the ship and their father, and followed him" (Matt 4:22). The Lord does not call everyone to full-time fishing as a missionary or evangelist, but He does call every believer to be willing to surrender all to reach souls for Him.

When most people go fishing for fish, they hope the rewards will offset any costs. While for some of us we have yet to experience that reality in physical fishing, it is always true when spiritually fishing for men. In evangelism, the benefits clearly outweigh the expenses. When you see fish in the net, as Peter did in Matthew 4 and in John 21, and when you see a fish on the hook as Peter did in Matthew 17, you immediately want to plan another fishing trip. Likewise, seeing God save a soul will only leave you like Peter: "he was astonished" (Luke 5:9). And the more you see the unique miracle of God saving souls, the more you will want to see Him do it again.

Normally, a fish in a net or a fish on a hook will either become supper or serve as bait for a bigger catch. Spiritual fishing for men, though, is different. You never know what God might do with what looks like a spiritual "throw-back" fish. God is not only in the business of catching fish, He also is interested in turning fish into fishermen. Maybe God will give you the joy of seeing the next George Whitfield or John Wesley saved. Don't limit God as to what He might do through your small evangelistic efforts. Andrew must have stood back on the day of Pentecost as he listened to his brother, amazed that he had been privileged to bring Peter to Christ three years previously. D.L. Moody appreciated the potential of souls so much that he once said there were two and a half souls saved in one of his meetings. Someone asked him if he meant two adults and one child. "No", he said, "Two children and one adult". When a child is led to Christ, a whole life is saved and the potential of how God might use that life is beyond our ability to calculate.

Another sweet recompense for fishing for men is that it provides an opportunity for communion and communication with the Lord. Listen to the following interaction: (Lk 5:4-8) Jesus "said unto Simon" (v.4), "Simon answering said unto him" (v.5), Simon Peter "...fell down at Jesus' knees saying..." (v.8), "and He "said unto them" (Mark 1:17); and the conversation continued as they walked down the beach together. One of the great joys of gospel work is that the Master loves to talk to fishers of men about evangelism. Communion in gospel work is a blessed privilege available to every believer with a heart for souls and an exercise to share the good news.

Fishers of men must be clear that they were once bottom-dwelling, contaminated fish too. One of the keys to proper evangelism is to maintain the Biblical perspective on your own heart. So, before the Lord would call Peter, He gave him a glimpse of divine purity, the high and lofty standard for all men. When Peter witnessed the miracle of Christ filling the nets so abundantly that the nets were stretching and the boats were sinking, he suddenly realized the greatness and holiness of the Lord. Undoubtedly his heart was pounding as he fell to his knees exclaiming, "Depart from me; for I am a sinful man, O Lord"

(Luke 5:8). Right at that moment, Peter understood that "there is no difference: For all have sinned, and come short of the glory of God" (Rom 3:22-23). He never forgot that standard either as he wrote about his Lord, "Who did no sin, neither was guile found in his mouth" (1 Peter 2:22). Effective evangelists must obtain and then maintain an understanding of the holiness of heaven and their own unworthiness to be involved in God's work.

One additional blessing was that, as Peter witnessed the Lord working in the miraculous filling of the net, he grew in his knowledge and appreciation of Christ. That day Peter learned more of Christ's supremacy as they became "labourers together with God" (1 Cor 3:9). Prior to the Saviour filling the nets, Peter saw Jesus as an important man. After seeing the miracle, he called Jesus, "Lord." He understood that Christ was placing a claim upon his life. Three years later, in the "Fishing for Men" review course on the shores of the Sea of Galilee in John 21, "Jesus shewed himself again to the disciples" (v.1). Evangelism provides great opportunities to see the Lord work and get to know Him better. When a soul receives eternal life, it makes you appreciate how great our God is, the only One who can give spiritual life to dead souls. Witnessing God work and the resulting joy in newly delivered souls makes you want to borrow the words of Thomas and declare, "My Lord and my God!". Evangelism would be one of the means by which Peter's final words to believers would be realized: "grow in grace, and in the knowledge of our Lord and Saviour Jesus Christ" (2 Peter 3:18).

The Lord Jesus had promised, "I will make you to become fishers of men" (Mark 1.17). And He did! Over the next thirty years, Peter developed a passion for lost souls, learned to evangelise in proper Biblical ways, and was privileged to see God work. Through it all, his appreciation and love for his God increased as he marvelled at the transformation the Lord had brought about in his life. And Peter was not the last case either. Thank God, He is still making fishers of men today.

CHAPTER 8

Peter the Water-Walker

Faith and difficulties are not mutually exclusive. The Bible does not teach that, as a believer, you either live by faith or you face trials. Instead, faith and trials are complementary, working together for our good and God's glory.

Circumstances and Faith

Our faith is often like a weak bone that will only be strengthened by putting weight on it. Wisely and caringly, the Lord allows circumstances in our lives to fortify our faith in Him. Peter and the disciples found themselves on the Sea of Galilee. In fact, this time, Jesus "made the disciples get into the boat and go before him to the other side" (Matt 14:22). Therefore, it is a complete falsehood that a Christian who has enough faith will not go through difficulties or trials. Look at the list of the men and women of faith in Hebrews 11, plus many others who "were tortured...And others had trial of cruel mockings and scourgings, yea, moreover of bonds and imprisonment: They were stoned, they were sawn asunder, were tempted, were slain with the sword: they wandered about in sheepskins and goatskins; being destitute, afflicted, tormented;...they wandered in deserts, and in mountains, and in dens and caves of the earth" (Heb 11:35-38). Look at Paul who said he was "in prisons more frequent, in deaths oft. Of the Jews five times received I forty stripes save one. Thrice was I beaten with rods, once was I stoned, thrice I suffered shipwreck, a night and a day I have been in the deep; In journeyings often, in perils of waters, in perils of robbers, in perils by mine own countrymen, in perils by the heathen, in perils in the city, in perils in the wilderness, in perils in the sea, in perils among false brethren; In weariness and painfulness, in watchings often, in hunger and thirst, in fastings often, in cold and nakedness" (2 Cor 11:23-27). Of course, the clearest example is "Jesus, the leader and completer of faith" (Heb 12:2, JND) who "endured the cross" and who "endured such contradiction of sinners against himself"(Heb 12.2-3). If the perfect man with perfect faith experienced trials, the notion that true believers will be exempt from trials if they have enough faith is both absurd and blasphemous. Peter himself faced at least three imprisonments and he wrote to believers to whom he said, "You have been grieved by various trials" (1 Peter 1:6, NKJV).

Turbulent experiences in life are often allowed and employed by the Lord as instructional tools. Sometimes He even allows similar or repeat experiences to reinforce our faith. Peter and the disciples had previously faced contrary winds, sea swells and dark clouds on the Sea of Galilee in Matthew 8:23-27. The experiences were similar when the 12 disciples faced two fierce storms on the same Sea of Galilee. In Matthew 8:26, Jesus "arose, and rebuked the winds and the sea; and there was a great calm". This time, "he got into the boat with them and the wind ceased" (Mark 6:51). Did the Lord not repeat a test of their faith in the similar feedings of multitudes of 5,000 and 4,000 respectively? The similarity and the repetition of experiences in life are intended to reinforce our reliance on God much like a muscle being strengthened through repeated exercise.

There were also differences between the two experiences on the Sea of Galilee. The first time, they doubted Jesus' care for them as He was with them in the boat, but "was asleep" (Matt 8:24). From their perspective, they were in a crisis, and the Lord was not doing anything about it. This time, they were also in a crisis, but the Lord appeared to be absent. On the first occasion, the Lord was with them. This time, He was not even there. What the disciples should have learned in the first experience was that the Saviour was caring for them even though He was not doing what they thought He should be doing. This time, they could not see Him as Jesus "went up on the mountain by himself to pray...alone" (Matt 14:23). They could not hear Him talking to His Father as they struggled in the storm. The lesson was that even when the Lord seems still or absent, His heart and His abilities remain unchanged. If He is the object of our faith, we must learn to evaluate trials from the starting point that He is the Immutable, the Almighty, "the only wise God" (Rom 16:27, Darby) who loves us — always!

These trials were not random coincidences, but instruments in the hand of God to mold and fortify their faith. Peter came to appreciate this great truth as he wrote "to the pilgrims of the Dispersion in Pontus, Galatia, Cappadocia, Asia, and Bithynia" (1 Peter 1:1). He said to them, "That the trial of your faith, being much more precious than of gold that perisheth, though it be tried with fire, might be found unto praise and honour and glory at the appearing of Jesus Christ" (1 Peter 1:7). God is constantly at work in our lives to remove the dross of unbelief and to make Christ-like faith shine in us like a precious metal.

Components of Faith

Faith is mentioned frequently in sermons and yet it is still a foggy notion to many. Here are three common errors that contribute to the confusion on this key Biblical truth:

- "Faith is an emotion".

  To most, "having faith" amounts to a feeling of serenity or confidence that something he or she desires will come to pass. The degree of calmness and positivity is equated to the amount of faith a person possesses. The focus is on the feeling. Therefore, I could have faith I am going to heaven and equally have faith that my dog will turn into a tomato in the morning. This concept of faith allows for both the serious and the absurd because it all depends on the feeling within a person created by any combination of physical, environmental, and mental factors.

- "Faith is a percentage game".

  The more I believe something, the greater the likelihood that it will be true or come to pass. Whether or not there is little reason, facts, or evidence to support the belief, is irrelevant. This error is manifest in statements like: "I have a lot of faith that I am going to pass this exam". Or, "I really believe she is going to get saved in these gospel meetings".

- "Faith is a crowbar".

  If I believe something and state my belief confidently, it will leverage God to respond and make what I believe come to pass. This idea is especially common in the charismatic movement where believers are taught to "name it and claim it". If their faith is sufficiently strong, it will be irresistible for God, and He will be forced to respond. Therefore, if a person has enough faith that their uncle Mel will be healed from colitis, God must work, and Mel will be well. Without consideration of all the teaching in Scripture on faith and prayer, they will support this erroneous thinking by using Biblical language such as "I have all faith, so that I could remove mountains" (1 Cor 13:2).

Biblical faith is very distinct, and Peter understood the difference. Warren Wiersbe, in his commentary on Hebrews entitled, "Be Confident", says that "True Bible faith is not blind optimism or a manufactured 'hope-so feeling'". He goes on to give the following definition: "True Bible faith is confident obedience to God's Word in spite of circumstances and consequences". This is more like the concept of faith upon which Peter operated and which the Saviour encouraged.

The Object of Faith

Sixteen specific spiritual heroes are mentioned in Hebrews 11 and all of them share the common denominator of depositing their trust in God. Knowing the attributes of God, they saw every reason to respond with reliance upon His person, His power, and His promises. So, as

Peter looked out over the stormy seas and felt the gusty wind, he knew that there was not even surface tension on the choppy waters to hold him up if he stepped out of the boat. Before he even expressed faith, he wisely said, "Lord if it is you..." (Matt 14:28). Peter had come to know Jesus enough to appreciate His omnipotence. Only a person with divine essence would be worthy of His trust in this matter.

The Basis of Faith

Mr. Wiersbe identified a key component in true Biblical faith:- "God's Word". Another common denominator to all the great models of faith in Hebrews 11 is the role the Word of God in their decisions and actions. For example, Noah built an ark because he was "warned of God", and Abraham went to the land of promise because "he was called" (Heb 11:7-8). Peter not only focused on the person of the Lord Jesus, he also said, "Command me to come to you on the water" (Matt 14:28). Faith does not occur based on favorable circumstances or a notable inner feeling of peace. It is based on the bedrock of divine revelation. So, just because the Lord can make something come to pass, that is not sufficient basis to exercise faith. Peter understood that in addition he must consider the Lord's will. Unless there was clear direction indicating that it was the Saviour's desire for him to walk on the water, he should not attempt it. Thus, he only swung his legs over the side when he heard Jesus say, "Come" (Matt 14:29).

The Response to Faith

Faith is the answer of obedience to the word of the Lord. Just knowing who God is and knowing what God wants is not faith. Heaven and earth admire the faith Abraham displayed on the mountain in Moriah as he prepared to sacrifice his son. Three times, the New Testament comments about him that "Abraham believed God" (Rom 4:3; Gal 3:6; James 2:23). The object of his faith was the eternal, Almighty God. The basis of his faith? "He that had received the promises offered up his only begotten son" (Heb 11:17). He was operating upon divine revelation. And, on the mountain that day, God commended Abraham's faith by saying, "thou hast obeyed my voice" (Gen 22:18).

Faith, then, is not the means to avoid trials nor is it something we exercise only when circumstances seem favourable towards the outcome we desire. Moses and the Israelites appeared to be trapped in a dead-end canyon. With the Egyptians closing in behind them, they had walls of rock on each side and the Red Sea in front of them. There appeared to be no escape route in any direction. So, how did they walk on dry land to the other side of the Red Sea? They had to believe in God, the only one who could make it possible. They responded with obedience when God gave them the command to march forward.

Peter understood that faith and obedience are inseparable concepts. He described unbelievers "which stumble at the word, being disobedient" (1 Peter 2:8), unsaved husbands "who obey not the word" (1 Peter 3:1), and the multitudes in Noah's day "who formerly were disobedient" (1 Peter 3:20, NKJV). Peter's general description of unsaved souls became evident in his question, "What shall the end be of them that obey not the gospel of God?" (1 Peter 4:17). While "unbeliever" is a word found often in Paul's writings, Peter prefers "disobedient" which emphasizes that it is an act of the will to not respond to the person of God upon the basis of His revealed Word. John captured that sentiment in the classic gospel text, John 3:36: "He that believeth on the Son hath everlasting life: and he that believeth not the Son shall not see life; but the wrath of God abideth on him". "Believeth not" in this verse is not the same Greek word (*pisteuō*) found in the first part of the verse with the negation provided by the prefix "a" (i.e. *apisteō*). Instead, it is the word *apeitheō* which means, according to Mounce: "to be uncompliant...to refuse belief and obedience". Thus, when the Lord Jesus gave the command to Peter to come to Him on the water, with confidence in the ability of Christ, he obeyed immediately. That was an act of faith.

Completion and Faith

Peter once witnessed the Lord suspend the Laws of Physics and

Chemistry when He turned water to wine. He also saw Him suspend the laws of nature when He calmed the winds and waves on the Sea of Galilee. He knew that the Law of Reproduction was suspended when the Son of God was conceived of a virgin. He even observed Him suspend the Law of Death when Jesus raised Jairus' daughter back to life (Matt 9:25). Now, he was witnessing the Lord suspend the Law of Gravity as He walked on the water. As Peter watched the stunning miracle unfold from his seat in the boat, he certainly could appreciate the deity and ability of the Son of God. However, what would make him think that he, a mere man, could do the same? Was his interest sparked only by curiosity? Or was it his carnal, competitive spirit propelling him to try and be one-up on all the other disciples?

Peter may have reflected in that moment upon the miracles the Lord had already done through him. He would remember the day on the shore of the Sea of Galilee when he had fished all night but had not caught a guppy. But when the Lord commanded him, "Launch out into the deep, and let down your nets for a catch" (Luke 5:4), Peter obeyed. That day he learned that the Lord would keep his promise and make "the catch" happen even if it required a miracle. He would also remember the day on the mountain when Jesus commanded His disciples by saying, "Heal the sick, cleanse the lepers, raise the dead, cast out devils" (Matt 10:8). They would be able to achieve these results because Jesus had "called unto him his twelve disciples, [and] he gave them power against unclean spirits, to cast them out, and to heal all manner of sickness and all manner of disease" (Matt 10:1). Therefore, Peter learned in his Christian experience, that the Lord never gives us a command without providing the means to accomplish it. Obediently, the disciples completed their commission and "they cast out many devils, and anointed with oil many that were sick, and healed them" (Mark 6:13). Thus, Peter admirably waited to hear the command of his Master. Peter even said, "Lord, if it is You, command me to come to You on the water" (Matt 14:28). Naturally, it was ridiculous to think Peter could defy gravity and walk on water. However, he trusted that if the Lord directed him to do it, he could depend on the Lord to make it possible.

This principle seems to have characterised Simon Peter as there were many things the Lord would do Himself which He would also make possible for Peter to do the same. Jesus "healed all that were sick" (Matt 8:16). Later, when Peter and the other disciples were in Jerusalem, people were "bringing sick folks, and them which were vexed with unclean spirits: and they were healed every one" (Acts 5:16). The Lord Jesus raised dead people such as the widow of Nain's son, Jairus' daughter, and His friend Lazarus. When Tabitha got "sick, and died" (Acts 9:37), Peter prayed and then "presented her alive" (Acts 9:41). Jesus spoke of Himself as opening doors as He said, "I have the keys of hell and of death" (Rev 1:18). He also said to Peter, "I will give unto thee the keys of the kingdom of heaven" (Matt 16:19). And on that stormy night on the sea, not only "Jesus went unto them, walking on the sea" (Matt 14:25), Peter [also] was come down out of the ship, [and] he walked on the water, to go to Jesus" (Matt 14:29).

Despite all these parallels between what Christ did Himself and what He did through Peter, there was one time when that was impossible. At the cross, only Christ could pay for our sins. Peter expressed this succinctly and humbly when he wrote about his Saviour "Who his own self bare our sins in his own body on the tree" (1 Peter 2:24). No one else was qualified and the Lord Jesus could not give authority or ability to anyone else to provide redemption. While the Lord Jesus could do many things through His disciples and even make Peter walk on water, the old hymn says it best: "Jesus alone, Jesus alone, Jesus alone can save".

Challenges to Faith

The human evaluation of Peter is astonishment – he actually walked on water! The divine evaluation was, "O thou of little faith, wherefore didst thou doubt?" (Matt 14:31). What happened? The Lord did not say, "O thou of no faith!". Unlike the other disciples, Peter had at least demonstrated faith. The problem was that his faith was short-lived.

The challenge of occupation

Focus is a key to faith. When Jesus came walking on the water towards the little boat, "the disciples saw him walking on the sea" (Matt 14:26), their eyes were locked on the Saviour. Peter maintained that focus as he conversed with the Lord and slipped over the side taking steps towards his Master. "But when he saw the wind boisterous...[he was] beginning to sink" (Matt 14:30). His focus wandered from the capabilities of the Lord Jesus to the circumstances around himself. Every honest believer reads those words and must humbly confess, "Been there, done that". The struggle when facing difficulties, pain, sadness, worries, uncertainties, etc. is to keep "Looking unto Jesus" (Heb 12:2). That was Moses' secret when it came to the history-changing decisions he made because he was "seeing him who is invisible" (Heb 11:27). He kept his focus on "the blessed and only Potentate, the King of kings, and Lord of lords; Who only hath immortality, dwelling in the light which no man can approach unto; whom no man hath seen, nor can see" (1 Tim 6:15-16). Obviously, we cannot physically lay eyes on the Lord Jesus, but mental and spiritual focusing are separate matters. Peter longed to encourage believers who had been exiled and scattered around five Roman provinces in Asia Minor. Recently, they had been uprooted from their communities and likely many were distanced from families. Peter speaks positively of their focus in trials as he spoke of Jesus Christ, "Whom having not seen, ye love; in whom, though now ye see him not, yet believing, ye rejoice with joy unspeakable and full of glory" (1 Peter 1:8). May the Lord help us not to let the awfulness of a situation distract our focus from being upon Him.

The challenge of emotion:

True faith is based on what we know, not what we feel. It is hard to trust when we are led about by our emotions. This happened to the disciples as a group. They were obediently headed across the Sea of Galilee when the storm descended. And when the Lord Jesus came towards them "they were troubled, saying, It is a spirit; and they cried out for fear" (Matt 14:26).

That happened as well when Peter, at the command of his Lord, started to walk on the water. "But when he saw the wind boisterous, he was afraid; and beginning to sink, he cried, saying, 'Lord, save me'". Very quickly, Peter went from fear to faith to fear. The Lord Jesus, the perfect man of faith, never felt fear. We normally feel afraid due to the uncertainty of a situation or when we sense our inability. The Lord Jesus, though, was never lacking knowledge or ability. Even on the cross, where was the emphasis of the Lord Jesus? His first and last words reveal His focus: "Father, forgive them" and, "Father, into thy hands I commend my spirit" (Lk 23:34, 46). Unlike the Saviour and more like us, Peter let emotion take over and he began to sink. Certain personalities, like that of Peter, are more prone to be led by feelings. However, all of us need to learn to let God be our guide rather than our emotions.

The challenge of timing:

Sometimes, if we are honest, we get frustrated with the Lord because He does not do what we think He should. In the first storm, the disciples looked at the still and sleeping form of Jesus and they said, "Master, carest thou not that we perish?" (Mk 4:38). Their question dripped with criticism as they jumped to the narrative that Jesus was not doing anything because He did not care. On this occasion, the night was dark, and the wind was pounding their faces. Time seemed to pass in slow motion as heaven waited to intervene until "the fourth watch of the night [when] Jesus went unto them, walking on the sea" (Matt 14:25). The Lord prayed on the mountain from dusk until sometime between 3:00am and 6:00am in the morning. Why? Often, we find it easier to trust God's word than we do to trust God's timing.

Think of the number of great men and women of God who had to wait upon the Lord. Abraham knew he would be the father of many nations, but he would not have Isaac until he was 100 years old. Moses knew he would function as redeemer in Egypt, but he would not be allowed to execute his role until he was 80 years old. Jesus knew He would be the Saviour of the World, but He waited through 4,500 years of human history, 30 years of life in Nazareth, and then an additional three years of public ministry until He would die on the cross. This experience was part of Peter's training as he would have to wait on the coming of the Spirit until Acts 2, and wait on the Lord for the use of the keys for the opening of stages of the evangelistic commission. He also knew he would die as a martyr, but he had to wait decades on the Lord's timing for that to occur. May God help us to be encouraged. If impetuous Peter learned through these trials to be patient and wait for God's timing, perhaps we can too. May we take the words of the Psalmist to heart: "Wait on the Lord: Be of good courage, and he shall strengthen thine heart: Wait, I say, on the Lord" (Ps 27:14). Peter never regretted waiting for God's timing and we won't either.

The Consequences of Faith

Faith builds upon the exercise of faith. How did Abraham have enough faith to trust God in what he thought was going to be the sacrifice of his son Isaac? God tested Abraham's faith on that occasion, and it proved to be already strong and developed. Previously, he had exercised faith when he left his homeland for the Promised Land. He had exercised faith in the battle with the kings to bring back Lot who had been captured. Clearly, Abraham´s life was a dot-to-dot of faith exercises. He learned the principle that trusting God in one experience will prepare us for greater trust in more difficult experiences ahead. The events on the sea were preparatory trials for even greater displays of faith on the land. One day Peter would preach a classic sermon to over 3,000 souls on the Day of Pentecost while trusting God for eternal results. Then, he would trust God to protect him as he preached the gospel even though the governing authorities had threatened him with consequences if he did. Later he trusted God to help him explain to Jewish Christians why he was preaching the gospel to Gentiles.

Faith produces greater faith, but it also generates adoration for the Lord: "Then they that were in the ship came and worshipped him, saying, Of a truth thou art the Son of God" (Matt 14:33). The New Testament speaks repeatedly of "the faith of Abraham" (Rom 4:16). Therefore, we should not find it surprising to read as well of Abraham building altars. He even came to view challenges and trials as opportunities to worship. In fact, when "God tested Abraham" (Gen 22:1, NKJV), Abraham responded in faith and obedience. At the same time he said to the servants, "I and the lad will go yonder and worship" (Gen 22:5). Abraham learned that the exercise of faith produces expressions of worship. So, when Peter operated on faith, even though it was small, it produced worship in him and others. This link is most clearly seen at the cross when the Lord Jesus expressed faith by saying, "Father, into thy hands I commend my spirit: and having said thus, he gave up the ghost." (Luke 23:46). And in so doing, He "through the eternal Spirit offered himself without spot to God" (Heb 9:14).

Faith in trials also allows for greater and closer communion with the Lord. Notice the progression in the proximity of the Lord Jesus. First, "he went up into a mountain" (Matt 14:23) while "the ship was... in the midst of the sea" (Matt 14:24). Then we read, "Jesus went unto them" (Matt 14:25). When Peter began to sink, the Lord drew even closer as "Jesus stretched forth his hand and caught him" (Matt 14:30-31). Finally, "they were come into the ship" (Matt 14:32). The Lord's knowledge of their situation, His care for their welfare, and His ability to work in their lives were not increased by His drawing near to them. It was their appreciation of Him that grew and that is what happens in trials. Like the young men in the fiery furnace, they appreciated the one like unto the Son of Man who was with them. Many believers look back on times of suffering and trials and they would not want to go through them again. And yet, the unmistakable enjoyment of the Lord's presence and closeness in a trial is something you always cherish.

CHAPTER 9

Peter the Debtor

"Everyone says forgiveness is a lovely idea, until they have something to forgive."

C.S. Lewis

The Context

Jesus was addressing interpersonal relationships in His spiritual kingdom. He recognized that, while all subjects under His reign would profess to be saved, they would continue to have a sinful nature actively working inside them. The flesh within would remain just as vile as before they were saved and would continue to be as wicked as the flesh in those who were not part of His kingdom. He understood that our sinful nature inclines us toward selfishness and stubbornness rather than sensitivity and consideration of others. Paul later identified over 15 specific "works of the flesh" (Gal 5:19-21) of which at least eight relate to interpersonal relationship problems (e.g. rivalries, dissensions, divisions, etc.). With that horrific potential wrapped up inside every Christian, Jesus taught, "It must needs be that offences come" (Matt 18:7). While offenses and sin among subjects in His kingdom would be inexcusable, they would also be inevitable.

In Matthew 18, the disciples challenged Jesus as to who would be "the greatest in the kingdom of heaven". This question follows two events in Matthew 17: The Mount of Transfiguration and the paying of the temple tax. As to the Mount of Transfiguration, Jesus selected only three disciples to go up with Him to see His majestic display of millennial glory. Although not mentioned, one wonders, "Did this in any way lead to a sense of pride in Peter, James and John or any feelings of jealousy in the other nine disciples because the Lord did not select them for that privilege? As to the paying of the temple tax, when tax-collectors approached Peter, they asked, "Doth not your (plural) master pay tribute?" (Matt 17:24). They addressed Peter on behalf of all 12 of the disciples. Again, it is not mentioned, but is there a possibility that this experience generated a feeling of superiority in Peter since he alone would catch the famous fish with the coin in its mouth? Perhaps as many as six others of "the 12" were also fisherman and yet they did not get to go fishing. Was there a competitive spirit in any of them resulting in jealousy?

The Saviour used the disciples' question over the qualifications for greatness in Christ's kingdom to address interpersonal relations. He knew they would not be the only disciples through the ages that would struggle with pride, self-pity, jealousy, covetousness, lust, envy, anger, etc. Thus, He first addressed the possibility of a believer offending others (Matt 18-1-14) and then the possibility of others sinning against a believer (Matt 18:15-35). The order of the two sections is intentional and significant. Before I concern myself with how others are treating me, I need to first consider my treatment of others. The teaching in this chapter seems to have left an indelible imprint on Peter. When he penned his first epistle he instructed believers to "love one another with a pure heart fervently" (1 Peter 1:22; 4:8), to "Use hospitality one to another" (1 Peter 4:9), to "minister the same one to another" (1 Peter 4:10), to "be subject one to another" (1 Peter 5:5) and to "Greet...one another" (1 Peter 5:14). He also uniquely uses the word "brotherhood" (*adelphotēs*) when he wrote, "Love the brotherhood" (1 Peter 2:17), and "your brotherhood in the world" (1 Peter 5:9). While he did struggle with selfishness at times, Peter clearly developed an appreciation for the Christ-like mindset of thinking of others first.

Then, Jesus used a child in all its defencelessness and vulnerability as an illustration of new or less mature believers. He first explained that all must enter His kingdom with humility and without the presumption of rights, just like children. He then balanced that teaching by warning about taking advantage of new or less mature believers as they are susceptible to being stumbled in their Christian lives and hindered in their Christian growth. His warning was strong. Rather than causing offence, it would be better to go swimming in deep water with a large upper millstone necklace which would make you sink like a stone. This extreme form of death penalty was employed by "ancient Syrians, Romans, Macedonians, and Greeks. It was inflicted on the worst class of criminals, especially on parricides (one who murders his or her mother, father, or near relative), and those guilty of sacrilege." (The New Manners and Customs of the Bible). However, the Lord Jesus used this to underline the repugnance of heaven at the deception, misleading, or damaging of vulnerable believers in the Kingdom of Heaven.

Therefore, citizens of His kingdom should have a zero-tolerance policy for sin in their own lives and equally seek to avoid provoking offense or sin in others. A desire to avoid stumbling others was the motivation for the Lord Jesus when it came to paying the temple tax. While He, being the Son of God, was exempt from the tax used for His Father's house (the temple), He did not insist on His right, but paid the tax so as not distract others or give cause for stumbling on spiritual matters (Matt 17:24-27). In Matthew 18, the Lord Jesus went on to confirm that Heaven notices when one believer is led astray by wrong teaching or treatment. And if offense occurs, we are to be like Christ who, with a shepherd's heart, pursues the recovery of straying believers (Matt 18:11-14) just as He seeks the salvation of lost souls (Luke 15:4-7).

Most believe that Peter was Mark's primary source of information when he wrote his Gospel. The first time we read of Mark was when Peter was released from prison and "he came to the house of Mary the mother of John, whose surname was Mark; where many were gathered together praying" (Acts 12:12). Mark was a promising young man whom Paul and Barnabas took with them on their first missionary journey. It started well, but then likely Mark began to struggle with the concept that Gentiles were being saved just like Jews. As a result, he abandoned Paul in Asia Minor (Perga in Pamphylia) and returned to Jerusalem (Acts 13:13). This led Paul to view Mark as being unqualified for evangelistic service and refuse to take him with him on his second missionary journey. Scripture tells us, though, that Barnabas differed with Paul on the matter and he chose to work with Mark following that incident. However, Peter's final commentary on Mark comes at the end of his first letter when he conveyed greetings from specific believers including "Marcus my son" (1 Peter 5:13). Being his father in the faith, undoubtedly Peter played a role in the encouragement, instruction, recovery and development of John Mark. As such, Peter demonstrated a little of the shepherd-heart of Christ when Mark stumbled.

In Matthew 18, Jesus addressed both the possibility that I could stumble others and that others could sin against me. Notice that when it comes to how others treat me, I am only to be concerned if someone actually sins against me. But as to my treatment of others, He spoke of "stumbling" others. Stumbling includes sinning plus anything else I might do or say to hinder, discourage or cause another believer to go astray from the teaching of Scripture. In other words, the standard is higher for my treatment of others which includes sacrificing what is within my rights, but not doctrinally essential. I am to develop that kind of sensitivity and be willing to make that level of sacrifice. But, when it comes to others toward me, Jesus only spoke about actual sin. He said, "Moreover if your brother sins against you ..." (Matt 18:15, NKJV). In that case, He provided a three-step process to try and win my brother (Matt 18:15-17).

In Matthew 18:15-20, Jesus taught that we must face sin, and in Matthew 18:21-35 He taught that we must forgive sin. He was not setting out a buffet of options from which we can choose. In the first section on facing sin He commands, "... go and tell him" (Matt 18:15). In the second, He said, "Should you not also have had compassion on your fellow servant" (Matt 18:33, NKJV). "Should you not" has the sense of being obligatory: "of that which one should do" (BDAG).

When Peter sinned, the Lord Jesus both faced him and forgave him. Luke tells us that when Peter denied the Lord the third time, "Immediately, while he was still speaking, the rooster crowed. And the Lord turned and looked at Peter. Then Peter remembered the word of the Lord" (Luke 22:60-61). Practicing what He preached, upon Peter's sin, the Lord confronted him with the intent to win Peter back to fellowship and usefulness for God. Also, as a repentant Peter remembered the word of the Lord and "went out, and wept bitterly" (Luke 22:62) and the Saviour forgave him.

What led the Lord Jesus to teach on forgiveness that day was Peter's question, "Lord, how oft shall my brother sin against me, and I forgive him? till seven times?" (Matt 18:21). Peter was trying to be both humble and generous, but he was not humble and generous enough. He anticipated the need and requirement to offer forgiveness which was commendable. He also knew that the standards of Christ were higher. Surely, he would remember the Sermon on the Mount in which Jesus said, "For I say unto you, That except your righteousness shall exceed the righteousness of the scribes and Pharisees, ye shall in no case enter into the kingdom of heaven" (Matt 5:20). The scribes in Peter's day taught that forgiveness was mandatory up to the third occurrence of the same sin. Taking that into account, Peter more than doubled their standard by proposing a forgiveness limit of up to seven times (the number of completeness and perfection).

The Challenge

The Lord Jesus responded with heaven's standard by declaring, "I say not unto thee, Until seven times: but, Until seventy times seven" (Matt 18:22). He was not suggesting that Peter keep a score card and gleefully anticipate passing from 489 to the final occurrence at number 490. His point was that there should be no limitation to the availability of forgiveness based on the repetition of a sin or the total number of sins.

Certainly, the Lord Jesus was taking Peter and the other disciples back to Genesis. When Cain sinned by killing his brother and the Lord God pronounced a curse on him, He balanced it by saying, "Whosoever slayeth Cain, vengeance shall be taken on him sevenfold" (Gen 4:15). The Old Testament begins with a promise of seven-fold vengeance upon anyone who killed Cain. Five generations later, a wicked descendant of Cain called Lamech killed an opponent who he claimed "wounded" him. He then arrogantly declared that he could make a better promise than God's for the killing of Cain. He said, "If Cain shall be avenged sevenfold, truly Lamech seventy and sevenfold" (Gen 4:24). What a contrast between the use of both the number seven and the number four hundred and ninety. Man has a twisted, unlimited threshold for vengeance, while the Lord Jesus has a transcendent, unlimited threshold for grace.

To explain forgiveness to Peter, the Lord Jesus told a parable which he introduced by saying, "The kingdom of heaven is likened unto a certain king, which..." (Matt 18:23). The king in the story was intended to illustrate the King who was speaking. The story-king had principles upon which his physical kingdom operated which paralleled the principles upon which Christ's spiritual kingdom operates.

The first principle was that of justice - the king "would take account of his servants" (v.23). Matthew, the former tax collector, uniquely uses the word meaning "to settle" (Matt 18:23, 24; 25:19). In the end, the books of heaven will be balanced, and every sin will receive a corresponding punishment because "the wages of sin is death" (Rom 6:23). With God, the punishment always fits the crime, so punishment will never be given without just cause. That also means that no sin will ever be overlooked. Peter wrote, "The Lord knoweth how to deliver the godly out of temptations, and to reserve the unjust unto the day of judgment to be punished" (2 Peter 2:9). He also wrote that all who sin "will give an account to Him who is ready to judge the living and the dead" (1 Peter 4:5, NKJV).

Jesus went on to tell in the story how, "one was brought unto him, which owed him ten thousand talents" (v.24). Upon hearing this number, Peter's jaw must have dropped. The Master had selected a massive number to illustrate a person's debt of sin.

Alexander the Great marched his troops east with his eyes on the prize of becoming King of all Asia. With one victory after another, he eventually approached Persia itself where King Darius III was awaiting the ominous arrival of the future world emperor. Just as Daniel had interpreted King Nebuchadnezzar's dream (Dan 2), the gold head of Babylon and its empire was long gone. It had been replaced by the Medo-Persian Empire pictured by the silver chest and arms of the large image. Now it was time for the bronze stomach and thighs, the Grecian Empire. In an attempt to save his own life, ransom the royal family which Alexander had already captured, and to save at least some of his dwindling kingdom, Darius III wrote up his proposal and sent it to Alexander the Great. He offered to pay 10,000 talents - the value he placed on his kingdom.

In the book of Esther, hatred for the Jews was consuming Haman. His diabolic animosity for God's people fuelled his scheme to eliminate all Jews from the face of the earth. To put his plan in motion, he had to obtain approval from King Ahasuerus. So, he prepared his slickly worded proposal and sugar-coated it with a stupendous offer of money. The king's coffers had likely dwindled recently due to funds being directed toward military battles, so Haman knew that the offer of funds would be hard for the king to refuse. Thus, upon being granted permission to stand before his majesty, Haman explained, "If it please the king, let it be written that they may be destroyed: and I will pay ten thousand talents of silver to the hands of those that have the charge of the business, to bring it into the king's treasuries" (Esth 3:9). To Haman, 10,000 talents was the value of a whole race of people.

In John 6, five thousand men plus women and children gathered to hear Jesus teach. Soon, as stomachs began to growl, Jesus sent his disciples to find food for everyone. Surveying the situation, Philip, one of the disciples, said, "Two hundred denarii worth of bread is not sufficient for them, that every one of them may have a little" (John 6:7, NKJV). While it was deemed not sufficient, if we allow that 200 denarii would have fed 5,000 people, and the commonly recognized currency value that 6,000 denarii equalled one talent, that means 10,000 talents would be enough money to buy food for 1.5 billion people.

At the time of Jesus, a denarius was the wage for one day of work (Matt 20:2). Since 6,000 denarii equalled 1 talent, the servant in the parable owed 60,000,000 days of work. Assuming a six-day working week (honouring the Sabbath), the average person would work 312 days per year. That means, this servant owed the equivalent of 192,307 years, 8 months, 1 week and 1 day worth of work – a truly astounding amount!

The Condition

Jesus' choice of this number was extreme, but not an exaggeration to describe Peter's sin – and ours. As for the quantity of our sin, we have no idea of the volumes of the detailed celestial record which John saw in his vision where "the dead were judged out of those things which were written in the books, according to their works" (Rev 20:12). And we equally lack the ability to evaluate the repulsiveness and offensiveness (i.e. the quality) of our sins against God. Job never claimed that he was perfect, but after God dealt with him and made him see a little of his prideful heart, Job exclaimed, "I abhor myself, and repent in dust and ashes" (Job 42:6). Likewise, when Peter compared himself with the holy and divine standard of the person of the Lord Jesus, he cried out, "Depart from me; for I am a sinful man, O Lord" (Luke 5:8). Like Peter, every person who receives God's forgiveness comes to appreciate the awfulness of both the quantity and quality of their sins before God.

In the Bible, forgiveness is prepared in the heart, but can only be received and enjoyed upon repentance. Peter had heard the Lord Jesus teach the need for repentance among believers when He said, "If thy brother trespass against thee, rebuke him; and if he repent, forgive him. And if he trespass against thee seven times in a day, and seven times in a day turn again to thee, saying, I repent; thou shalt forgive him" (Luke 17:3-4).

Also, when the Lord Jesus commissioned Peter and the other disciples, He said, "that repentance and remission of sins should be preached in his name among all nations, beginning at Jerusalem" (Luke 24:47). Thus, Peter preached to Jews, "The God of our fathers raised up Jesus, whom ye slew and hanged on a tree. Him hath God exalted with his right hand to be a Prince and a Saviour, for to give repentance to Israel, and forgiveness of sins" (Acts 5:30-31). Later, to Gentiles he equally proclaimed, "that everyone who believes in him receives forgiveness of sins through his name" (Acts 10:43).

In the Parable, then, upon hearing of his immense debt, the servant humbly states, "Lord, have patience with me, and I will pay thee all" (Matt 18:26). The condition of genuine repentance appeared to be met when the servant spoke of both personal responsibility ("I will pay") and total responsibility for his debt ("all"). He did not present any excuses, justifications, or disputes over what he owed. The servant appears genuinely to agree completely with the king and that is true repentance. Whether sinner or saint, repentance is not feeling sorry that we got caught (like Judas), but rather a full acceptance of God's viewpoint about our debt of sins and the punishment we deserve for them.

The Cost

The Lord Jesus went on to say that "the lord of that servant was moved with compassion, and loosed him, and forgave him the debt" (Matt 18:27). Forgiveness always has a price tag, and someone has to absorb the cost. The principle the Saviour taught that day was - the one who pardons, pays. Peter could recall the time when four friends brought a paralyzed man to Peter's house and Jesus said to him, "Man, thy sins are forgiven thee" (Luke 5:20). Peter knew that the One who pardoned the paralytic would have to pay. And when he looked in the mirror and considered his own sins, he could equally appreciate that the One who forgave him would have to pay his debt as well. Not surprisingly, then, Peter often includes himself when he refers to the suffering and sacrifice of the Lord Jesus. He wrote, "Christ also suffered for us" (1 Peter 2:21) and, "Who his own self bare our sins in his own body on the tree" (1 Peter 2:24), and that He is "our Saviour Jesus Christ" and "Jesus our Lord" (2 Peter 1:1-2). And today, we, as forgiven sinners, can express our immense gratitude in the words of Elvina Hall:

> "And when, before the throne,
> I stand in Him complete,
> "Jesus died my soul to save,"
> My lips shall still repeat.

Jesus paid it all,
All to Him I owe;
Sin had left a crimson stain,
He washed it white as snow".

The Concept

D. L. Moody once said, "Forgiveness is not to bury the hatchet with the handle sticking out of the ground, so you can grasp it the minute you want it". And, "Forgive and forget" is not a biblical principle either. The Lord Jesus never has and never will forget that Peter denied Him. Even more, Peter once said, "Lord, thou knowest all things" (John 21:17). As the Omniscient One, God cannot forget our debt of sin. However, what He does promise is that "their sins and iniquities will I remember no more" (Heb 10:17). That means that upon forgiving Peter for having denied Him three times, the Saviour never raised the point again. Upon forgiveness, the debt had been resolved and the issue would never be resurrected – ever! Thus, the apostles and even Peter never spake of his denial from that point forward. Therefore, what is true in the vertical forgiveness that we have received from God, should also be true in the horizontal forgiveness we extend to one another.

The Contrast

In the parable, the servant who was offered forgiveness, immediately went and found a man who owed him 200 denarii. It is interesting that the Lord did not use the amount of two mites, the two small copper coins the widow put in the temple offering (Mark 12:42). Had He done that; it might have indicated that He did not think sins of one citizen in His kingdom against another are not that serious. In this chapter, He had already taught that interpersonal sin is so grave that it can even result in the need to be disciplined and removed from church membership (Matt 18:17). Thus, the Saviour selected an amount that conveys His viewpoint that sins against one another are both offensive and hurtful.

Sadly, though, the servant confronted the man and grabbed him by the throat. The word Matthew used to describe this action is the same word Mark used to describe what happened when Jesus cast out the legion of demons in the man of Gadara. On that occasion, "the unclean spirits went out, and entered into the swine: and the herd ran violently down a steep place into the sea...and were choked in the sea" (Mark 5:13). The servant made this man feel like a drowning pig. Incredibly, even when the fellow genuinely repented and used the exact same words, "Have patience with me, and I will pay thee all" (Matt 18:29), the servant still "would not [forgive]: but went and cast him into prison, till he should pay the debt" (Matt 18:30).

The Lord Jesus concluded the parable by directly addressing Peter's question about how often he should forgive if his brother repeatedly sinned against him. The Saviour told how the king "was wroth, and delivered him [the unforgiving servant] to the tormentors, till he should pay all that was due unto him" (Matt 18:34). Jesus then added the broad warning, "So likewise shall my heavenly Father do also unto you, if ye from your hearts forgive not every one his brother their trespasses" (Matt 18:35). Was Jesus suggesting that God will take sinners whom He has forgiven and cast them into hell? Never! Salvation cannot be lost as Jesus Himself said, "him that cometh to me I will in no wise cast out" (John 6:37). Just as in the parables of the wheat and the tares (Matt 13:24-30) and the good and bad fish in the net (Matt 13:47-50), Jesus was teaching about the danger of profession without reality. The king had offered forgiveness to the servant, but, in the end, the servant's obsession and pursuit of vengeance provided full proof that he had never genuinely repented and thus had never received forgiveness.

When Paul described the works of the flesh that reside in every believer, he also warned that, "those who practice such things will not inherit the kingdom of God" (Gal 5:21). While sin can occur in a believer, the habitual practice of sin with seemingly little conscience is the common attitude and behaviour of people who are not saved. John agreed as he wrote, " No one born of God makes a practice of sinning" (1 John 3:9, ESV). In the parable, the Lord was not focusing on a person habitually sinning, but rather habitually holding a grudge and being unwilling to forgive. Therefore, one of the evidences of a person having truly received the forgiveness of sins from God is that he will then be able to forgive others. The opposite is also true. Professing Christians who refuse or are not able to forgive are potentially giving evidence that they have never truly received the forgiveness of their sins by the Lord. Peter likely recalled that, in the Sermon on the Mount, the Lord Jesus gave the disciples a model for prayer that included the statement: "And forgive us our debts, as we forgive our debtors" (Matt 6:12). Jesus also added: "For if ye forgive men their trespasses, your heavenly Father will also forgive you: But if ye forgive not men their trespasses, neither will your Father forgive your trespasses" (Matt 6:14).

Peter learned that day that God expected him not to put a limit on the number of times he would forgive his brother. The motivation and ability to offer such forgiveness would come from a constant and deepening appreciation for the forgiveness he had received for his own sins. As Paul wrote, "Be ye kind one to another, tenderhearted, forgiving one another, even as God for Christ's sake hath forgiven you" (Eph 4:32). The impact of the Lord's teaching was not lost on Peter either. Focusing more on the attitude that lends toward a forgiving spirit, Peter wrote, "And above all things have fervent love for one another, for 'love will cover a multitude of sins'" (1 Peter 4:8, NKJV). In this verse, Peter quoted the words of Proverbs 10:12 to show that true love will demonstrate itself in the response of a believer when someone has sinned against him. It is interesting that "the Hebrew verb for 'covers' is sometimes used in the Old Testament to mean 'atone' for (Ex 29:36), 'forgive' (Ps 32:1), 'appease' (Prov 16:14)" (Louw-Nida). Combining that commentary with the text, Peter the Debtor appears to have learned a great lesson: love will enable us to forgive an endless number of sins — again, and again, and again.

CHAPTER 10

Peter the Eyewitness

Mark Twain once said, "Nothing ruins a good story like the arrival of an eyewitness". Matthew, Mark and Luke were inspired reporters who told the amazing story of the day when Jesus took Peter, James and John up to a high mountain, known as the Mount of Transfiguration. There, the Lord would be transformed before them and display His glory just as He will be when He returns to earth to establish His Kingdom. Later, Peter picked up his pen to write his second epistle. He was not just another writer who would relate the story he had investigated to the best of his ability. Peter said that on that day, "we...were eyewitnesses of his majesty" (2 Peter 1:16). Peter would not ruin the story told by the three evangelists. Instead, he would confirm every detail giving us confidence in the accounts of the gospel writers.

Consciousness of Grace

This is the only time this word "eyewitness" (*epóptes*) is found in the New Testament. Thayer says it refers to a spectator and BDAG gives it as having "first-hand acquaintance with something, with implication of special privilege". This word was known by Greeks to describe the highest mysteries of the Eleusinian religious cult. The few advanced members in the cult who had supposedly experienced the revelation of the highest secret mysteries, were called "*epóptes*". Peter was not claiming he had had a vision in a drug-induced state. He and James and John were real eyewitnesses who "saw...Jesus" (Matt 17:8; Mark 9:8). Luke adds that they "saw his glory" (Luke 9:32). In addition to providing ocular testimony, Peter provides auditory testimony by saying, "we heard" the voice from heaven. With that real and unforgettable experience etched forever in his mind, Peter wrote, "For we did not follow cleverly devised myths when we made known to you the power and coming of our Lord Jesus Christ, but we were eyewitnesses of his majesty" (2 Peter 1:16, ESV). What a privilege given by our gracious Lord!

This was one of three occasions that we know of when the Lord selected Peter, James, and John for a special honour. The other two were when He took the three men to witness the raising of the daughter of Jairus and when He called the same three apart to witness His intense agony in the Garden of Gethsemane. This was not a case of favouritism, but of divine favour. The Lord was not showing partiality, but He was giving undeserved privilege. The disciples must have come to view it that way too. While they did argue over the places they would have in the coming Kingdom, not one of these three men claimed priority because they had been chosen to be eyewitnesses of the transfiguration of Christ. Grace allows no room for bragging, nor does grace allow room for envy and competition. Selection for privilege was by grace, therefore there were no grounds for complaint or conceit. For example, Andrew could have complained that James and John were brothers, so why couldn't he go up the mountain since he was a brother to Peter? While none of the three ever claimed superiority because of this experience, none of the other nine disciples ever whined about not being chosen to witness this unique event either. Yes, Peter does speak 15 times of the essential glory of Christ, or Christ being glorified by God and man. At the same time, Peter also writes of grace 10 times in his epistles. His last recorded words in the book of the Acts are, "But we believe that through the grace of the Lord Jesus Christ we shall be saved, even as they" (Acts 15:11). His last recorded words in Scripture are, "But grow in grace, and in the knowledge of our Lord and Saviour Jesus Christ. To him be glory both now and forever. Amen" (2 Peter 3:18). So, when God gives us privilege, it should make us humble and thankful. When God gives privileges to others, it should make us equally grateful and in awe of His grace.

Contemplation of Glory

Matthew says that Jesus' "face did shine as the sun, and his raiment was white as the light" (Matt 17:2). The sun is the brightest, constant light in the sky. Mark has us look at the ground as he records (likely from Peter's testimony) that Jesus' "raiment became shining, exceeding white as snow" (Mark 9:3). If they were on the highest mountain in Israel, Mount Hermon, it is usually covered with pristine snow. Luke records that Jesus' "face was altered, and His robe became white and glistening" (Luke 9:29). The NASB provides the footnote that glistening means "flashing like lightning." Lightning is a blinding light that runs across the heavens and it also runs from earth to sky and from sky to earth. Comparing His glory with the brightest whites in heaven, on earth and between heaven and earth, the purity of Christ outshines them all.

The three synoptic writers use the greatest and brightest "whites" God made to try to explain the radiance of the glory of Christ. Mark searches for the brightest white that man can produce. He describes Jesus' clothes as being bright "such as no launderer on earth can whiten them" (Mark 9:3, NKJV). Every writer stretches to compare the radiance of the glory of the Lord Jesus to the most extreme things in their experience. About thirty years later, Peter simply describes what he saw as the "excellent glory" of Christ. Excellent, as it excelled everything made by God and man; excellent, as it excelled everything in the heavens above and the earth beneath. Truly, His glory is majestic, a glory that is out of this world.

Some modern scholars believe that the Eleusian mysteries were secrets "to elevate man above the human sphere into the divine and to assure his redemption by making him a god and thus conferring immortality upon him". If that were true, then it was just a Greek version of Satan's promise in the Garden of Eden, "ye shall be as gods" (Gen 3:5). The Mount of Transfiguration, though, had nothing to do with the majesty of a man becoming a god. Peter and his fellow-disciples must have stood in awe as they realized the sublime truth - God had become a man.

Veiled in flesh, the Godhead see;
Hail, the incarnate Deity:
Pleased, as man, with men to dwell,
Jesus, our Emmanuel!

John shared that clear impression as he wrote, "the Word was made flesh, and dwelt among us, (and we beheld his glory, the glory as of the only begotten of the Father,) full of grace and truth" (John 1:14). Only when we are personal eyewitness of His glory will we be able to appreciate more fully the tremendous miracle of the veiling of His effulgence when "he was made in the likeness of men" (Phil 2:7).

That day, Peter witnessed a metamorphosis that was far more memorable and beautiful than any caterpillar transforming into a butterfly. Matthew and Mark report that "he was transfigured before them" (Matt 17:2; Mark 9:2). The Greek word "transfigured" is *metamorphaō* which gives us our English word *metamorphosis*. It is a compound word made up of *meta*, implying change, and *morphe*, form. It is not a change produced by an outside force, but an inward reality being brought to external manifestation. Paul confirmed this as he wrote about Christ: "For in him dwelleth all the fulness of the Godhead bodily" (Col 2:9). Therefore, Peter and his friends did not see the Lord Jesus become something new, but rather radiating out what He already was.

It certainly appears that the transformation of Christ that day impacted the three witnesses greatly and created in them a longing to have more of the moral character of Christ in themselves. That is what seeing the glories of Christ always does. John looked forward in his writings to the dramatic transformation that awaits us because "when he shall appear, we shall be like him; for we shall see him as he is" (1 John 3:2). Paul, who saw the same blinding glory of Christ on the road to Damascus; wrote to the Corinthian Christians that even now God has begun the slow transformation of our character. How? "And we all, with unveiled face, beholding the glory of the Lord, are being transformed into the same image from one degree of glory to another. For this comes from the Lord who is the Spirit" (2 Cor 3:18, ESV). As we behold Christ in the Scriptures, the Spirit slowly brings more Christlikeness into our lives. Peter showed with enthusiasm that we need not wait until the rapture to begin to experience a transformation of character. Toward the end of his life, likely Peter was reflecting back on the change God had produced in him when he wrote that God has given unto us "all things that pertain unto life and godliness" (2 Peter 1:3). The promises and instruction of the Word of God open up the possibilities for a transformation by the Spirit from the inside out so that we "might be partakers of the divine nature" (2 Peter 1:4). We will never be God, but the Lord longs to work in us even now to make us "to be conformed to the image of his Son" (Rom 8:29).

Completeness of the Gathering

The scene on the Mount of Transfiguration was a major meeting point. The first arrivals came from the bottom of the mountain when "Jesus took with him Peter and James and John" (Mark 9:2). Then, from Heaven "behold, there appeared unto them Moses and Elias talking with him" (Matt 17:3). So, when the Lord Jesus would be transformed and display His glory, two witnesses from heaven and three witnesses from earth would be there to see it. This would meet the divine standard for something to be unquestionably true which was that "in the mouth of two or three witnesses every word may be established" (Matt 18:16). This unique moment when Christ manifested His glory as the eternal Son of God and the King of glory would be indisputable in heaven and on earth. The witnesses present would represent the Old Testament with the law (Moses) and the prophets (Elijah), as well as the New Testament (Peter and John). All Scripture unitedly establishes the present and future glories of Christ.

The Mount of Transfiguration also was the meeting place of men from both sides of death. Peter, James and John were alive. Moses and Elijah had already left this world: Moses by way of death (Deut 34:5) and Elijah by way of a whirlwind that took him up to Heaven (2 Kings 2:1). At that scene, there were living saints, a saint who died, a saint who was raptured, and the eternal Son of God. It was a mini conference picturing the brief time when only believers will be on earth after the arrival of the King of Glory at the beginning of His millennial rein. The raptured church (pictured by Elijah) will be there as Paul said, "When Christ, who is our life, shall appear, then shall ye also appear with him in glory" (Col 3:4). At the same time, the 144,000 Jewish witnesses and all other true believers who have survived the horrific seven years of Tribulation judgments will be welcomed alive by Christ into His Kingdom just as He had escorted Peter, James and John to that millennial mountain scene. Also, Moses, who had gone through death, would represent Old Testament saints (Dan 12:2) and Tribulation martyrs (Rev 20:4) who will be brought to life at the resurrection of the just so they can join in the glorious establishment of the Millennial Kingdom.

But this was not a conference of equals. Mark tells us that the three disciples were "with him [Christ]" (Mark 9:2), and the two Old Testament worthies were "with Jesus" (Mark 9:4). This was not a conference like the one in Jerusalem in Acts 15 where equal minds met to discuss and decide a spiritual matter. All five men were privileged to be "with him."

In his coming Kingdom, it will be amazing to be united with New Testament and Old Testament heroes of the faith as well as family and friends. However, the greatest joy will be just to be "with him". Scripture gives us the guarantee that even if we die, "them also which sleep in Jesus will God bring with him" (1 Thess 4:14). In the millennium, we will witness the Creator eliminating diseases and developing agriculture such that there will be "corn in the earth on the top of the mountains" (Ps 72:16). We will stand in awe as "Behold, a king shall reign in righteousness" (Isa 32:1) and "we shall also reign with him" (2 Tim 2:12).

It is equally thrilling to notice who was not at the Mount of Transfiguration – Satan! He was permitted to be at the temptation of Christ (Matt 4:1-11), in the Garden of Gethsemane (John 14:30), and at the cross (Gen 3: 15; Heb 2:14; Col 2:14-15). John, in the Revelation, saw that the Lord Jesus "laid hold on the dragon, that old serpent, which is the Devil, and Satan, and bound him a thousand years, And cast him into the bottomless pit" (Rev 20:2-3). Just as it was on the mountain that day, for 1,000 years, Christ will reign in righteousness with no Satanic attempts to impede His purposes and oppose His glory.

This gathering also provides insight and answers to a number of questions about the future. Clearly, like Moses and Elijah, we will not experience soul-sleep after death. We will maintain our identities, enjoy consciousness, and be fully able to communicate even though our bodies will go to dust in the graves of earth. We know that Moses died, and his body was left on earth. When he and Elijah appeared on the mountain with Christ, Luke says they were "two men" (Luke 9:30). They were not just generally identifiable as human beings, but their gender is also noted as they were men (*aner*). Yes, Jesus taught that after the resurrection believers will "neither marry, nor are given in marriage; but are as the angels which are in heaven" (Mark 12:25), but that refers to a ceasing of marriage relationships, not to the removal of gender. In addition, there were no introductions recorded, so they were not nameless, faceless, generic spirits. Just like the living disciples, the two who appeared from heaven were distinguishable to the human eye by their being (human), gender (men), and the unique features of their personhood (Moses and Elijah). The rich man in Hell and Abraham and Lazarus in Luke 16, no longer had bodies after death either, and they did not lose any of their uniqueness or identity. This should settle questions and worries about what we will be like after death, resurrection or the rapture. We will be transformed and morally "we shall be like him" (1 John 3:2). As Peter himself wrote, truly we have a "lively hope by the resurrection of Jesus Christ from the dead" (1 Peter 1:3). Physically, we will have bodies "like unto his glorious body" (Phil 3:21). So, while you should never be content with failure and flaws in your life, be thankful for your personality. God made you unique and He plans to keep you as you forever.

Commitment of Gaffes

In Matthew's gospel, there are seven mountain scenes with Christ: Matt 4:8 – a mountain of temptation; 5:1 – a mountain of teaching;

14:23 – a mountain of prayer; 15:29 – a mountain of healing; 17:1 - a mountain of transfiguration; 24:3 – a mountain of prophecy; 28:16 – a mountain of commission. The Saviour graciously included at least some of the disciples by allowing them to share with Him on five of those seven significant experiences. But privilege itself is never a protection from failure. If we ever think that because we are in the assembly or being used of God we are exempt from failure, we are greatly mistaken.

Peter was full of energy and did everything with gusto – including sleeping. Later in Gethsemane, the same three would be found "sleeping for sorrow" (Luke 22:45). Also, Peter, enjoying the peace of knowing God was in control, would be found "sleeping between two soldiers" in the prison (Acts 12:6). On the Mount of Transfiguration though, Luke, the physician notes that "Peter and they that were with him were heavy with sleep" (Lk 9:32). He would miss much of seeing the agony of Christ in the garden and miss the glory of Christ here in the mountain. Clearly, we have been damaged by sin and perhaps Christ allowed them to sleep to show, as J.C. Ryle said in his Expository Thoughts on the Gospels, "Our physical constitution must be greatly altered before we could enjoy heaven". Because of our limitations, we equally need divine enablement to enjoy the glories of Christ just as much as we do to resist the temptations of sin and Satan. We need to recognize that our human limitations do not naturally incline us towards spiritual discernment and activities. Thus, Paul wrote to the Romans, "...now it is high time to awake out of sleep: for now is our salvation nearer than when we believed" (Rom 13:11).

To Peter's credit, he understood the significance of the Feast of Tabernacles, the annual Jewish Festival to celebrate the glorious kingdom of the Messiah. However, Peter spoke, "not knowing what he said" (Luke 9:33). At the same time, Mark says, "They were terrified!" (Mark 9:6). When a lack of information and understanding intersects with a surge of emotion, watch out! The wise man warned, "Be not rash with thy mouth, and let not thine heart be hasty to utter any thing before God" (Eccl 5:2).

Thinking about the Feast of Tabernacles, Peter went on to say, "Let us make three tents, one for you and one for Moses and one for Elijah" (Mark 9:5 ESV). What a mistake! Excitement and enthusiasm clouded his comprehension and his expression. What an insult to the Lord to be put on the same level as Moses and Elijah. Peter had to relearn the lesson that in all things Christ must have the pre-eminence (Col 1:18).

Communication of His Greatness

There was a complete group on the mountain: three disciples, two Old Testament saints, the Lord Jesus, and the Father who was also observing. Seven is a number of totality, so the event was a complete revelation and confirmation of the person of Christ.

Moses, on Mount Sinai (Ex 34:6), and Elijah, on Mount Horeb (1 Kings 19:11) had both had an experience of wonder when "the Lord passed by". They recognized that they were in the presence of the Supreme and glorious Sovereign of the universe. But, at the Mount of Transfiguration, Peter showed his ignorance and failed to distinguish Christ from the prophets. Despite Peter's failure, while "he was still speaking" (Matt 17:5) the cloud surrounded them. The failure of a saint will never stop the purposes of God. We are told, "behold, a bright cloud overshadowed them" (Matt 17:5). This was undoubtedly the pillar cloud; the *shekinah* glory of Jehovah which Peter would see again on a different mountain. After His resurrection, the Lord Jesus ascended to heaven from the Mount of Olives "and a cloud received him out of their sight" (Acts 1:9). When Solomon built the temple, "the cloud filled the house of the Lord, So that the priests could not stand to minister because of the cloud: for the glory of the Lord had filled the house of the Lord." (1 Kings 8:10-11). Similarly, Peter described the cloud on the mountain that day as "the excellent glory" (2 Peter 1:17). The cloud "overshadowed them". They were not now observing the presence of God from a distance that Moses had witnessed on Mount Sinai, they were submersed in the outshining of the glory of God.

In confirmation that it was the presence of God, "a voice came out of the cloud" (Mark 9:7). The Father was about to speak about His Son. First, He put His divine approval upon the Lord Jesus as He had at His baptism by saying, "This is my beloved Son" (Matt 17:5; Mark 9:7). Some modern translations see a difference in Luke's recording of the voice which said, "This is my Chosen one" (Luke 9:35, NASB, HSCB, ESV). Peter remembered the event more specifically and records that the Father said, "This is my beloved Son, in whom I am well pleased" (2 Peter 1:17). God never spoke of Moses, Elijah or any other man as His Son, the Chosen One, and the One who fully pleased Him. To further the distinction, the Father added, "Hear him!" He did not say, "Hear them!" As the writer to the Hebrews said, "God, who at sundry times and in divers manners spake in time past unto the fathers by the prophets, Hath in these last days spoken unto us by his Son" (Heb 1:1-2). Putting the word of any angel, man, woman, church or organization on equality with the word of Christ would be an insult to His Sonship and glory. The challenge Peter would face for the rest of his time on earth would be to keep his ear attuned strictly to the words of his Lord. Yes, he would soon lose focus and listen to the words of a young maid leading to his denial of Christ and later to the voices of men who confused Judaism with Christianity (Gal 2). With a Peter-like tendency toward distraction and loss of focus in all of us, may every believer take to heart personally the command of the Father on the Mount of Transfiguration, "Hear ye him!"

Coming in His Grandeur

Peter does not focus much on the rapture in his preaching and writing. He knew he was not going to be raptured, as the Lord had said, "... when thou shalt be old, thou shalt stretch forth thy hands, and another shall gird thee, and carry thee whither thou wouldest not" (John 21:18). He would leave this world like Moses rather than like Elijah. Prior to the Mount of Transfiguration experience, the Lord had said, "Verily I say unto you, There be some standing here, which shall not taste of death, till they see the Son of man coming in his kingdom"

(Matt 16:28). So, when Jesus on the beach in John 21 predicted Peter's death, Peter did not question whether he would "see the Son of man coming in his kingdom" as the Lord had promised. Why? Because he had already seen the glory of the Son of Man that will radiate from Him when He comes to set up His Millennial Kingdom. So, Peter was not focused on escaping earth's problems and persecutions, but rather on the glorious, future revelation of Christ at His coming. Thus, Peter later wrote to believers expressing great anticipation and confidence in the coming Kingdom. He said, "For thus shall the entrance into the everlasting kingdom of our Lord and Saviour Jesus Christ be richly furnished unto you" (2 Peter 1:11, J N Darby).

Peter wrote about "the revelation of Jesus Christ" (1 Peter 1:7), "when his glory is revealed (1 Peter 4:13), and "the glory that is going to be revealed" (1 Peter 5:1). As Peter penned his last words, he looked out beyond the executioner's block and sword, beyond the persecution of believers and the building by Christ of His church and he says, "To him be glory both now and to the day of eternity. Amen" (2 Peter 3:18, J N Darby). Rome would flex its muscles and reveal its power and glory by silencing the voice of God's servant Peter. That would be a mere speed bump on the road to the global kingdom of Christ his king. Peter likely never forgot the promise of Christ who said, "When the Son of man shall sit in the throne of his glory, ye also shall sit upon twelve thrones, judging the twelve tribes of Israel" (Matt 19:28).

Peter preached with passion and conviction about the future. Nothing for him was foggy or "iffy" about God's plans for our world. To over 3,000 Jews he proclaimed, "The times of refreshing shall come from the presence of the Lord; And he shall send Jesus Christ, which before was preached unto you: Whom the heaven must receive until the times of restitution of all things, which God hath spoken by the mouth of all his holy prophets since the world began" (Acts 3:19-21). For Peter, the Mount of Transfiguration was a mental Mount of Transportation to the future of Christ on earth. As a result, he then lived the rest of his days longing for the return of the Son of Man to earth as he and the others had seen Him go in Acts 1. "Restitution" is the word *apokatastasis* (*apo*, "back, again," *kathistemi*, "to set in order) and Peter employs this word in his sermon in Acts 3 to describe the Millennium. Christ's coming will bring about, as Mounce describes it, "the renovation of a new and better era". Thayer says the coming of Christ in glory will produce "the restoration not only of the true theocracy but also of that more perfect state of (even physical) things which existed before the fall". But it will also be a time of refreshing, *anapsuxis*, which Vine says refers to as "obtaining relief". BDAG says the earth will enjoy the "experience of relief from obligation or trouble, breathing space". The Dictionary of Biblical Languages says it will provide "relaxation from burdensome circumstance". It is hard for us to imagine what creation will be like during the Millennium with the Creator here on earth. Creation's groan will turn to joy and the world will know prosperity and peace as it has never known before.

The transfiguration experience took place on a high mountain. Traditionally, Mount Tabor has been labelled as the Mount of Transfiguration. However, "The unnamed location was probably a southern ridge of Mount Hermon (ca. 9,200 feet) about 12 miles northeast of Caesarea Philippi (cf. 8:27; 9:30, 33). This is preferable to Mount Tabor in Galilee" (Bible Knowledge Commentary). The event recorded in Matthew, Mark, and Luke prior to the Transfiguration is the confession of Peter which took place at Caesarea Philippi at the foot of Mount Hermon. Therefore, it is reasonable to consider Mount Hermon as the high mountain where the Transfiguration took place.

Peter does not call it a high mountain, but rather "the holy mount" (2 Peter 1:18). The Transfiguration and what it prefigures stand out in the plans of the Almighty. Its occurrence on the high and holy mountain reminds us of the exalted and lofty place the coming of Christ will have in the Divine program of the ages. Dr. David Jeremiah writes, "In the Old Testament, Christ's return is emphasized in no less than 17 books and the New Testament authors speak of it in 23 of the 27 books. Seven out of 10 chapters in the New Testament mention His return. In other words, one out of every 30 verses in the New Testament teaches us that Jesus Christ is coming back to this earth. The Lord Himself referred to His return 21 times." (https://davidjeremiah.blog/the-second-coming-of-christ). Therefore, this was a pinnacle experience in the life of Peter. As an eyewitness, he saw and heard a little of what we will witness in what could be as little as seven years from now. At that time, Christ will return in glory to the Mount of Olives to set up His kingdom and we will "be glorified with him" (Rom 8:17). Then, along with Peter and all other saints, we will eternally praise the Almighty, "the God of all grace, who hath called us unto his eternal glory by Christ Jesus" (1 Peter 5:10).

CHAPTER 11

Peter the Servant

Peter and the twelve disciples had only one thing written in their agendas – Passover. The night before the sacred Jewish festival began they sat in the upper room of a house in Jerusalem witnessing the Lord Jesus operate in three different roles.

- Jesus, the consummate Priest (John 17)

  Hearing the Lord pray had to be one of the highlights of Peter's time with the Master. That night, he listened to Him referencing all His activities for the good of others (glorify, manifest, give, pray, come, keep, speak, send, consecrate, desire, know, etc.). He is the Great High Priest always seeking the blessing of God's people.

- Jesus, the consummate Prophet (John 14-16)

  Peter listened to Jesus speak being the great Prophet of Jehovah that Moses had promised (Deut 18:18). In these three chapters, the Saviour uses two verbs a total of 22 times in ways such as "I have spoken" or "I have said". The Son of God is the great Prophet who was speaking both for God and as God.

- Jesus, the consummate King (John 13)

  Rehoboam suddenly found himself sitting on the throne. The people of Israel were peppering him with questions as to what his policies were going to be and how he would treat the citizens of Israel. In his bewilderment, Rehoboam consulted with older men. Their advice was, "If thou wilt be a servant unto this people this day, and wilt serve them, and answer them, and speak good words to them, then they will be thy servants for ever" (1 Kings 12:7). Those wise gentlemen understood what the attitude and approach of a godly king should be. If he were to be the best servant he could be, he would become the best king he could be. A true leader does not see others working for his good, but rather he sees himself working for the good of others. So, when Peter and the disciples saw the Lord of Glory washing their feet like a humble slave that evening in John 13, they must have realized that they were in the presence of the King of Kings.

As the Saviour confidently and determinedly mounted the stairs to the upper room, the 12 disciples wearily dragged their feet behind Him. They thought they were going there to celebrate Passover, and they were. However, little did they know that they were about to hear intercession by the perfect Priest (Ch. 17), receive instruction from the perfect Prophet, and see a living illustration of service from the perfect King. Tired and hungry, they took their places looking forward to eating with their Master.

But, before the Saviour would fill them with food, He would load them up with homework. He was about to share His recipe for a full and blessed life.

Ingredient 1: Holiness

The Lord Jesus waited for the perfect moment. Right when the disciples were focused on food, Jesus stood up, walked toward the basin at the entrance and took off His outer tunic. He then took the towel lying there and tied it around His waist just as a household slave would do. Then, He filled the basin with water and moved from disciple to disciple washing the dust off their feet. When He came to Simon Peter, Peter muttered incredulously, "Lord are you going to wash my feet?" (v.6 HSCB) Peter couldn't wrap his head around it. Was the one Peter had called, "the Christ, the Son of the living God" really going to stoop down and clean his filthy feet? The Lord Jesus said, "What I do thou knowest not now; but thou shalt know hereafter" (v.7). In that moment, Peter may not have grasped it fully, but later he would understand as he reflected on this unforgettable object lesson. That night, the Saviour taught him, and the others, about the contamination we pick up simply from moving about in a sinful world. This was not so much a lesson about personal sin and failure, but about the subtle pollution that infiltrates our minds and hearts in everyday activities.

Absence

The first lesson Peter learned was that no record is given that night of the Lord Jesus or anyone else washing the feet of the Saviour. On a previous occasion, the Saviour went into Simon the Pharisee's house, and He tried to reveal Simon's pride to him (Luke 7:36-50). A sinful woman had entered and bathed the feet of the Saviour with her tears, kisses and with expensive ointment. By contrast, He pointed out to Simon, "Thou gavest me no water for my feet". There, where the lesson was about appreciation and devotion, Jesus allows for the possibility that He had dust on His feet. It certainly would not be sinful if He did have.

However, in the upper room, the lesson was about spiritual contamination. Therefore, there is not the slightest implication, much less a mention, of the Saviour's feet and the need to wash them. Of course, there was no consideration of a whole-body cleansing for Christ either. Peter got it! He made it very clear when he described the Lord Jesus in his first epistle as one "Who did no sin, neither was guile found in his mouth" (1 Peter 2:22). He certainly appreciated that the Saviour picked up no contamination in life and even in death. In his first sermon in Acts 2, he quoted the words the Lord Jesus could say: Psalm 16: "For thou wilt not leave my soul in hell; neither wilt thou suffer thine Holy One to see corruption". He learned from the upper room illustration that the Lord Jesus was "holy, harmless, undefiled, separate from sinners" (Heb 7:26). Neither defilement nor death could ever pollute the mind and heart of the "just" one (1 Peter 3:18).

Assurance

The second lesson became clear when Peter went from a question to exclaiming, "Thou shalt never wash my feet". The Saviour then explained, "If I wash thee not, thou hast no part with me". Yes, even Peter, who had received the keys to the Kingdom, was regularly in need of the ministry of the Lord Jesus to remove contamination in his mind that he picked up by simply living in a Galilean society. One of the signs of a true believer is an increasing awareness and desire for the cleansing ministry of the Lord in our hearts and lives.

The pendulum then swung to the other side in Peter's thinking, and he announced, "Lord, not my feet only, but also my hands and my head". His motives were great, but his understanding was lacking. Jesus explained to him, "He that is washed needeth not save to wash his feet, but is clean every whit: and ye are clean, but not all". The Lord distinguished between Peter being washed (saved) once and having his feet cleaned regularly (daily cleansing from contamination from this world).

That night, the Saviour settled the question about eternal security once and for all. Even though all the disciples would shortly become defiled as they heard the foul language of an unruly mob in the Garden of Gethsemane, and even though Peter would soon deny him, the Saviour declared, "Ye (plural) are clean!" He did not declare, "Ye WERE cleaned!" referring to the moment of salvation. Nor did He think of their future in Heaven and tell them, "Ye WILL BE clean!". Instead, He employed two verbs to explain it. First, he said, "He that is washed" - a perfect, passive participle meaning, "has been washed...". Then, in the same sentence he says, "...ye are clean" — a present, active indicative verb. So, He covers from the past to the present showing our position of having been forgiven by God once and forever. Those would soon bring Peter great comfort. After he sinned and denied the Lord Jesus, was he so guilt-stricken that he wondered if he was still saved? Thank God, as John wrote, "The blood of Jesus Christ, his Son, cleanseth us from all sin" (1 John 1:7). By contrast, talking specifically about Judas, Jesus said, "Ye (plural) are not all clean". Judas had never been saved so he was still as an "unclean thing" (Isa 64:6).

Thank God for eternal security! Peter must have believed it otherwise he could never have claimed to be "preaching peace by Jesus Christ" (Acts 10:36). He uniquely implied this confidence in his two letters as he used the greeting, "Grace and peace be multiplied" (1 Peter 1:2; 2 Peter 1:2). If you truly believed you could lose your salvation you would live with fear not peace. It would be better not to get out of bed in the morning in case you sinned and died. Peter was clear that because God saves us there is no way we can lose our standing in Christ. He wrote that we "are kept by the power of God through faith unto salvation ready to be revealed in the last time" (1 Peter 1:5).

Availability

Since the disciples had picked up contamination, they only needed to turn to the Lord, and He would have all the resources to cleanse them. Some have wondered if the water in the story is picturing the Holy Spirit since water is used to symbolise the Spirit elsewhere in John's Gospel (John 3:5; 4:14; 7:38-39). Others have taken this as a symbolic representation of the Scriptures, so that the Lord Jesus approaches us in the way He does His church, "That he might sanctify and cleanse it with the washing of water by the word" (Eph 5:26). The Psalmist did say, "Wherewithal shall a young man cleanse his way? by taking heed thereto according to thy word" (Ps 119:9). A third option is a combination of the first two which is not just the mechanical reading of the Word, but a fresh Word from God applied by the Spirit to our hearts. At a minimum we can appreciate that there is no excuse for us to be carting around in our hearts an accumulation of contamination from this world. We must realise that there is no substitute for spending personal time alone with Him who has all the resources to keep us clean. May we never forget that we require His cleansing – frequently!

Therefore, the first ingredient to true happiness for Peter and the disciples was to learn to "love righteousness and hate iniquity" (Heb 1:9). Even if a believer avoids sin, he inevitably will sense the effects of being surrounded by the "corruption that is in the world through lust" (2 Peter 1:4). Uninvited contamination bombards us through all forms of media, social media, office conversations, school lectures, ambient music in stores, billboards, unsaved people conversing, and through innumerable other means. Sadly, our world loves to swim in the putrid, moral muck of life without God. Before conversion, we would have been comfortable in a world dominated by "the former lusts" (1 Peter 1:14), "fleshly lusts" (2:11); "lusts of men" (4:2) and "lust of uncleanness" (2 Peter 2:10). But that was then, and this is now. In Peter's own words, "we, being dead to sins, should live unto righteousness" (1 Peter 2:24).

Ingredient 2: Humility

At the same time as Jesus was teaching His disciples about holiness, He was also teaching them about humility. Andrew Murray, the prolific writer and minister in South Africa, once said, "The lack of humility is the sufficient explanation of every defect and failure". It certainly was lacking in the fall of Lucifer and in the first sin of mankind. The tendency towards pride was bound up in all its lethal potential in each of the disciples sitting around the table. Pride had already shown its ugly face a few times including in the heated discussion over who would be the greatest (Luke 9:46-48). Pride also appeared in their competition to cast out demons (Luke 9:49-50), and in dealing with the Samaritans who would not receive the Saviour (Luke 9:51-56).

Please ban all ideas from your mind that humility is putting yourself down, pointing out your failures, or thinking badly about yourself. The Lord Jesus said, "I am meek and lowly in heart" (Matt 11:29). He never pointed out His failures because He had none nor could He. He always thought correctly about Himself because He always viewed His value, roles, character, and everything else through the eyes of His Father. John tells us, "Jesus [was] knowing that the Father had given all things into his hands, and that he was come from God, and went to God" (John 13:3). He appreciated that the Father would have such confidence in Him that He would put "all things into his hands". Jesus also lived with divine perspective on His Father's great plan for His life. He knew He had "come from God" and thus spoke of His being sent by the Father over 50 times. This is the key to authentic humility: appreciating from God's perspective who you are and why you are on earth – no more and no less.

The Lord had already taught them in words that, "The Son of Man came not to be ministered unto, but to minister, and to give his life a ransom for many" (Mark 10:45). Now He would teach them with a basin, a towel, and some water. He would drill into these disciples that true happiness is not found in asserting your rights and manipulating others to meet your needs and desires. True happiness is found in genuine humility, where self-centeredness is replaced by a life filled with serving others.

Who can I Serve?

In the group that day, there were eleven Christians. Calmly and consistently the Lord Jesus moved from the feet of one disciple to another. If there was any doubt, the Lord even said afterwards, "Ye also ought to wash one another's feet" (John 13:14). What a counter-culture mindset! In our world of "selfies" and self-absorption, the Lord Jesus calls us to have the mind of Christ and "Look not every man on his own things, but every man also on the things of others" (Phil 2:4). Our lives should be dot-to-dot of acts of service for our fellow saints. That was the way He lived, and He said about this lesson in the upper room, "I have given you an example, that ye should do as I have done to you" (John 13:15).

But Peter likely noticed that Judas was at the table and the Lord Jesus washed his feet as well (13:5). Judas was not "clean" (v. 10), because Judas was not saved. Here the Lord Jesus taught Peter that we must also serve those who are not believers and even those who may never be saved. Just as His service for Peter did not hinge on Peter being faithful, His service to help Judas was not conditional upon Judas believing in Him for salvation. The service of the Saviour was truly unconditional. Peter clearly learned the need for proper motives in service. He wrote, "...if any man minister, let him do it as of the ability which God giveth: that God in all things may be glorified through Jesus Christ, to whom be praise and dominion for ever and ever. Amen" (1 Peter 4:11).

In What Ways can I Serve?

See the problem

Ever come across one of those optical illusion pictures where you look at it one way and you see an old lady? Then you keep looking and suddenly you see a young lady looking in a different direction? John 13 is really a contrast between what we would see around the table and what the Saviour saw. Most of us see a group of "dull skulls" who perhaps stepped right over or around a basin as they marched straight to the table. How inconsiderate and how could they miss such an obvious opportunity to serve? When you read the story, you almost want to reach in, grab a couple of disciples, and give them a shake.

Instead of sternly correcting their insensitivity though, the Lord Jesus focuses on the problem of their filthy feet. He moves in to address that issue first. Oh, to be more perceptive like the Saviour and see what the real or primary need is in the lives of those around us.

Once, I gently tried to give correction to a believer who was arriving late for meetings. I thought the problem was a lack of respect for the Lord. I had to apologise to the dear brother when I found out that the reason he was arriving late was because he had no money for fuel for his car and was dependent on public transport. I realised that his devotion was not lacking. I had shamefully not seen the true need and had jumped to a false conclusion.

Sense the possibilities

It is easy to be critical of the owner of the house for not providing a servant or slave to wash everyone's feet. It is equally easy to be hard on the 12 men who all but stumbled over a basin and a towel. Everything was right there, but they let the opportunity slip. Similarly, the Lord looks down at us often and has to say, "They missed it!". But the Lord Jesus never missed an opportunity to serve others. He saw the basin, the towel, and the water and He saw the potential for blessing that was in them. Peter seemed to appreciate the principle that we should seek to use what God has given us rather than dreaming about what we don't have. He wrote, "As each has received a gift, use it to serve one another, as good stewards of God's varied grace" (1 Peter 4:10). Whether it is spiritual ability, possessions, wisdom, knowledge, or natural talent, may we see what God has put in our hands and may we use these gifts for the blessing of others and the glory of God. Really, we do not need the Lord to give us more opportunities to serve, we need to pray that He will help us to take advantage of more of the ones we already have.

When should I Serve?

Jesus did not wait for ideal circumstances. First, there was unimaginable and unseen stress upon Him. We can't comprehend the weight of knowing that He would soon suffer the wrath of God for our sins. No one else could sense the tremendous pressure He must have been feeling in His soul. It was a deep, holy anticipation, because "Jesus knew that his hour was come that he should depart out of this world unto the Father" (John 13:1).

In addition, there was the pressure of the impending assault of the enemy against Him. He was fully aware that, "The devil...now put into the heart of Judas Iscariot, Simon's son, to betray him" (v.2). Sometimes, people can be experiencing great sources of concern and stress that remain unseen to the eyes of their closest friends. In this case, the enemy couldn't be worse. But even though the incalculable trial of the cross would soon produce in his body sweat "as it were great drops of blood falling down to the ground" (Luke 22:44), and Satan himself would attack him through Judas, the Saviour still showed humility and served others.

There would also be the sadness of having to interrupt the supper. Giving up something enjoyable can generate feelings of disappointment and loss. How many times had the Saviour dined with the disciples and enjoyed special moments with them? This was the last. However, the joy and fellowship of the moment would not be a deterrent to the Saviour displaying His humble heart in service to others.

The unworthiness of the 12 men did not limit Him either. These men should have been full of thankfulness just to participate in any service for God. Instead, they appear to be ungrateful and egotistical. However, as mentioned, humble service does not depend on the worthiness or the merit of the recipient of the service. The Saviour had already shown grace as multitudes of people had been blessed by His healing power and yet they had never turned and trusted Him for salvation. He knew they would reject Him. Despite that, He served them. On that night, "he knew who should betray him" (v.11), he knew Peter would deny Him, and He knew all the disciples would forsake Him. They were not worthy of His service, but He humbly met their need.

Washing filthy feet is a demeaning and revolting task, especially to a Western mind. John G. Butler points out in his book "Peter – the Illustrious Disciple", that this event in John 13 was not a model for a "feet washing service" in a New Testament Church as we never read of feet washing again in either the book of Acts or the Epistles. Additionally, what is practiced in modern feet-washing services is not what happened in the upper room. Today, people wash their feet to be clean and presentable for the feet washing service. That night, the Saviour was using feet washing as an illustration to show how He was willing to serve in the most menial ways for the benefit of saints and sinners. Now **that** is a truly humble mind.

Of course, this was just a picture of what Paul would eventually write to the Philippians about humility. He told them, "Let this mind be in you, which was also in Christ Jesus: Who, being in the form of God, thought it not robbery to be equal with God: But made himself of no reputation, and took upon him the form of a servant, and was made in the likeness of men: And being found in fashion as a man, he humbled himself, and became obedient unto death, even the death of the cross" (Phil 2:5-8). As awful as cleaning the dust-covered feet of the disciples seemed, this was just a very small sample of the humility of the Lord Jesus. He was about to perform the greatest act of service ever, in the worst circumstance ever, for the benefit of the worst people ever. That is the mind of Christ!

I wonder if Peter remembered as he observed the scene or reflected on it later, that the Lord Jesus had said, "I am meek and lowly of heart" (Matt 11:29). He never heard the Saviour complain in the upper room with the towel in His hands, or on the cross with nails through His hands. Peter captured the spirit of the Saviour when he said, "Use hospitality one to another without grudging" (1 Peter 4:9). One secret to success in a Christian testimony is that we "be all of one mind, sympathising, full of brotherly love, tender hearted, humble minded" (1 Peter 3:8 Darby).

How should I Serve?

Sadly, when we hear the word "humility", our word association skills give us the image of a hunched-over slave staring at the floor until his master shouts a command at him. That is the picture of someone who has been humiliated, not a person who was humble. The Lord Jesus, by contrast, was humility personified. He did not wait for the owner of the house or the disciples to ask Him to wash their feet. He took the initiative. True servants do not act independently of their masters, yet they show creativity and ingenuity to meet needs. Because Peter saw his family at home and his fellow disciples with no source of income, he said, "I go a-fishing" (John 21:3). True humility translates into having a greater sensitivity to the needs and possibilities around us. Humility also promotes rather than impedes initiative and ingenuity to help others.

Humility also leads a person to want to do quality work. Never once did the Lord Jesus do a "half-healing" or do less than a complete and perfect work. At Creation, "all things were made by him" (John 1:3), "God saw every thing that he had made, and, behold, it was very good" (Gen 1:31). When He completed the great work of the cross, Jesus would declare without any exaggeration, "It is finished!". All was done; every detail was perfect. Humility motivates a servant to achieve excellence to the delight of his master. In the upper room, the disciples' feet were both washed and dried. They could not have been cleaner. The Perfect Servant was teaching His disciples to discharge their duties with diligence and to the best of their ability.

Why should I Serve Others?

The expressions we use

Jesus reminded Peter and the disciples, "You call Me Teacher and Lord, and you say well, for so I am." (v.13). How interesting that when Peter first addressed the Saviour directly, he had called him "Teacher" (John 1:38). Now, twice in one night, Peter calls the Saviour, "Lord" (John 13:6,9). At salvation, we enter a new relationship with the Son of God, although we perhaps did not appreciate this aspect. Paul said, "That if thou shalt confess with thy mouth the Lord Jesus, and shalt believe in thine heart that God hath raised him from the dead, thou shalt be saved" (Rom 10:9). There is no option given in the Scriptures to have Christ as Saviour and not as Lord. He must be both! It is an immense privilege to call Him Lord and Master, but, as always, great privileges bring great responsibilities. Since He is our Lord, we should seek to do His will and serve as He wishes us to serve.

The example we follow

Jesus said to the disciples in the upper room, "For I have given you an example, that ye should do as I have done to you" (John 13:15). With a basin of water and a towel, Jesus showed them how to be "givers" instead of "getters". That was the way Christ lived all through His life and He would continue to demonstrate the heart of a servant even in His death. Between the upper room and the cross, He gave warnings to women who followed Him, He sought forgiveness for ignorant soldiers, He showed care for His mother, He gave salvation to a repentant thief, and He demonstrated trust by placing Himself in the hands of the Father. The standard is very high: He said, "Do, as I have done to you". In the upper room, He gave His time, His attention, His love, and His effort. At the cross, He gave all He had - He gave Himself. We have no excuse, then, as we could not have been given a better model of selflessness than that of our Master, our Lord Jesus Christ. The command to follow His example obviously stuck with Peter as, years later, he wrote, "be clothed with humility!" (1 Peter 5:5). Even as an older believer he was still seeking to imitate the self-less example of Christ in the upper room and exhorting others to follow that example.

The expectations we have

The Saviour gave Peter one last word about expectations: "Verily, verily, I say unto you, 'The servant is not greater than his lord; neither he that is sent greater than he that sent him'" (v.16). The Master was putting His students on "Full Pride Alert". If we ever have the mindset of expecting others to serve us, we are considering ourselves to be superior to the Lord Jesus. That would be grossly insulting and blasphemous. Since He is greater than us and He served others, we should set our expectations accordingly and feel the burden to serve others.

The Lord Jesus promised blessing for disciples who learn to think and serve like Him. He said, "If ye know these things, happy are ye if ye do them" (v.17). The blessing is not some kind of a euphoric feeling or bubbly sentiment. Happy (*makarios*) is the same word the Lord Jesus used when He said, "Thomas, because thou hast seen me, thou hast believed: blessed are they that have not seen, and yet have believed" (John 20:27). He used this word nine times in the Sermon on the Mount in the section often called "The Beatitudes". It means favoured, blessed, fortunate, happy, or privileged. It is not then so much a feeling, but a fact that one receives the smile, favour and blessing of God. Peter made enough money to survive in his fishing business, but now the Saviour is giving him the secret to a true and lasting fortune.

It appears that Peter understood that this kind of blessing is independent of feelings and circumstances. He later wrote, "But and if ye suffer for righteousness' sake, happy are ye" (1 Peter 3:14). He then added, "If ye be reproached for the name of Christ, happy are ye; for the spirit of glory and of God resteth upon you" (1 Peter 4:14). If holiness + humility = happiness, the Son of God was truly the happiest man to ever live on earth. He uniquely "loved righteousness, and hated iniquity" (Heb 1:9), and "he came not to be ministered unto, but to minister" (Mark 10:45). Peter witnessed the linking of holiness and happiness that night in the upper room and again the next day when the Saviour hung on the cross.

But let us not forget that Jesus said, "IF ye do these things....". While He made it clear that the life of holiness and humility is the most fulfilling life possible, this "blessedness" does not randomly occur in the lives of a few who "get lucky". It requires an intentional decision before God, and Peter evidently made that choice. When he lifted his pen to write his second and last epistle, he began, "Simeon Peter, a servant and an apostle of Jesus Christ" (2 Peter 1:1). May God help us to learn what Peter learned and to choose what Peter chose. The Lord Jesus did not regret that choice nor did Peter. You won't regret it either!

CHAPTER 12

Peter the Petitioner

"The first and last stages of holy living are crowned with praying. It is a life trade."

E. M. Bounds

Peter the fisherman knew that to be good at any trade it requires commitment, hard work, and discipline. He became so good at fishing that, while many of us are surprised when we catch something, Peter was shocked when he fished all night and caught nothing. In the same way, he developed a beautiful and consistent habit of prayer – a priceless spiritual life trade.

Peter is well-known for his first recorded prayer, a prayer of confession when "he fell down at Jesus' knees, saying, Depart from me; for I am a sinful man, O Lord" (Luke 5:8). He is also well-known for one of the shortest prayers in the Bible and one of the very few directed to the Lord Jesus instead of the Father. At the command of the Lord on the Sea of Galilee, "Peter got out of the boat and walked on the water and came to Jesus" (Matt 14:29, ESV). However, when he saw the wind and waves, he began "to sink [and] he cried, saying, Lord, save me!" (Matt 14:30).

Of course, as E.M. Bounds also said, "None but praying leaders can have praying followers". And that is exactly what Peter experienced as he spent three years with the greatest leader and the greatest man of prayer ever – Jesus, the Son of God. Peter must have taken mental notes when the Master gave His followers a guide commonly known as the "Lord's Prayer" (Matt 6:9-13; Luke 11:2-4). Because it contains the confession of sin, the Lord could never have prayed those words as a personal prayer. Instead, it is a model of how to approach God so that prayer can be enjoyable both for disciples and for the Father. That model includes the discipline of learning to speak to God about His things ("thy name", "thy kingdom", and "thy will") before ours ("our bread", "our debts", and "our debtors"). We see that model in action when the believers met for prayer in Acts 4 and Peter was present. Before they requested boldness (Acts 4:29) for the apostles, they spent five verses in worship (Acts 4:24-28) speaking about the character and works of God.

When it came to prayer for themselves, the model the Lord Jesus presented to His disciples included three requests: two were spiritual (temptations and forgiveness) and one was material (daily bread). We, too, need to learn to spend more time in prayer conversing with God about His person, works, and interests, and we also need to pray more about spiritual needs than about physical needs.

They also heard the Lord articulate parables packed with lessons about prayer: the friend at midnight (Luke 11:5-13); the widow and the judge (Luke 18:1-8); and the Pharisee and the publican (Luke 18:9-14). Luke, who presents Christ as the perfect man, gives us 13 occasions when the Lord spoke to God in prayer:

- At His baptism (Luke 3:21)
- At times in wilderness places (Luke 5:16)
- At the selection of the 12 disciples (Luke 6:12)
- At the Transfiguration (Luke 9:29)
- At the giving of instruction about Prayer (Luke 11:1)
- At the feeding of the 5,000 (Luke 9:16)
- At Caesarea Philippi (Luke 9:18)
- At the return of the 70 (Luke 10:21)
- At Gethsemane (Luke 22:41-46)
- At the beginning of the six hours on the cross (Luke 23:34)

- At the end of the six hours on the cross (Luke 23:46)

- At the Passover and the institution of the Lord's supper (Luke 22:17,19)

- At the meal in Emmaus (Luke 24:30).

Peter was present on at least nine of these, including the one when Jesus "was praying in a certain place, [and] when he ceased, one of his disciples said unto him, 'Lord, teach us to pray, as John also taught his disciples'" (Luke 11:1). If Peter didn't ask the question, he was certainly interested in the answer and the instruction of the Master about prayer.

Peter would have learned the difference between saying prayers, as was the habit of the Pharisees, and genuine communication with God. He was physically present to hear Jesus preach the Sermon on the Mount in which He warned of dry, mechanical prayers using vain repetition (Matt 6:7). This was the typical style of pagan worshipers who employed repetitive words or phrases to try and gain the attention and favour of their gods. Jesus taught that, instead, the disciples should enjoy transparent and authentic communication with Heaven. To guide them, He provided the model which begins: "Our Father which art in heaven" (Matt 6:9). Father? This was revolutionary as there are less than a dozen occasions in all the Old Testament when people addressed God as Father. But now, Jesus was going to teach His disciples, "Whatsoever ye shall ask the Father in my name, he will give it you" (John 16:23). This privilege would not be exclusive to Jewish Christians alone. Paul would explain that for Jews and Gentiles, "through him [Christ] we both have access by one Spirit unto the Father" (Eph 2:18). Thus, in the New Testament, there are over 250 references to the Father. Because we have been born into God's family, we can now talk with Him openly and from the heart. Peter enjoyed that privilege often. He recognized both the awesome character of his God to whom he was approaching and yet the comfort he enjoyed while speaking to his heavenly Father. Later in life, he wrote about God who says, "I am holy" (1 Peter 1:16). He appreciated the need for reverence, but Peter went on to say, "If you call on the

Father..." (1 Peter 1:17). Thus, while maintaining full respect for the holy character of our God, we can have honest and open communication with Him as our Father.

This is what Peter witnessed and heard (1 John 1:1) as he was present on two of the three times when the Father spoke from Heaven about His Son (Matt 3:17; John 12:28; Matt 17:5). On all three occasions, we are told the Lord Jesus was praying. As He spoke to God, the Father spoke to Him. Likewise, when Peter was praying on the roof of the house of Simon the Tanner in Joppa, the Lord gave him the vision of the sheet full of unclean animals coming down from heaven. And as Peter was speaking to God, the Lord spoke to him saying, "What God hath cleansed, that call not thou common" (Acts 10:15). Today, we do not hear His audible voice from Heaven, nor does God speak to us in dreams and visions. Instead, He speaks to us through the Bible. But it is still true: we can and should participate in the circle of communication in which we speak to God in prayer, and He speaks to us through His Word.

On at least a couple of occasions, Peter heard the Lord Jesus say, "When you pray..." (Matt 6:5,6,7; Luke 11:2), not "If you pray". The Lord was assuming that the disciples would have an interest in regular interaction with their Father in Heaven. He also said His disciples "always ought to pray and not lose heart" (Luke 18:1, NKJV). While prayer can be spontaneous, there needs to be regular and scheduled times of communion with the Lord. To help develop the discipline of programmed and sacred times of communication with God, Jesus taught the need to have a specific place to pray. He referred to it as one's closet where the Father would be waiting to communicate with His child. While as desirable as that sounds to believers, Jesus also knew that our lives would be full of distractions that can impede communion with the Lord. Thus, He taught, "Shut thy door" (Matt 6:6) – we must intentionally and actively guard our location and times of communication with Heaven, and actively limit distractions. Peter would know exactly where the "closet" was for the Lord Jesus when He was near Jerusalem, because often Jesus "went, as was his custom, to the Mount of Olives" (Luke 22:39). "Judas ... [also] knew the place: for Jesus ofttimes resorted thither with his disciples" (John 18:2). Did Peter ever get up early and hear the holy communications between the perfect Servant of Jehovah and His Master? The Lord Jesus said about His God, "He wakeneth morning by morning, He wakeneth mine ear to hear as the learned" (Isa 50:4). Peter obviously witnessed at first-hand the holy habits of the Perfect Man and he made it his goal to imitate his Lord.

It appears that Peter personally followed a regular schedule of prayer much like Daniel who "kneeled upon his knees three times a day, and prayed, and gave thanks before his God" (Dan 6:10). In Joppa, "Peter went up upon the housetop to pray about the sixth hour" (Acts 10:9). In Jerusalem, "Peter and John went up together into the temple at the hour of prayer, being the ninth hour" (Acts 3:1). Later, when Peter and the disciples delegated the administration of funds to care for Christian widows, they handed over that responsibility with clear intentions. They said, "We will give ourselves continually to prayer, and to the ministry of the word" (Acts 6:4). Likely, Peter kept the practice from his Jewish background that included set times of prayer during the day. What a holy and helpful discipline to establish - regular, personal times of communion and conversation with the Lord.

Peter also believed in the value of prayer in marriage. This is evident in his first epistle when he wrote, "Likewise, ye husbands, dwell with them [your wives] according to knowledge, giving honour unto the wife, as unto the weaker vessel, and as being heirs together of the grace of life; that your prayers be not hindered" (1 Peter 3:7). Note that he does not consider the hypothetical possibility of a married couple not praying. Instead, he assumes it will be a normal and routine (plural) practice. Is it so in your marriage? Prayer has a uniting and binding effect upon a couple as together they focus on the same Lord and present to Him their joint thanksgivings and their shared concerns.

Upon the formation of the first assembly in Jerusalem, Peter, the rest of the apostles, and all the other believers "devoted themselves to the apostles' teaching and the fellowship, to the breaking of bread and the prayers" (Acts 2:42, ESV). This was not a commitment by each believer to pray alone at home, but rather a specific devotion to "the" prayers – the prayer meeting of the local church (Acts 4:23-

31; 12:12). Peter would have taught and practised the need for equal commitment to attend and participate in the Breaking of Bread and the prayer meeting as the believers did in the first local church.

Peter was part of the church leadership in the first assembly in Jerusalem. So, when they faced their first crisis over the care of widows, they delegated the responsibility to select men. The congregation carefully chose fit men "Whom they set before the apostles: and when they had prayed, they laid their hands on them" (Acts 6:6). In order to lead the assembly in Jerusalem through that transition period, Peter and the other apostles made time to take matters before the Lord in prayer.

Peter not only learned from his Master the trade of how to pray, but he also learned that there are specific times when prayer is advisable or required. Notice the parallel occasions in which both the Lord Jesus and Peter prayed.

After Times of Success

Jesus:

"Great multitudes came together to hear, and to be healed by him of their infirmities. And he withdrew himself into the wilderness and prayed" (Luke 5:15-16). Jesus was enjoying great popularity and triumphing over every disease. Even though He was not capable of pride or sin, Jesus taught His disciples by example of the need to spend time in prayer when God was evidently working.

Peter:

Peter had just had some memorable experiences. At Lydda, he healed Aeneas, a man who had been bedridden and paralyzed for eight years. Shortly thereafter, messengers arrived from the nearby town of Joppa on the coast because a well-respected sister named Tabitha (Dorcas) had become sick and died. Peter responded to their request by going to Joppa and raising her from the dead. He remained in Joppa, and we are told, "Peter went up upon the housetop to pray, about the sixth hour" (Acts 10:9). Following great exploits for God, Peter also bowed in prayer before God.

In Times of Trial

Jesus:

On the night before His crucifixion, Jesus entered the Garden of Gethsemane with His disciples "And he was withdrawn from them about a stone's cast, and kneeled down, and prayed" (Luke 22:41). The anticipation of the cross was so intense that "being in an agony he prayed more earnestly: and his sweat was as it were great drops of blood falling down to the ground" (Luke 22:44). And on the cross? The first words of Christ were a prayer: "Father, forgive them for they know not what they do" (Luke 23:34). His final words in life were a simple but sublime prayer to God: "Father, into thy hands I commend my Spirit" (Luke 23:46).

Peter:

John and Peter had been arrested by the Jewish leaders for preaching the gospel of Jesus Christ. Perhaps they thought their ministry and lives were coming to an end. Eventually, though, they were let go and they immediately "went to their own company", the Christians in the local church in Jerusalem. Together, "they lifted up their voice to God with one accord" (Acts 4:23-24). The two apostles had just been through an awful experience, and they knew that continued preaching of the gospel would generate more trials ahead. Thus, Peter and the other believers turned to God in very difficult and uncertain times.

In Times of Decision

Jesus:

One day, "he went out into a mountain to pray, and continued all night in prayer to God. And when it was day, he called unto him his disciples: and of them he chose twelve, whom also he named apostles" (Luke 6:12-13). The omniscient Son of God first spoke to His Father before making the crucial selection of twelve men to be His special followers.

Peter:

After the ascension of Christ, Peter spoke to the remaining disciples about finding a replacement for Judas who had committed suicide. He led them in the decision-making process and, in the end, "they appointed two, Joseph called Barsabas, who was surnamed Justus, and Matthias. And they prayed" (Acts 1:23-24). The 12 would be God's leadership in His plan for worldwide evangelism after the descent of the Holy Spirit. One key component to that vital selection process of which Peter was the leader was to pray about the matter in the presence of God.

At Times of Temptation

Jesus:

At the Jordon River, He also was "being baptized, and [was] praying" (Luke 3:21). Immediately following, "Jesus being full of the Holy Ghost returned from Jordan, and was led by the Spirit into the wilderness, Being forty days tempted of the devil" (Luke 4:1-2).

Peter:

In the Garden of Gethsemane, Peter was exhausted. At that very vulnerable moment, the Lord Jesus tried to teach him a lesson. He said to him, "Pray that ye enter not into temptation" (Luke 22:40). Peter also learned the importance of prayer in view of temptation as he recalled the tender words of the Saviour, "Simon, Simon, behold, Satan hath desired to have you, that he may sift you as wheat: But I have prayed for thee, that thy faith fail not" (Luke 22:31-32). The Lord had also given the model of prayer to the disciples which included, "Lead us not into temptation, but deliver us from evil" (Matt 6:13). Reflecting on both the example and teaching of the Lord about the importance of prayer in temptation, Peter understood that the devil "as a roaring lion, walketh about, seeking whom he may devour" (1 Peter 5:8). He and his agents are still lurking around believers, and they work together with the world and the flesh to tempt us into sin and disobedience. Peter learned the reality of temptation and trial through personal experience. Thus, he exhorts believers to live, "Casting all your care upon him; for he careth for you. Be sober, be vigilant...". Notice the balance. In prayer, we should place every concern in the capable hands of our Lord and yet vigilantly be on guard for the next temptation and trial to come our way.

At Times of Evangelistic Opportunity

Jesus:

He had specifically arranged the time and place to speak to men about the identity of the Messiah. Jesus began by asking, "Whom say the people that I am?" (Luke 9:18). He then asked the disciples, "But whom say ye that I am?". Peter led the response when he said, "The Christ of God." (Luke 9:20). This gospel discussion grew out of the fact that Christ "alone [was] praying, [and] his disciples were with him" (Luke 9:18).

Peter:

Philip the evangelist launched north of Jerusalem with the gospel. Soon, the apostles and the church in Jerusalem "heard that Samaria had received the word of God" (Acts 8:14). As a result, "they sent unto them Peter and John: Who, when they were come down, prayed for them, that they might receive the Holy Ghost" (Acts 8:14-15). Salvation is a work of God, and we are completely dependent on Him for it. Thus, the apostles prayed as they gave full credit to God for the salvation of Samaritan souls. We must do the same.

At Times of Need

Jesus:

Although He was omnipotent in Himself, when faced with a hungry crowd of 5,000 men plus women and children, the Saviour took five little barley loaves and two small fish in His hands. Then, "he looked up to heaven and blessed..." (Mark 6:41). When the need was overwhelming, He showed His disciples that they could take the crisis to their God in prayer.

Peter:

When Peter arrived in the room to see Dorcas lying there with women weeping at her passing, Peter was confronted with a deep need. Luke tells us that at that point, "Peter put them all forth, and kneeled down, and prayed" (Acts 9:40). Thank God, we too can flee to Him in critical times that are beyond our abilities and resources.

One surprising reality in Scripture is that we never read of Peter or any other disciple praying until after the death, burial, resurrection, and ascension of Christ. Perhaps this silence is intended to highlight the incalculable cost to the Lord Jesus so that we might "come boldly unto the throne of grace, that we may obtain mercy, and find grace to help in time of need" (Heb 4:16). Another possibility is that the equivalent of prayer was their interactions directly with the Lord Jesus while He was with them on earth. As noted, Peter communicated more with the Lord Jesus than any of the other disciples. Look at the types of interactions he had with the Saviour which we can also have with the Father in prayer:

- Ask a question

  "Then answered Peter and said unto him, 'Behold, we have forsaken all, and followed thee; what shall we have therefore?'" (Matt 19:27). Also, "Simon Peter said unto him, 'Lord, whither goest thou?'" (John 13:36), and, "Peter said unto him, Lord, why cannot I follow thee now?" (John 13:37).

- Proclaim love and loyalty

  "Peter said unto him, 'Though I should die with thee, yet will I not deny thee'" (Matt 26:35). Also, "Peter said to him, 'Lord, I am ready to go with you both to prison and to death'" (Luke 22:33).

- Make a request

  "Then answered Peter and said unto him, 'Declare unto us this parable'" (Matt 15:15).

- Clarify a point

  "Then Peter said unto him, 'Lord, speakest thou this parable unto us, or even to all?'" (Luke 12:41).

- Share an observation

  "And Peter calling to remembrance saith unto him, 'Master, behold, the fig tree which thou cursedst is withered away'" (Mark 11:21).

- Review your past

  "Peter said, 'Not so, Lord; for I have never eaten any thing that is common or unclean'" (Acts 10:14).

- Express a doubt

  When the woman with the personal issue touched His tunic and was healed, "Peter and they that were with him said, 'Master, the multitude throng thee and press thee, and sayest thou, Who touched me?' (Lk 8:45)".

- Present worship

  "Peter answereth and saith unto him, 'Thou art the Christ'" (Mark 8:29).

- Discuss what you have learned

  "Simon Peter answered him, 'Lord...we have believed, and have come to know, that you are the Holy One of God'" (John 6:68-69).

- Dialogue over what the Lord is doing:

  "He came to Simon Peter, who said to him, 'Lord, do you wash my feet?' Jesus answered him, 'What I am doing you do not understand now, but afterward you will understand.' Peter said to him, 'You shall never wash my feet.' Jesus answered him, 'If I do not wash you, you have no share with me.' Simon Peter said to him, 'Lord, not my feet only but also my hands and my head!' Jesus said to him, 'The one who has bathed does not need to wash, except for his feet, but is completely clean. And you are clean, but not every one of you'" (John 13:6-10).

Sadly, many of us suffer from monochromatic prayer lives that too often consist of a laundry list of requests. Peter's communication with his Lord was varied, natural and genuine. While He is a holy God who deserves reverence, at the same time He is our Father. He is interested in every detail of our lives, and He delights in His children approaching, conversing, and sharing with a diversity of communications just as Peter did with the Lord Jesus during His life and ministry.

The one question everyone considers at some point is: Why should I pray if God is sovereign, and He is going to work out His plans anyway? When Peter was sinking in the Sea of Galilee, he called out to the Lord because he was facing his own inability to walk on water. When Jesus spoke of His betrayal, "Simon Peter therefore beckoned to him [John], that he should ask who it should be of whom he spake" (John

13:24). He had John speak to Jesus about the matter as neither knew what was ahead for the Saviour. In the same conversation, the Lord Jesus informed the disciples of His impending death and exodus from this world. Again, because Peter was ignorant of what was ahead, he asked, "Lord, whither goest thou?" (John 13:36). Peter did not know what was in his own future either. Thus, he added, "Lord, why cannot I follow thee now?" (John 13:37). Similarly, his lack of knowledge and understanding showed when he, James, John, and Andrew were on the Mount of Olives and Jesus told them about the eventual destruction of the temple. They didn't understand so they had to ask, "Tell us, when shall these things be? and what shall be the sign when all these things shall be fulfilled?" (Mark 13:4). Thus, when Peter found himself in a situation where he was not able to do something, he spoke to the Lord. Likewise, when he did not know something about his life, the future of the Lord Jesus or the future of the world, he spoke to the Saviour.

And yet, even though the Lord Jesus never lacked knowledge or ability, He often spoke to God in prayer. Why? Peter was standing nearby when Jesus prayed by Lazarus' tomb: "Father, I thank thee that thou hast heard me. And I knew that thou hearest me always" (John 11:41-42). He was not praying for power, nor for God to tell him something He did not know. He prayed simply because the Father deeply enjoys communication and fellowship with His Son. Peter wrote that spiritually we are "obedient children" and that we, too, can "call on the Father" (1 Peter 1:17). So, even if prayer does not change the outcome, the fact that communication in prayer delights our Father's heart should be sufficient motivation to pray frequently and to pray more.

Peter could remember how much of a priority prayer was to the Lord Jesus. One morning Simon and the disciples woke up and the Saviour was gone. They eventually learned what happened: "And in the morning, rising up a great while before day, he [Jesus] went out, and departed into a solitary place, and there prayed" (Mark 1:35). Did Peter reflect on that experience later when the Lord taught them: "... when thou prayest, enter into thy closet, and when thou hast shut thy door, pray to thy Father which is in secret" (Matt 6:6). They witnessed the Saviour intentionally making time for prayer and intentionally limiting distractions by rising early and going to a solitary place to speak to His Father.

And more lessons were to follow. "Simon and they that were with him followed after him [Jesus]. And when they had found him, they said unto him, 'All men seek for thee'" (Mark 1:36-37). While they were focusing on an ideal opportunity for service, their Lord was enjoying an ideal time to pray. His response must have shocked them. He said to them, "Let us go into the next towns, that I may preach there also: for therefore came I forth" (Mark 1:38). Why would He leave if the current crowd was interested? This must have left Peter and the others with the clear lesson that, if we want to be on the same page as Heaven, we need to keep in touch and in tune with our Heavenly Father.

Peter must have also noted that the Lord Jesus expressed emotions in prayer. He likely heard Him say, "Now is my soul troubled; and what shall I say? Father, save me from this hour: but for this cause came I unto this hour. Father, glorify thy name." (John 12:27-28). Later, in Gethsemane, Jesus said, "My soul is exceeding sorrowful unto death" (Mark 14:34). Then "he went forward a little, and fell on the ground, and prayed." (Mark 14:35). And yet, while it is perfectly normal to experience and share our emotions with our Father in prayer, prayer is a time for clear-headed thinking. Peter once wrote to believers who were likely experiencing great emotions as they faced persecution. He said, "The end of all things is at hand; therefore be self-controlled and sober-minded for the sake of your prayers" (1 Peter 4:7, ESV). Like the Lord Jesus that morning in the solitary place, or later when He was in Gethsemane, prayer is a time for careful thought, reflection to discern God's will, and to form convictions according to Scripture.

In the trial of Gethsemane, the Lord Jesus told his disciples to pray for themselves when He said, "Pray that ye enter not into temptation" (Luke 22:40). At that time, He Himself presented a personal request in prayer to His Father asking that He might allow the cup of suffering to pass from Him. On the cross, His final prayer was to the Father to whom He was entrusting His Spirit. So, it is acceptable and necessary to pray about matters in our own lives. However, never once did the Lord Jesus request that the disciples or anyone else pray for Him. Instead, to Peter He said, "I have prayed for thee" (Luke 22:32). In the upper room, Jesus said about His disciples, "I pray for them" (John 17:9), and on the cross, He prayed for His enemies. Therefore, one of the features that can make prayer interesting and vibrant is the proportion of His focus on others versus a focus on ourselves.

Peter had learned from Christ how to pray, and he honed his trade during years of service for God. He had seen the clear connection between the spiritual condition of the one praying and the joy that communication through prayer brings to the Father. Undoubtedly, Peter would agree that there is no one who is more righteous than the Lord Jesus and no one who has prayed more. The prayer life of the holy Son of God was especially fragrant and delightful to His Father. So, while an Omniscient God hears all prayers, Peter appreciated the words of Psalm 34 which he quoted in his first epistle in the section on maintaining righteousness in interpersonal interactions. Peter wrote that we should "turn away from evil and do good" (1 Peter 3:11). It is in that context that Peter concludes, "For the eyes of the Lord are over the righteous, and his ears are open unto their prayers" (1 Peter 3:12). This was 100% true of Peter's Lord, "Jesus Christ the righteous" (1 John 2:1), and it appears that Peter made it his goal to be like Him. He wanted to reflect the Saviour's character and imitate His habits in prayer. With a well-honed life-trade of communication with God, Peter longed that for him, too, the ears of the Lord would be open to the prayers of a righteous man.

CHAPTER 13

Peter the Shepherd

The Metaphor of a Shepherd

Peter's eyes must have bulged, and his mouth dropped open. The risen Christ had just told a fisherman three times to shepherd his sheep. Three years before, on the same shore of the Sea of Galilee, Jesus the Carpenter, had told Peter the fisherman and his brother Andrew, "I will make you fishers of men" (Matt 4:19). Peter may have thought then, "No problem. I have been fishing for years. Fish? Men? It's all the same". Yes, finding fish and finding souls are parallel tasks requiring similar skill sets: patience, timing, proper bait, and hard work. But, to be clear, the Lord was not now guilty of "bait and switch." He was not shutting down Peter's evangelism career; He was adding shepherding to Peter's responsibilities.

But, why would the Lord pick a completely unfamiliar task to describe Peter's future work with believers? Peter wouldn't have a clue where to begin and he wouldn't be able to access "shepherding sites" on Google or obtain a Master's degree in church leadership at a Galilean seminary. Moses was raised as a palace prince in Egypt, and he had no knowledge or experience of leading sheep because "every shepherd is an abomination to the Egyptians" (Gen 46:34). But when he was called to shepherd in the back side of the desert, at least he had Jethro, his father-in-law, to teach him. The normal custom in ancient times was that the youngest son in the family would shepherd the sheep. Being the youngest, surely David learned something of the trade from his seven older brothers. But Peter was a first-generation shepherd of saints and he had no one to teach him and no role models to follow in the Jerusalem church. The Lord selected the motif of shepherding and sheep fully cognizant of Peter's ignorance. Clearly, Peter would have to look to the Lord to equip him and develop his abilities for this new task. And he did.

The New Testament makes it clear that God's plan for church leadership remains the same today. While organizational, communication, and management skills can be valuable, the work of spiritual shepherding in a local church is very different. Every shepherd must look to the Lord to equip, train and direct in this vital work. What the Saviour said about fruit-bearing is also true of shepherding: "...without me, ye can do nothing" (John 15:5).

The Model of a Shepherd

The Lord Jesus knew that Peter was from a fishing family and had lived almost all his life in Bethsaida on the northern shore of the Sea of Galilee. Peter probably had had limited exposure to the art and responsibilities of shepherds. It may have been that the only shepherd Peter had ever met was the One who said, "I am the good Shepherd" (John 10:11). Peter's role model and standard for shepherding would always and only be the Lord Jesus. Possibly, for the rest of his life, he reflected often on the teaching of the Saviour in John 10. On that occasion, he learned fundamental lessons from the consummate Shepherd, the one the writer to the Hebrews eventually called "the Great Shepherd" (Heb 13:20). He grew in his appreciation of this ability and the role that he saw the Saviour execute with such wonderful skill. Three decades later he called the Lord Jesus "the Shepherd and Overseer of your souls" (1 Peter 2:25, NKJV). Personally, Peter had experienced the tender care of the Master Shepherd and would seek to emulate His example.

The Motivations of a Shepherd:

Three times Jesus called Peter to become a spiritual shepherd and each time He preceded the call with a question. Jesus did not ask him, "Are you trained?" or "Are you capable?" He didn't even ask him, "Are you willing?" He simply asked, "Simon, son of Jonas, lovest thou me?" (John 21:15,16,17). When you love someone, that person's interests become your interests. If Peter truly loved the Lord, interest and concern for the Lord's sheep would be automatic. Once Peter had confessed, "Lord, thou knowest that I love thee" only then was the Lord going to give him the privilege and responsibility of caring for His people.

Peter would have known that not all people who interact with sheep have healthy motives. He once heard his Master speak about "robbers" (John 10:1) and "the thief [who] cometh not, but for to steal, and to kill, and to destroy" (John 10:10). Sadly, there are men who view God's people as sources, not sheep. Paul gave qualifications for shepherds twice and both times he included "not greedy for money" (1 Tim 3:3; Titus 1:7). After three years of serving and preaching with Judas Iscariot, Peter learned that Judas was a thief, and from the money bag of Jesus and the disciples, Judas used to steal what was put in it (John 12:6, NKJV). Never having forgotten that experience, he later exhorted men to "Shepherd the flock of God...not for dishonest gain but eagerly" (1 Peter 5:2, NKJV).

Peter also heard the Lord speak about "hirelings" or hired hands. Hired hands care for the sheep out of a sense of duty just to fulfil a contract. But when danger comes (e.g. a wolf), Jesus said, "The hireling fleeth, because he is an hireling, and careth not for the sheep" (John 10:13). Peter later warned about the possibility of "taking the oversight thereof", "by constraint", rather than "willingly" (1 Peter 5:2). Shepherding is not to be a role foisted on some poor Christian by pressure, nor is it a role determined by vote, family connections or simply because there is a need. Paul spoke of a Christian brother who would "desire the office of a bishop" (1 Tim 3:1). "Desire" is a Greek word meaning to stretch out for something. A true Biblical leader reaches out to give to the flock, not take from the flock. Caring for believers becomes such a burden that a man is willing to wear himself out and stretch himself thin to see others prosper spiritually.

Peter identified a third danger when it comes to the motivation of a shepherd. He may have heard of specific cases like Diotrephes in 3 John, a leader who loved pre-eminence and abused authority. Anticipating this possibility, Peter wrote that men should "Feed the flock of God ... Neither as being lords over God's heritage, but being ensamples to the flock" (1 Peter 5:2-3). John MacArthur says that Diotrephes-type men have an approach to the church in which they "lead by dominating someone or some situation. It implies leadership by manipulation and intimidation". To them, church administration becomes a means by which they boost their own egos and enjoy a sense of importance. Money, ego, and power are what drive men who want to "get" from the flock. By contrast, Jesus said, "I am the good shepherd the good shepherd giveth his life for the sheep" (John 10:11). A true shepherd thinks about what he can provide for sheep, not what he can take from them. That is why the Saviour touches on the issue of motivation before He gives the mandate to shepherd.

For everyone involved in shepherding believers, we need to constantly evaluate our motives. The key to more Biblical and effective leadership in assemblies is not greater organisation, more effective use of social media, or more activities to keep everyone involved. All of that may be useful if done Biblically. However, if any one of us met Christ today, would He ask, "Why aren't you using Instagram more?" or, "Why don't you have more activities for young people?" or, "Why don't you have a five-year plan for the assembly?". Likely, one by one, He would look us straight in our eyes and simply ask, "_____ (fill in your name), Do you love me?".

The Mentality of a Shepherd

Jesus never envisioned one man leading a congregation with the title of "pastor" nor one man presiding over various congregations with the title of "bishop". Eventually, a collective local testimony in the New Testament would be called a "Church of God" (1 Cor 1:2). Other figures would be employed to feature different functions of the church such as "temple of God" (1 Cor 3:16), "house of God" (1 Tim 3:15), and "flock of God" (1 Peter 5:2). Each description clearly conveys the concepts of the distinctiveness, possession, and ownership of each assembly. No church leader can ever claim that the people are "his sheep" or that it is "his church". Every New Testament assembly belongs exclusively to God. Peter learned this great truth that day on the beach when Jesus told him three times to tend and feed "My lambs" (John 21:15) and "My sheep" (John 21:16,17). Those words stuck in his mind and moulded his perspective in his approach to believers. He later described sheep in assemblies as "those allotted to your charge" (1 Peter 5:3, NASB) or "those entrusted to you" (1 Peter 5:3, HCSB). The word "kleros" is translated as "lot" (Acts 1:26), "part" (Acts 1:17), and "inheritance" (Col 1:12). It is the portion that is assigned to someone - in this case the Chief Shepherd assigns to elders the responsibility to care for certain sheep. The Theological Dictionary of the New Testament agrees by stating, "kleros is the portion allotted to each individual elder". This completely prohibits any sense of personal ownership, despotic authority or independent control of the type shown by Diotrephes in 3 John. The assembly is the Lord's flock and the individual believers that comprise the assembly are His sheep. Every elder is simply a "steward of God" (Titus 1:7).

Having received this stewardship from the Lord, Peter would sense that he was working on behalf of the Chief Shepherd to care for and feed His sheep. Just as in any modern assembly missionary work, Peter would have functioned as part of the leadership in the new assembly when it was first planted in Jerusalem in Acts 2. This is confirmed by the fact that we do not read of elders in the Jerusalem assembly until Acts 11:30. In addition to shepherding in the local assembly, the Lord's commissioning of Peter to shepherd included a broader ministry for the establishment of the Church, the body of Christ. Paul described to the Ephesian Christians how Christ had given certain men to the church for specific purposes. He said, "And he gave some, apostles; and some, prophets; and some, evangelists; and some, pastors and teachers; For the perfecting of the saints, for the work of the ministry, for the edifying of the body of Christ" (Eph 4:11-12). Peter fulfilled the roles of apostle, evangelist, pastor, and teacher (or pastoring teacher). At the same time, towards the end of his life, he wrote, "The elders which are among you I exhort, who am also an elder" (1 Peter 5:1). Through both his preaching and written ministry, Peter cared for sheep in the assembly in Jerusalem and he also provided spiritual food for sheep in other assemblies.

The Mandates for a Shepherd

The Lord did not hand Peter a title, a badge, and keys to an office with a view. He simply and soberingly entrusted him with an immense work to do. Peter eventually came to appreciate three primary duties of a church leader.

Be an Elder!

Peter was very familiar with the Jewish concept of elders. In the culture, seniors deserved respect as "the beauty of old men is the grey head" (Prov 20:29). It was assumed that chronological age generally reflected years of experience in life resulting in practical wisdom. Beyond that, he would remember times when "all the chief priests and the elders and the scribes" came together (Mark 14:53). They met in Caiaphas's house "and Peter followed ... at a distance, right into the courtyard of the high priest" (Mark 14:54). There, in front of his eyes, he saw the Great Sanhedrin calling a meeting to order. The priests carried out the ceremonial law, the Scribes copied the law and interpreted it, and the elders, according to Gill, "were the civil magistrates". They applied the law for the people. Jewish history recounts the story of Moses telling God's plans to "all the elders" (Ex 12:21). Later, Boaz worked out the redemption of some fields and his marriage to Ruth "in the presence of the elders" (Ruth 4:4). Historically, in the city of Jerusalem the elders were respected for being mature, such that residents in the city would have confidence in their judgment. But, by the time of Christ, the "elders" had become political men forming part of the 71-member Great Sanhedrin which condemned the Son of God to death. After the resurrection of Christ, Peter preached the gospel to the same "rulers of the people, and elders" (Acts 4:8).

The word "elders" was carried over and sanctified by the Lord to describe those responsible for a New Testament church. The term is not describing a political position or a civil role. Rather, it is a trait of every man to whom the Lord has given the role of leadership in a local assembly. There are three key concepts involved with the term "elder".

Maturity:

The word implies progression. In their Christian lives, they have grown spiritually by feeding on the Word of God and their character and convictions are known and respected. As "ensamples to the flock" (1 Peter 5:3), they are role models whose example is Biblically sound. In addition, their counsel is trustworthy as they are "apt to teach" (2 Tim 2:24), and "they have spoken unto you the word of God" (Heb 13:7).

Responsibility:

Unlike children, mature adults assume responsibility for their decisions and actions. Church leaders are called elders because they are accountable to God for the direction and condition of the local church. The writer to the Hebrews said, "Obey them that have the rule over you, and submit yourselves: for they watch for your souls, as they that must give account" (Heb 13:17).

Stability:

Leaders will be tested through problems arising from within and without. Paul met with the elders of the assembly in Ephesus, and he warned them, "For I know this, that after my departing shall grievous wolves enter in among you, not sparing the flock. Also of your own selves shall men arise, speaking perverse things, to draw away disciples after them" (Acts 20:29-30). It wasn't long until Peter and the first assembly in Jerusalem were facing internal tension and conflict over the handling of funds for widows (Acts 6). The assembly also faced the external problem of Saul of Tarsus and his cronies persecuting believers. Luke noted that "at that time there was a great persecution against the church which was at Jerusalem; and they were all scattered abroad throughout the regions of Judaea and Samaria, except the apostles" (Acts 8:1). While others could pick up and leave, Peter and the other leaders "stayed by the stuff" to continue caring for the remaining sheep in their flock. Their own health and lives were at risk, but a "sheep-first" mentality continued to be their guiding principle.

So, in crisis moments, the Jerusalem assembly turned to their leaders knowing they would be there to guide them. In general, aren't older people usually more stable and predictable in life than younger folks? So, this is a great word to describe what God expects of leaders in his churches. Believers need to see consistency in assembly government. As the writer to the Hebrews said about leaders, ... whose faith follow, considering the outcome of their conduct" (Heb 13:7, NKJV). How impressive, then, that Peter should write, "I ... am also an elder." (1 Peter 5:1). The impetuous, unpredictable, constantly shifting Simon, had truly become Peter, the rock.

Be an Overseer!

Peter said that leaders are to be "taking the oversight" (1 Peter 5:2). This verb, *episcopeo*, is translated "serving as overseers" (1 Peter 5:2, NKJV) and "exercising oversight" (1 Peter 5:2, ESV). It only occurs one other time in the New Testament in Hebrews 12:15 where it is translated "looking diligently". The noun form is *episkopos*, a compound word combining *epi*, "over", and *skopeo*, "to look or watch". It is found five times in the New Testament and refers to the men who take on this role as overseers ("bishops" in the King James Version). Thayer gives the definition: "A man charged with the duty of seeing that things to be done by others are done rightly". Therefore, an overseer has the duty to make sure things in an assembly are done in an orderly way, according to Scripture.

Paul directed his Philippian letter to "all the saints in Christ Jesus which are at Philippi with the bishops and deacons" (Phil 1:1). These men were not secret agents, clandestinely scheming to control the church. They were known and recognized by all in the assembly. They were not voted into the role of elders nor did they force themselves into leadership positions. Paul reminded the Ephesian elders: "the Holy Spirit hath made you overseers" (Acts 20:28). Paul also gave the prerequisites to become a church leader and each time he said, "An overseer...must be..." (1 Tim 3:2; Titus 1:7). Overseers must pursue and meet a high standard of character which was fully and perfectly met by the model for church leaders, our Lord Jesus Christ. Peter reminded assembly believers of this when he wrote, "For you were straying like sheep, but have now returned to the Shepherd and Overseer of your souls" (1 Peter 2:25).

There is a third related word, *episcope,* which is a noun referring to the work done in this role. Paul wrote, "This is a true saying, If a man desire the office of a bishop, he desireth a good work" (1 Tim 3:1). Darby translates this verse, "if anyone aspires to exercise oversight, he desires a good work". This word, "office of a bishop" in the AV occurs just four times in the New Testament including twice where it is translated as "visitation". BDAG gives the definition: "the act of watching over with special reference to being present (visitation)". Peter also used this word when he exhorted believers, "Keep your conduct among the Gentiles honorable, so that when they speak against you as evildoers, they may see your good deeds and glorify God on the day of visitation" (1 Peter 2:12, ESV).

Therefore, the role of an overseer involves two main activities:

Observation:

The wise man said, "Be thou diligent to know the state of thy flocks, and look well to thy herds" (Prov 27:23). Paul warned the elders of the assembly in Ephesus of problems coming from outside and inside the assembly. He said, "For I know this, that after my departure savage wolves will come in among you, not sparing the flock. Also, from among yourselves men will rise up, speaking perverse things, to draw away disciples after themselves. Therefore watch ..." (Acts 20:29-31). Overseeing means to be watching over the assembly. Even the Lord Jesus warned about "the wolf coming ... and the wolf catcheth them, and scattereth the sheep" (John 10:12). Wrong doctrine can divide and devastate an assembly very quickly, so elders must be constantly on guard.

Vigilance is especially necessary when it comes to doctrine that is being taught both publicly and in private discussions. Peter had developed sensitivity to the importance of accuracy when it comes to teaching. In his last letter, he warned believers, "There will be false teachers among you, who will secretly bring in destructive heresies" (2 Peter 2:1, NKJV). Sadly, he added, "And many will follow their destructive ways" (2 Peter 2:2). He had seen a Judas secretly working among the disciples. He had sniffed out the fraudulent Simon Magus among the believers in Samaria (Acts 8:14-24). He was present at the great conference in Jerusalem to discuss men who had left that city wrongly preaching to Gentiles: "Except ye be circumcised after the manner of Moses, ye cannot be saved" (Acts 15:1). Peter himself experienced intimidation by slick operators who deceived him when he visited Antioch. Unwittingly, Peter began to espouse doctrinal error such that Paul had to confront him face to face. Paul later described what occurred when he said, "For before that certain came from James, he [Peter] did eat with the Gentiles: but when they were come, he withdrew and separated himself, fearing them which were of the circumcision" (Gal 2:12). If errant Judaizing teachers intimidated an apostle and elder like Peter, what could they do to the rest of us?

The writer to the Hebrews said that "them that have the rule over you ... watch for your souls" (Heb 13:17). How? "Praying always with all prayer and supplication in the Spirit, and watching thereunto with all perseverance and supplication for all saints" (Eph 6:18). Prayer and watching are essential activities for overseers. Is that how Peter knew Simon the Sorcerer was fraudulent? Is that how he knew Ananias and Sapphira were infected with the virus of greed? Like cancer, early detection is the key to the treatment of spiritual ailments among the sheep and to thwart spiritual attacks against them. So, may God give all who seek to lead God's flocks a greater burden for watchfulness and increased discernment for problems within the assemblies.

Administration:

The second activity of overseers is the management of the assembly.

They are responsible to God for the condition, activities, and decisions of the church. The very first mention of elders is when, in the assembly in Antioch, "every man according to his ability, determined to send relief unto the brethren which dwelt in Judaea: Which also they did, and sent it to the elders by the hands of Barnabas and Saul" (Acts 11:29-30). The introduction of elders is not when they are teaching or confronting problems, but when they are receiving funds. While they would obviously encourage input from assembly believers as to how to distribute the offerings received, the administration of those funds was the elders' responsibility.

Peter and the other apostles, who functioned in leadership at the beginning of the assembly in Jerusalem, assumed a very practical responsibility. "As many as were possessors of lands or houses sold them, and brought the prices of the things that were sold, And laid them down at the apostles' feet: and distribution was made unto every man according as he had need" (Acts 4:34-35). Their first problem also had to do with money. "Now in those days, when the number of the disciples was multiplying, there arose a complaint against the Hebrews by the Hellenists, because their widows were neglected in the daily distribution" (Acts 6:1). In that case, the church leaders decided to delegate the distribution of funds to men of good character and reputation. They said to the assembly, "Therefore, brethren, seek out from among you seven men of good reputation, full of the Holy Spirit and wisdom, whom we may appoint over this business" (Acts 6:3, NKJV). Choosing to delegate duties was a wise decision just as it was for Moses when he faced the overwhelming responsibility of making decisions and guiding the Israelites (Ex 18:13-27). While a group of reliable men would handle the practical responsibilities of gathering and administering the funds in the church in Jerusalem, the elders would remain accountable to God for all decisions and the practical execution of them. Financial matters are just some of the very practical judgments and activities in an assembly for which elders are responsible, whether they make the decisions themselves or assign them to others. May God give leaders today what the leaders in the first assembly of over 5,000 needed:

stamina, wisdom, courage, and the grace to know when to delegate responsibilities.

Be a Shepherd!

Through Interaction:

You cannot effectively shepherd sheep remotely from your study or office. You must get out and have contact with them. Peter heard Jesus teach about a shepherd: "... the sheep hear his voice; and he calleth his own sheep by name, and leadeth them out" (John 10:3). As the Good Shepherd, said, "My sheep hear my voice, and I know them, and they follow me" (John 10:27). So, when Peter wrote approximately 30 years later, he spoke of "The elders which are among you" (1 Peter 5:1). To them he repeated the point: "Feed the flock of God which is among you" (1 Peter 5:2). Peter is the only apostle that specifically identifies himself as a shepherd in an assembly. While other apostles took the gospel to distant lands, Peter appears to have stayed primarily in Jerusalem and the surrounding area, thus allowing him locally to shepherd the sheep for which he was responsible.

Remember that the term "overseer" involves the concept of visits. Communication with believers is easier now than ever before. It is not a case of just shaking hands with them at meetings, it is keeping in touch with when things are going well and when there are difficulties. Through communication and interaction, the goal is to get to know the sheep. Praying for each one by name is a great way to care for the flock. If there is communication with the sheep on a personal level first, this will guide an overseer when he bows to pray about them before God.

Hospitality is also a requirement for elders. Paul listed "given to hospitality" (1 Tim 3:2) and "a lover of hospitality" (Titus 1:8) as characteristics of all church leaders. When the assembly was formed in Jerusalem, Peter was already in the habit of using his home to help and bless others. It was likely in Peter's house in Capernaum that the multitude gathered to hear the Lord Jesus teach and there He healed the paralytic. The Saviour was a frequent guest in Peter's home in Galilee, and undoubtedly Peter continued that practice with believers in Jerusalem. Thus, with years of this healthy habit in place, Peter wrote, "Be hospitable to one another without grumbling" (1 Peter 4:9). Interaction with believers over a private meal or a cup of coffee is a great way to understand the thinking, convictions, activities, problems, needs and burdens of each believer in the flock.

When the Lord Jesus commissioned Peter to care for believers, He said, "Tend my sheep" (John 21:16). Paul used this word when he told the Ephesian elders that the Holy Spirit had made them overseers and they were to "shepherd the assembly of God" (Acts 20:28, Darby), or, as the ESV gives it, "care for the church of God". Sheep are needy creatures and depend on those who care for them to lead them, help them find food, resolve issues when they are sick, defend them when they are in danger, and seek them out when they stray. That is the exact mission the Lord gave to Peter, and he then relayed that commission to others when he wrote, "shepherd the flock of God" (1 Peter 5:2, ESV). It requires long hours, much energy, and great sacrifices to care for God's people. They have varied and constant needs which can tax the most able shepherd. But, if "the good shepherd giveth his life for the sheep" (John 10:11), assembly shepherds should stretch themselves out in sacrificial care for God's people as well.

Through Instruction:

Jesus also told Peter, "Feed my lambs" (John 21:15) and "Feed my sheep" (John 21:17). In the synoptic Gospels, the word *bosko* is used to describe a person providing food for a herd of animals (e.g. pigs). While he likely had no heart for hogs, the prodigal son ended up feeding swine before he repented and returned home (Luke 15:15). The idea is to provide nutrition which will stimulate growth in young ones (lambs) and maintain health in older ones (sheep). David wrote, "The Lord is my shepherd; I shall not want. He maketh me to lie down in green pastures: he leadeth me beside the still waters" (Ps 23:1-2). Jesus told Peter and the disciples that, as the Good Shepherd, He assures that His sheep "shall go in and out, and find pasture" (John 10:9).

Therefore, a nutritious diet is critical for the health and growth of sheep. Shepherds, by divine mandate, are to be "apt to teach" (1 Tim 3:2). They should seek to follow Paul's example in Ephesus. He reminded the elders there: "I have not shunned to declare unto you all the counsel of God" (Acts 20:27). Consecutive ministry and contextual ministry will be the greatest means through which we will see spiritual prosperity in both the lambs and the sheep in the assembly.

But this takes sensitivity as the diet must be appropriate to the developmental stage of the sheep. The Saviour distinctly said that Peter was to feed lambs and feed sheep. He was recognizing that, while they are both part of the same flock, they are at different stages of spiritual maturity. If teaching in an assembly consists solely of the exposition of deep truths in Scripture, older believers may be happy and healthy, but the spiritually immature will be unable to digest it. If the teaching in an assembly is limited to only the basics of baptism and Christian living, less mature believers will grow, but more mature ones may become stagnant, weak, and sick.

Through intervention:

Young David once said to King Saul, "Thy servant kept his father's sheep, and there came a lion, and a bear, and took a lamb out of the flock: And I went out after him, and smote him, and delivered it out of his mouth: and when he arose against me, I caught him by his beard, and smote him, and slew him" (1 Sam 17:34-35). A shepherd keeps an eye out for enemies of the sheep who might do them harm. When he senses danger, he will courageously confront the threat.

As evangelists, Peter and his fellow apostles required great valour to speak to unbelieving and hostile Jewish audiences. Peter and John were infused with such conviction that even the Jewish leaders "saw the boldness of Peter and John" (Acts 4:13). As they served the Lord and preached the gospel, "they spake the word of God with boldness" (Acts 4:31). But Peter would also require courage to confront fraudulent believers and errant teachers.

It was Peter who discerned that Simon Magus had deceived Philip the evangelist and it was Peter who confronted Simon with the truth when he said, "Thou hast neither part nor lot in this matter: for thy heart is not right in the sight of God" (Acts 8:21). It was Peter who wrote to believers and warned, "There shall be false teachers among you, who privily shall bring in damnable heresies … And many shall follow their pernicious ways" (2 Peter 2:1-2). Peter went on to detail the twisted motives and flawed character of these men and their deceptive modes of operation. Then he concluded, "be on your guard so that you are not carried away by the error of unprincipled men" (2 Peter 3:17, NSAB). Sheep depend on shepherds for their safety. Thus, a shepherd needs the discernment and courage of a Peter to spot and confront threats to the health and welfare of the flock.

Be a leader!

The writer to the Hebrew Christians was very conscious of Jewish admiration for the patriarchs, Abraham, Isaac and Jacob, and the long list of leaders in their history including Joseph, Moses, David, "Gideon, Barak, Samson, Jephthah, of David and Samuel and the prophets" (Heb 11:32). He reminds them of their national history replete with outstanding examples of faith found in generations of leaders raised up by God. In Chapter 12, he takes them to the Consummate Leader, "the author and finisher of our faith" (Heb 12:2), our Lord Jesus Christ. Then, in chapter 13, he tells them, "Remember them which have the rule over you, who have spoken unto you the word of God: whose faith follow, considering the end of their conversation" (Heb 13:7). Lest anyone misunderstands, this text is no justification to "rule over" in a despotic manner of the kind that marked Pharaoh's rule over the Hebrew slaves. Scripture never envisions red-faced, out-of-control, verbal bat-wielding despots. In fact, Peter himself prohibited elders from "being lords over God's heritage, but [rather] being ensamples to the flock" (1 Peter 5:3). This word "rule over" is better understood as "leader" as in the Darby translation. It is a participle used to describe men by their habitual action – leading. Thus, the NASB translates it, "Remember those who led you, who spoke the word of God to you; and considering the result of their conduct, imitate their faith". This is a call to actively learn from the teaching of previous leaders who had perhaps been martyred for their faith. They were men who had led God's people by teaching and example; men whose practice agreed with their preaching.

Then, the writer focuses his letter to Hebrew Christians on current assembly government when he says, "Obey them that have the rule over you, and submit yourselves: for they watch for your souls, as they that must give account, that they may do it with joy, and not with grief: for that is unprofitable for you" (Heb 13:17). Especially in tough times, it is easy to find fault with leaders and to rebel against them. The writer combines both concepts and tells the sheep to respond to the shepherds with obedience and submission so that when they speak to God about them, they can do it with a smile and not a heartache.

One prominent feature of true Biblical leaders in this chapter is that they have convictions based on Scripture, not tradition. Peter exemplified this as he led the other disciples in finding a replacement for Judas in Acts 1. He explained his clear Biblical basis for the action by quoting from Psalm 69:25 and Psalm 109:8, and with an implied connection to Psalm 41:9. Peter also learned of the tremendous danger when a leader acts without Biblical basis. As mentioned, Paul once had to confront him on his view on the treatment of Gentile Christians who were not circumcised (Gal 2). The worst part is that because he was a leader, "The rest of the Jews joined him in hypocrisy, with the result that even Barnabas was carried away by their hypocrisy" (Gal 2:13, NASB).

Another characteristic of true leaders is that they are willing both to make decisions and to be quick to accept responsibility for them. Peter was likely a natural leader, and the Lord sanctified the skill for His purposes. For example, the Lord gave the responsibility to Peter to lead in the sharing of the gospel with Gentiles, like Cornelius. At the conference in Jerusalem, the first to stand up and speak in favour of the commission to evangelize every creature was Peter. He preached the first sermon to the Jews (Acts 2) and the first sermon to the Gentiles (Acts 10), and we are still following his example today. Peter proved to be a fantastic leader in his home, in the fishing business, among the 12 apostles, and in the assembly in Jerusalem.

Leadership is best seen in the person of the Lord Jesus. The wise men used this word when quoting Micah 5:2 to describe the child, Jesus. They said, "...for from you [Bethlehem] shall come a ruler who will shepherd my people Israel". Therefore, as shepherds, our role model is the "Good Shepherd" (John 10:11, 14). As overseers, our role model is Christ, "the Overseer of your souls" (1 Peter 2:25, NKJV). Likewise, as leaders, our role model is the perfect leader, the King of Kings and Lord of Lords. In following His example, we have the opportunity to display a little of His character as we serve others in the assembly.

Be a Messenger!

The Lord Jesus wanted to communicate with seven assemblies in Asia Minor. To do that, He commanded the Apostle John to write and send mini letters to each one. These letters are compiled in the second and third chapters of the book of Revelation. John was to address each letter to what the AV calls, "the angel of the church in ....". Much debate has occurred over the centuries as to whom this refers. Many knowledgeable and spiritual men have taught that the angel is a literal angel as that is consistent with the vast majority of the 175 uses of the word *angelos* in the New Testament. In addition, in the 58 times the word is used outside of these mini letters in the book of the Revelation it always refers to literal angels. However, Matthew, Mark, Luke, Paul, James, and the writer to the Hebrews all use the same word at least once in their writings to describe a person sent on a mission which is the precise meaning of *angelos*. The preferred translation in all versions on those occasions is "messenger". I suggest, therefore, that the Lord instructs John to write to the leadership of each church - the elders or oversight. The "messenger" is part of the church, and five of the seven churches are told to repent. An angel, if literally understood, would not have a need to repent of sin. So, if we allow the interpretation that "the messenger" refers to the element of leadership in an assembly, that means that the responsibility of local church leaders is to keep in touch with Heaven and relay messages from the Lord at the right time, to the right people, in the right way and about the right issues. The duty of church leaders then is to have a Haggai-type ministry and be "the Lord's messenger in the Lord's message unto the people" (Hag 1:13).

Peter demonstrated that spirit when the first Gentiles were reached with the gospel in the book of Acts. Fairly quickly afterward, "the apostles and brethren that were in Judaea heard that the Gentiles had also received the word of God" (Acts 11:1). When questions were raised, Peter returned to Jerusalem and "rehearsed the matter from the beginning and expounded it by order unto them" (Acts 11:4). He did not just quote random or favourite Bible verses. Instead, he reported to the men in Jerusalem and presented a word from God. Yes, the activities of distributing funds, planning meetings, and organizing activities can consume much time and energy. However, the greatest need for overseers is to be in touch with God and have messages for the moment. May God help us to learn this art from our Saviour whose secret He revealed when He said, "The Lord God hath given me the tongue of the learned that I should know how to speak a word in season to him that is weary: he wakeneth morning by morning, he wakeneth mine ear to hear as the learned" (Isa 50:4).

The Measuring of a Shepherd

Shepherding work can be wearisome and discouraging. Often shepherds become the focus of criticism as their work and judgments are public and their decisions impact individuals and families. Any wrong decisions are subject to great scrutiny. Peter knew what it was like to face conflict as a leader when there was dissension over the treatment of widows in the assembly in Jerusalem in Acts 6. He knew what it was like to face a crisis as he and the other leaders confronted a major issue at the great conference in Jerusalem. He knew what it was to take heat for his belief that Gentiles could also be saved. Luke records, "Now the apostles and the brothers who were throughout Judea heard that the Gentiles also had received the word of God. So, when Peter went up to Jerusalem, the circumcision party criticized him" (Acts 11:1-2, ESV). Peter also knew what it was like as a leader to fail publicly. He would never forget that he had denied his Lord and years later he let men with wrong doctrine influence his behaviour toward other Christians (Gal 2:12). It is always embarrassing to fail, but it is worse when a leader fails because his error in judgment is more readily seen, discussed, and criticized by others.

Perhaps someone would ask, "Why bother putting yourself in a position for so much stress and scrutiny?" It does make you wonder what kept Peter going as an elder and shepherd among God's people. He was certainly not interested in being voted "Elder of the Year". Although he acted as a gentleman and tried to be as careful and kind as he could, what mattered most was not his approval ratings among believers. He clearly had the conviction that the Lord had entrusted His sheep to him (John 21:15-17). Therefore, even the numerical quantity of sheep in the assembly did not interest Peter because the Saviour does not grade shepherds based on the size of their flocks. The Lord's greatest desire for shepherds is faithfulness to His Word and obedience to His will. Thus, Peter exhorted fellow elders to complete their mission faithfully because "when the chief Shepherd shall appear, ye shall receive a crown of glory that fadeth not away" (1 Peter 5:4).

Peter reminded shepherds in God's assemblies that they are working for Christ as delegated extensions of His great care for His people. Christ is the Good Shepherd (John 10:11) who sacrificed his life, the "great shepherd" (Heb 13:20) who succeeded in his death, and the "chief Shepherd" who will give rewards (1 Peter 5:4). Peter once heard the Saviour say, "And whosoever shall give to drink unto one of these little ones a cup of cold water only in the name of a disciple, verily I say unto you, he shall in no wise lose his reward" (Matt 10:42).

CHAPTER 14

Peter the Doorkeeper

It was a stunning announcement! The Lord Jesus had taken His disciples 25 miles north of the Sea of Galilee to Caesarea Philippi at the base of Mount Hermon. The Old Testament names and references to this mountain reflect the long history of idolatry in the most northerly region of Israel. It is referred to as Baal-Hermon (Judges 3:3) and Baal-Gad, the name of a god of fortune (Joshua 13:5). Centuries later, the Greeks named the city Panium or Paneas, after their god Pan, the god who watches over flocks, forests, mountains and the wild. It became a famous place for the worship of Pan and many other gods. Eventually, the Roman Empire spread, and the area was given to Herod the Great who built a pagan temple there. Later, his son, Philip, showing both his desire to please Emperor Augustus and stroke his own ego, renamed the city, Caesarea Philippi.

To the Jews, this place was infamous as a consummate example of pagan and pantheistic worship of many Greek and Roman gods. Perhaps that is why the Jewish historian Flavius Josephus, in his *Antiquities of the Jews* (written in about AD 93), still refers to the city as Caesarea Paneas. The specific place of worship was a large cave out of the mouth of which water had flowed for centuries forming the beginning of the Jordan River. It was similar to Pergamos in Asia Minor, a place "where Satan's seat is ... where Satan dwelleth" (Rev 2:13).

The Lord Jesus did not take Peter and the disciples to the temple of the Jews in Jerusalem. Nor did He take them to Mount Gerizim, the revered mountain of worship of the Samaritans. Instead, He led his followers to Panias, a recognized command and control centre of Satan. As they approached Panias, He asked His disciples, "Whom do men say that I the Son of man am?" (Matt 16:13). They reported that some Jews were thinking that He was John the Baptist, others thought He was Elijah, and still others that He was Jeremiah or one of the Old Testament prophets. The diversity and ignorance in their views showed that, "He [Christ] was in the world, and the world was made by him, and the world knew him not. He came unto his own, and his own received him not" (John 1:10-11).

The Lord then asked for the disciples to give their opinions as to who He was. Peter immediately declared, "Thou art the Christ, the Son of the living God" (Mathew 16:16). What a confession! This was a deep conviction in Peter's heart which he emphasizes with the articles "THE Christ", THE Son, and "THE God" preceded by the most definite affirmation, "Thou art". This is the second person way of saying "I AM", the great identity of Jehovah to Moses (Ex 3:14) and of Christ as seen in the seven "I AM" statements in John's gospel.

Ironically, at some point, a Greek myth developed about a goddess called Echo. Greeks believed that Echo had previously been punished and her voice was taken so that she could only repeat the words of others. Later, Echo refused the love of the god Pan. So, supposedly, in an act of vengeance, Pan had Echo brutally destroyed and had her body distributed to all parts of the world. Her body was gone, and yet the myth was that her voice continued to speak. Perhaps it was with that in the background, that the Lord appreciates Peter's confession which is now recorded in Scripture and resounding throughout the world. Thank God, the identity of His Son will continue to sound and be appreciated throughout eternity.

As we know, Greeks and Romans sincerely believed in their mythological gods which were nothing more than diabolical explanations of natural events as a way to capture and control the hearts of pagans. Against that background, Peter makes his great confession about the one, true living God and His unique Son, Jesus the Christ. His statement was a contradiction of Pan, which came to mean all or multiple; it was an affront to the plurality of gods of Pantheism. His confession contrasted Jehovah, the one true God, with all false pagan gods. He claimed that God was alive, unlike all idols of wood and stone made by men. For, "Their idols are silver and gold, the work of men's hands. They have mouths, but they speak not: eyes have they, but they see not: They have ears, but they hear not: noses have they, but they smell not: They have hands, but they handle not: feet have they, but they walk not: neither speak they through their throat" (Ps 115:4-7). Finally, unlike the complex and intertwined Greek and Roman gods with multiple partners and multiple children, Peter's thrilling claim was that Jesus was THE Son of THE God. Peter's grasp of the person of God and the person of Christ was outstanding; truly a unique appreciation among the disciples. The Greeks had Eros, the god of love; Rhea, the god of comfort; Penelope, the god of patience, etc. Peter believed that all divine attributes were equally found in the one living God and His Son, Jesus Christ.

Against the background of a massive stone cliff and cave, Jesus announced, "Thou art Peter, and upon this rock I will build my church" (Matt 16:18). There is a divergence of opinions among Bible scholars and commentators as to what Jesus was referring when he spoke of "this rock". The Catholic interpretation is that He was referring to Peter as the first pope and Jesus was introducing papal or apostolic succession. However, Peter never referred to himself as a rock nor did any of the other apostles or New Testament writers in the sense of him being a pope or having papal authority as defined by the Roman Catholic Church.

Perhaps to avoid any association with Peter, many commentators have pointed out what appears to be a play on words in Greek with a subtle difference between Peter (*petros*) and rock (*petra*). Thus, based on that distinction, some have thought the Lord was describing Himself as the true Rock. Undeniably, "rock" is a common metaphor to describe Jehovah in the Old Testament. Moses wrote, "He is the Rock, his work is perfect" (Deut 32:4). David similarly said, "The Lord is my rock, and my fortress, and my deliverer, my God, my rock, in whom I take refuge" (2 Sam 22:2-3). Isaiah (Isa 44:8), Ethan the Ezrahite (Ps 89:26), Asaph (Ps 78:35), and the sons of Korah (Ps 42:9) also refer to God with the title of "Rock". In the New Testament, Paul clarified an Old Testament symbol when he wrote that the Israelites "drank of that spiritual Rock that followed them: and that Rock was Christ" (1 Cor 10:4). Peter also used the same Greek word, *petra*, to describe Christ when he wrote that Christ was a "stone of stumbling, and a rock of offense" (1 Peter 2:8). Therefore, describing the Church again, Paul wrote, "For other foundation can no man lay than that is laid, which is Jesus Christ" (1 Cor 3:11). Without any question, using the word "rock" to describe Christ and His immutable character has a clear Biblical basis.

Another common view is that the Lord was referring to the content of Peter's confession as being the solid, foundational truth of the church. Considering Matthew 16:17, the view is that it is truth revealed by the Father that forms the basis of Peter's statement. No-one would contend the reality that belief in the deity of Christ is essential for a person to have eternal life (1 John 5:10-13). The opposite is also true: "This is the antichrist, he who denies the Father and the Son" (1 John 2:22). Paul later wrote that the Church is "built on the foundation of the apostles and prophets, Christ Jesus himself being the cornerstone" (Eph 2:20). What the apostles and prophets confessed and taught about Christ became the very basis for the formation of His church.

A further suggestion that seems most valid is that He could actually have been referring to Peter, but clearly not in the sense of him becoming the first pope or to papal authority and succession as taught by the Roman Catholic Church. The Lord said, "thou art Peter (*petros*), and upon this rock (*petra*) I will build my church" (Matt 16:18). Much is made by commentators about the difference between *petros* and *petra* with the distinction being made that the former refers to a loose rock and the latter to bedrock or a large rock shelf or face. In John 1:42, the Lord had laid out His plan to transform a very unstable, impetuous, (Simon) into a firm, unchanging rock (*kephas* in Aramaic, meaning rock). At times, the Lord refers to Peter by his natural name Simon, or Simon, son of John, especially when Peter acts in a natural, fleshly way. Even here, the Lord points out that naturally he is Simon Barjona. By contrast, this would be a pinnacle spiritual moment for him when making this great confession. So, it is fitting that at this moment the Lord exclaims, "Thou art Peter!" He was truly acting and speaking with solid, Biblical basis. It is upon a man with that character, conviction and confession that He would initiate the building process of His church. In other words, He is pointing out the character of the instrument He would use to initiate His great construction plans. In this interpretation, the Lord is not the rock then, but the architect and builder. He was a carpenter in Nazareth who likely worked with both wood and stone. For this project, the first tool in His hand would be Peter in Acts chapter two. We must not let our fear of assigning him papacy keep us from seeing the clear focus on the man called Peter in the Lord's statement in Matthew 16:18.

The Lord asked the disciples (plural) who they thought He was. Peter steps forward and stands out with a personal confession in Matthew 16:16. Andrew had recognized that Jesus was the Messiah (John 1.41), but Peter is the first to be convinced and audibly declare the deity of Christ. Before introducing His plan to use Peter, "Jesus answered and said unto him, Blessed art thou, Simon Barjona: for flesh and blood hath not revealed it unto thee, but my Father which is in heaven" (Matt 16:17). Some people had taken Herod's view that Jesus was John the Baptist (Matt 14:2), or the popular view promoted by some Jewish leaders that He was at best one of the prophets. However, rather than finding his belief in popular opinions of mere men ("flesh and blood") or his own personal opinions or feelings, Peter's understanding of the deity of Christ, came directly from the Father through Old Testament Scripture. Clearly, it was a conviction and confession based on divine revelation.

Truth revealed by God through Scripture is always the foundation of our beliefs. Hearing the Lord speak about the rock, surely Peter's mind would dart back to the Lord's teaching in what is often called His Sermon on the Mount. Jesus taught in the Parable of the Two Builders, "Therefore whosoever heareth these sayings of mine, and doeth them, I will liken him unto a wise man, which built his house upon a rock" (Matt 7:24). Here was a divinely given and unchanging revelation to Peter's heart that would anchor him spiritually for the rest of his life and for eternity. No wonder, then, that the Saviour says, "Blessed art thou!" (Matt 16:17). It was true for Christ himself as "Blessed is the man ... [whose] delight is in the law of the LORD; and in his law doth he meditate day and night" (Ps 1:1-2). Isn't that still true today? The Scripturally based life is truly the blessed life as it is the life Christ lived on earth.

The Lord Jesus immediately follows by saying, "upon this rock (*petra*), I will build my church" (Matt 16:16). As Vincent puts it, "The word refers neither to Christ as a rock, distinguished from Simon, a stone, nor to Peter's confession, but to Peter himself, in a sense defined by his previous confession, and as enlightened by the "Father in Heaven". In verse 17, the Lord praises Peter and explains His conclusion as to the identity of the Saviour being due to divine revelation. The immediate context when the Lord said in Matthew 16:18, "upon this rock" is Peter. Verse 18 even begins with the Lord referring to His disciple by saying, "thou art Peter". The words "upon this" usually would refer to the closest antecedent, which is *petros*. Edersheim adds, "The word πέτρα was used in the same sense [as petras] in Rabbinic language". Louw-Nida admits, "As can be seen from the transliteration of the Greek words, the masculine derivative form Petros (Peter) has a different ending from the root word *petra*, which is feminine and means rock". Aramaic, however, would not distinguish between masculine and feminine forms, so that the result would be "You are *kefa*, and on this *kefa* I will build ..." Because Jesus would have generally spoken in Aramaic to His Jewish followers, they likely would not have even thought of a difference between Jesus as a rock face and Peter as a small crumbling of shale. Some English translators have made the Aramaic statement abundantly clear. For example, Phillips in his New Testament translation gives it as "You are Peter the rock, and it is on this rock ...". Young's Literal Translation reads, "And I also say to thee, that thou art a rock, and upon this rock I will build my assembly".

Peter would understand that "the church", by definition, as a called-out company, would be distinct from Israel. He would also sense that Christ's building plans had been eternally drawn, but the project had not yet begun. Christ said, "I will   " (future, active, indicative, first person, singular). This statement clearly emphasizes that this is the

Son of God's church and its construction would depend uniquely on Him. Peter would have no authority in himself; he would solely be an instrument in the hand of the divine architect and builder, the Lord of Glory.

Whenever something is pronounced as belonging to Christ or being used by Christ, Satanic opposition and fury are aroused. In the Parable of the Sower and the Soils, Jesus identified that "the seed is the word of God" (Luke 8:11). Having identified that the seed of Scripture belongs to God and that God uses it when it is sown by the sower, Jesus continued, "then cometh the devil, and taketh away the word out of their hearts, lest they should believe and be saved" (Luke 8:12). At Jesus' baptism, the Father declared from heaven, "This is my beloved Son, in whom I am well pleased" (Matt 3:17). Immediately afterwards, "Then was Jesus led up of the Spirit into the wilderness to be tempted of the devil" (Matt 4:1). This time would be no exception. Jesus anticipated the Satanic attempts to ruin His plan to build His church. "The gates of Hell (*hades*)" (Matt (16:18) is an expression referring to the demonic forces led by their leader, Satan himself. Gates in Scripture are where the leaders and authorities did business. For example, Lot sat in the gate, and Boaz worked out his plan of redemption at the gates of Bethlehem with the elders (Ruth 4:1-13). The Lord brought the disciples to Panias and He made this great announcement right there in a command and control centre of infernal hosts. Despite their location, Jesus never experienced fear that day or on any occasion. Instead, He confidently stated His promise, "the gates of hell shall not prevail against it" (Matt 16:18). The Devil and his cohorts could pour out from Hell like waters out of that cave of Panias and roll down in attack on Christ's church, but they would have zero success. He would build "His church" – and He continues to build it today!

It appears that Satan also understood that Peter would be Christ's instrument to initiate the building project of His church. Immediately following this dialogue, just four verses later, we are told that Peter began rebuking the Lord for speaking about the imminent suffering and death on the cross. The Lord then had to say to Peter, "Get thee behind me, Satan" (Matt 16:22). Without his awareness, Peter was being influenced by Satan to try to stop the Lord Jesus from going to the cross and thus prevent the formation and construction of His church. We know Satan only backed off temporarily. It was not long until he came after Peter again. While he did succeed in influencing Peter to deny the Lord three times, he could never stop the Saviour from going to the cross. Nor could he impede the Lord's plan and promise to use Peter to begin the great construction project of His church.

But, how would Peter be used if the Lord was the builder? Jesus went on to say to him, "I will give unto thee the keys of the kingdom of heaven: and whatsoever thou shalt bind on earth shall be bound in heaven: and whatsoever thou shalt loose on earth shall be loosed in heaven" (Matt 16:19). As certainly as the Lord would build His church, He would also assuredly provide means through which Peter, as a doorkeeper, could open significant gates on behalf of heaven. Thus, the Lord would give him the "keys of the kingdom of heaven". The expression, "kingdom of heaven" occurs 32 times and is only found in Matthew's Gospel, the Gospel of the king. At times it seems to refer to the physical kingdom of Christ on earth that is still to come in the Millennium, but, also it refers to the spiritual, invisible reign of Christ in the hearts of believers on earth while He is heaven. Both aspects of His kingdom currently have and will have the same character and requirements.

The keys were for distinct openings of opportunities and plans relative to the kingdom, where heaven's authority is recognized, and heaven's character is put on display. The Lord promised that He would give Peter more than one key (plural), which implies different phases (doors) which He would initiate relative to the reign of divine authority. In Matthew 16, the Lord did not identify when Peter would use the keys or what doors he would open. One thing would be clear, the Lord would do the building, but Peter would open doors.

This would be an incredibly humbling privilege for Peter. Just 50 days before the day of Pentecost in Acts 2, Peter had slipped into Caiaphas, the high priest's house where Jesus was detained. Jesus' accusers gathered around a fire, "But Peter stood at the door without. Then went out that other disciple, which was known unto the high priest, and spake unto her that kept the door, and brought in Peter" (John 18:16). It was that doorkeeper who mentioned Peter's connection to Christ, but Peter denied it. As he thought on the Lord's promise to open doors through him, Peter would never forget his failure at a door that he should have left shut.

To add to his humbling, Peter also would have to recognize that the Lord did not need him. Later, when Peter was in prison in Jerusalem, he was awakened by an angel and miraculously led out. "When they were past the first and the second guard posts, they came to the iron gate that leads to the city, which opened to them of its own accord; and they went out and went down one street, and immediately the angel departed from him" (Acts 12:10, NKJV). The Lord is capable of opening doors all by Himself. As to a sheepfold gate, Peter heard Jesus say, "I am the door. If anyone enters by me, he will be saved and will go in and out and find pasture" (John 10:9). The Lord Jesus himself said, "I have the keys of Death and Hades" (Rev 1:18). To the angel of the church in Philadelphia, Christ described Himself with the promise of Isaiah 22:22 by saying, "The words of the holy one, the true one, who has the key of David, who opens and no one will shut, who shuts and no one opens ... Behold, I have set before thee an open door, and no man can shut it" (Rev 3:7-8). Clearly, Christ could open any door necessary - He did not need Peter.

When the Lord brought him out of prison, Peter went to Mary's house where the assembly was holding a prayer meeting. "And as Peter knocked at the door of the gate, a damsel came to hearken, named Rhoda. And when she knew Peter's voice, she opened not the gate for gladness, but ran in, and told how Peter stood before the gate" (Acts 12:13-14). Rhoda, in her excitement, failed as a doorkeeper. Peter had come to know the perfect Doorkeeper who would always open the right doors at the right time. He clearly did not need Peter as a doorman, and He had already shown him that He did not need him as a fisherman either. Nor did the Lord need Peter to look after sheep or be an overseer because He alone is the Good Shepherd and the "Overseer of our souls" (1 Peter 2:25). How humbling, then, for Peter to think that the Lord did not need him to fish, but He wanted to use him to fish for men. The Lord did not need him to shepherd, yet He commanded Peter to "Feed my sheep!" He did not need him to oversee, yet He gave him the opportunity to oversee the flock in Jerusalem. Likewise, although He did not need Peter to open doors, the Lord longed to use him, and kindly placed the keys of the Kingdom in Peter's hands. And may we apply the same truth to our roles and activities as well. In whatever we are called to do for Him, may we never lose sight of the fact that we are unworthy of such a privilege because of our failure and limitations. In addition, may we never forget that, while the Lord is able to complete His purposes without us, He longs to use us.

As the work of building the Church is taken forward, we watch Peter execute his role with divine help. On the Day of Pentecost in Acts 2, the Kingdom of Heaven was particularly opened first to the Jews when Peter preached in Jerusalem and 3,000 souls were saved. Then, in Acts 8, when Peter heard of Philip preaching in Samaria, he travelled there. While traditionally "the Jews have no dealings with the Samaritans" (John 4:9), this was the next door to be opened and he confirms the divine plan by preaching to the Samaritans. Jesus had told his disciples, "ye shall be witnesses unto me both in Jerusalem, and in all Judaea, and in Samaria, and unto the uttermost part of the earth" (Acts 1:8). Step one (Jerusalem and Judea) and step two (Samaria) had been completed as the Lord used Peter to open door one and door two. All that was left now was the door to the Gentiles.

Peter was praying on the roof of Simon the Tanner's house in Joppa, when suddenly he had the vision of the sheet full of clean and unclean animals being let down from Heaven three times. Peter understood the Lord's instruction and later explained it to others by saying, "God hath shewed me that I should not call any man common or unclean" (Acts 10:28). Following the vision, the Lord directed Peter to Caesarea to the house of Cornelius, a Gentile Roman centurion. When Peter declared, "through his name (Jesus) whosoever believeth in him shall receive remission of sins" (Acts 10:43), the door to world-wide evangelism of Gentiles was also flung open. Later, at the great church conference of apostles and elders in Jerusalem, "Peter rose up, and said unto them, 'Men and brethren, ye know how that a good while ago God made choice among us, that the Gentiles by my mouth should hear the word of the gospel, and believe.'" (Acts 15:7). Yes, the very mouth that had once denied the Lord was now used of God. A man who had once failed to keep a door closed, by God's grace, now faithfully and obediently opened three great doors of evangelistic outreach for which we will all be eternally grateful.

CHAPTER 15

Peter the Citizen

The Lord Jesus had a way of teaching without saying a word. In the Garden of Gethsemane, He took Peter, James, and John a little distance from the other disciples. Then, "he withdrew from them about a stone's throw, and knelt down and prayed" (Lk 22:41, ESV). By the distance of His position, He was demonstrating that even the closest of His disciples could not share in His sorrow, nor could they comprehend it. Before speaking a word, His very posture (knelt) and purpose (prayed) showed that even in intense suffering, He would continue in communion with the Father.

Likewise, a simple choice by the Sovereign Saviour would convey a clear lesson to Peter and his co-disciples. Mark tells us that Jesus "went up on the mountain and called to him those whom he desired, and they came to him. And he appointed twelve" (Mark 3:13-14). In the mix of men who were privileged to form part of His select servants were the unlikely choices of Matthew and the other Simon. Matthew himself records the event and he adds that one of the young men was "Matthew the publican" (Matt 10:3). While no one else would bring up his pre-conversion life, Matthew never forgot the sinful pit from which the grace of God had lifted him. Before he met Christ, he was a Jew working for the Roman government as a tax collector. Publicans were renowned for abusing their position by overcharging tax bills to line their own pockets. However, as a Jew, his employment was more than a job; it was an endorsement, or at least a tacit approval, of Roman occupation and control of the land promised to Israel.

In all four lists of the twelve disciples, the other Simon is distinguished by Luke as Zelotes, "the Zealot" (Luke 6:15; Acts 1:13), or as "the Canaanite" by the other writers (Matt 10:4; Mark 3:18). Marvin Vincent explains the difference when he says that this Simon pertained to a "sect which stood for the recovery of Jewish freedom and the maintenance of distinctive Jewish institutions. From the Hebrew *kanná*, zealous; compare the Chaldee *kanán*, by which this sect was denoted". This man was a Jewish purist and loyalist having joined a fanatical and aggressive group that sought to promote Jewish revolution against the Roman government. Perhaps the most well-known sub-group were the 960 Zealots whom Josephus calls the *sicarii*. They had taken up residence in Masada, a fortified palace on the top of a high mesa with limited access. The Romans set siege at the bottom and slowly prepared to charge upward and subdue the Zealots. After a valiant effort to defend the fortress and as they sensed their doom, the whole group killed each other carrying out a suicide pact to avoid capture by the Romans.

Therefore, Peter must have been astounded that day when the Lord picked Simon the Zealot, a man who had opposed the Roman government, and Matthew, a man who supported and worked for the Roman government. He was calling them to be part of the same team in service for their Master. The Lord knew this would be possible due to the transforming power of His salvation which both men had experienced. On that day, He explained their new mission and message when "he ordained twelve, that they should be with him, and that he might send them forth to preach" (Mark 3:14). He specifically told them, "Go not into the way of the Gentiles, and into any city of the Samaritans enter ye not. But go rather to the lost sheep of the house of Israel. And as ye go, preach, saying, 'The kingdom of heaven is at hand'" (Matt 10:5-7). As for politics, the choice of Matthew the publican and Simon the Zealot provided clear parameters for Peter and for us today. We are neither to get involved in the promotion of a government that we approve of, nor are we to oppose one with which we do not agree. Our mission is higher and better — we are called to spread the gospel and win souls for eternity.

When the Lord Jesus was here on earth and during the apostolic age, the Roman Empire was full of activities, customs and laws that were against Scripture. Slavery, oppression, mistreatment of women, "exposing" or abandonment of unwanted children, institutional racism and corruption abounded. One might argue that these were moral issues not political. Perhaps, but even so, the Lord Jesus fulfilled the prophesy of Isaiah: "He shall not strive, nor cry; neither shall any man hear his voice in the streets" (Matt 12:19). The Saviour's mission was to affect spiritual change, not social change. Thus, neither He nor His disciples were active in political parties, attended social protests, ran for office, or made strong statements against social evils. Their goal, as was Peter's, was to spread the gospel and wisely so. When a person is changed from spiritual darkness to light, their beliefs and conduct will slowly be adjusted on social questions as well.

Even more important than voting "the right way" on issues, is living on the right side of issues. Before Peter ever touched the relationship between Christians and government, he wrote, "Beloved, I beg you as sojourners and pilgrims, abstain from fleshly lusts which war against the soul, having your conduct honourable among the Gentiles" (1 Peter 2:11-12, NKJV). Peter had learned the lesson well from the sovereign selection of the disciples. If we view ourselves as permanent residents in this world, of course we will focus on improving society through governmental and political processes. However, if we see ourselves as "travellers and pilgrims," we will view our time here as temporary. We are not going to be here long, and Peter went on to show before he laid down his pen that "the earth also and the works that are therein shall be burned up" (2 Peter 3:10). This world will not be here for long either.

As horrific as international conflicts can be, Peter recognized that our chief concern should be what is going on inside us rather than what is going on around us. He warned of "fleshly lusts, which war against the soul" (1 Peter 2:11). In the Garden of Gethsemane, Peter saw the temple police arriving to arrest Jesus and he went on the attack. A short time later, he learned a tough lesson when he denied his Lord: the bigger battle is within us. Thus, he warned of desires and passions which are our greatest enemies. So, as believers, we should endeavour to keep our "conduct honourable among the Gentiles" (1 Peter 2:12). So, let us do a self-evaluation by asking, "Do I get more worked up about political failure out there or about personal failure in my heart? Am I more motivated to talk to others about government or the gospel?" Searching, isn't it!

Peter calls his readers to understand that by default, people around us are going to speak badly about us as Christians. He does not say, "If they speak against you" but that, "whereas they speak against you as evildoers" (1 Peter 2:12). Because they are already inclined to speak negatively about us and our gospel, we should not provide them with ammunition. We should be extremely careful to not afford any reason for moral criticism against us. But, what if Neighbour A (a believer) makes a Facebook or Instagram post in favour of a political candidate or party, and Neighbour B (an unbeliever) is an ardent supporter of a different candidate or party? When Neighbour A then tries to share the gospel with Neighbour B, the likelihood that Neighbour B will recall the post and use it to filter or block out the gospel message is much higher. In other words, politics and evangelism do not mix well. Political statements and involvement can hinder evangelism and the reception of the gospel message.

It is obvious that the unsaved are watching us. Peter said, "they observe" (1 Peter 2:12). That can be a liability leading to a negative mark on our testimony, or it can work in our favour. Peter talked about honourable conduct and good works. "Honourable" and "good" are the same Greek word. Our general conduct and specific works we do, if they are good, will speak to them. So, whether God works with them (day of visitation), and they come to salvation, or judges them (a day of condemnation), they will have to admit before God that the character, conduct, and works of believers were correct. A few verses later, Peter added, "For so is the will of God, that with well-doing ye may put to silence the ignorance of foolish men" (1 Peter 2:15). In the end, all will recognize that God's will for how we should live is both right and best.

The Role and Responsibility of Government

Peter recognizes that there will be different levels and branches of government and believers are to respect them all. Pilate was the governor of Jerusalem (a city), and Herod was the King of Galilee, the most northerly region of Israel where Nazareth is located and where Jesus was raised. It is interesting, then, that Peter teaches that our civil responsibilities to respect and submit apply "whether it be to the king, as supreme: Or unto governors" (1 Peter 2:13-14).

Peter addresses the role and responsibility of government in a succinct way. First, he speaks of "them that are sent by him". Human government was ordained by God after the flood when he said to Noah, "Whoso sheddeth man's blood, by man shall his blood be shed: for in the image of God made he man" (Gen 9:6). Man as a government was to maintain justice on the earth according to God's word. Paul wrote nearly 2,500 years later, "For there is no power but of God: the powers that be are ordained of God" (Rom 13:1). It is not that God approves of the character and choices of every man in a leadership position, but God has allowed human government and governmental positions to be established. Therefore, we are to respond to human government "for the Lord's sake" (1 Peter 2:13).

Peter also very clearly defined the role of government at all levels. God allows men and women to take up positions in government "for the punishment of evildoers, and for the praise of them that do well" (1 Peter 2:14). Their duties are two: to impede injustice and evil, and to promote good and righteousness. It is hard to imagine what a society would look like if a government evaluated every decision in the light of their responsibility before God. One day, we will no longer have to wonder as the King of Righteousness will establish His millennial government on earth. Then, true justice will prevail and good will abound.

Peter once tried to take on the duty of government. A massive injustice was unfolding before his eyes as he saw the temple police arrive at the Garden of Gethsemane with the intent of arresting an innocent man. Peter immediately reacted by taking out his sword and going on the attack. Later, as already noted, Paul wrote, "But if thou do that which is evil, be afraid; for he beareth not the sword in vain: for he is the minister of God, a revenger to execute wrath upon him that doeth evil" (Rom 13:4). The government was to use the sword to punish injustice, not Peter. So, may we thank God for government and pray for "kings, and for all that are in authority" (1 Tim 2:2) as their responsibility is great before God.

The Role and Responsibility of Citizens

It is amazing how the Spirit can use one word to sum up a lifetime of responsibilities. To husbands He just says: "love your wives" (Eph 5:25). What kind of a husband can stop loving his wife? Only a dead one. When Paul says we are to love our wives that embraces every area of life and our work to complete that role will continue until the Lord calls us home.

Likewise, to citizens or those visiting in a region, Peter provides one single requirement: "Submit yourselves to every ordinance of man" (1 Peter 2:13). The Greek word for submit is *hupotasso*, with the two meanings of *hupo* (under) and *tasso* (arranged) compounded together. The word implies an existing scheme or organization like that of the military with different roles and ranks. It is as if there were a chart on the wall laying out a divinely given hierarchy. Our duty is to locate ourselves on the chart and to respond to others accordingly. We are to accommodate ourselves under powers that be as God has prescribed. In this case, citizens and visitors to any given area on earth are called to place themselves under the appropriate and prescribed governmental authorities.

Peter lived for several years in Capernaum where a Roman centurion had funded the construction of a synagogue. Likely he was there the day the centurion came to the Lord Jesus and asked Him to speak a word so his servant would be healed. He went on to explain, "For I also am a man set under authority, having under me soldiers, and I say unto one, Go, and he goeth; and to another, Come, and he cometh; and to my servant, Do this, and he doeth it" (Luke 7:8). Being a military man, he understood the true meaning of submission - to accommodate oneself under an authority. Peter uses that word in 1 Peter to describe the responsibility of wives to husbands (3:1), sheep to shepherds (5:5), workers to employers (2:18), and citizens to government (2:13).

Although the Lord did not use the exact word, He taught the same truth about paying taxes. Peter would readily recall the time when some Pharisees asked Jesus, "Tell us, therefore, what do You think? Is it lawful to pay taxes to Caesar, or not?" (Matt 22:17, NKJV). The Lord Jesus then asked for a denarius coin with Caesar's image on it. That was when He spoke the famous words: "Render therefore unto Caesar the things which are Caesar's; and unto God the things that are God's" (Matt 22:21). Taxes are a government requirement which Peter included when he taught, "Submit yourselves to every ordinance of man" (1 Peter 2:13).

The other occasion that would remain fixed in Peter's memory was the time the Jews came and asked him if the Lord Jesus was going to pay the annual temple tax of two denarii per person. Knowing his Lord, Peter affirmed that He would. Later, the Lord Jesus explained that fathers do not levy taxes on their sons. Therefore, seeing as the temple was His Father's house and He is God's Son, the Lord Jesus was exempt from having to pay the tax. However, He instructed Peter to go fishing and promised that the first fish he would catch would have a coin in its mouth worth four drachma. That would cover the two-drachma temple tax bill for the Lord Jesus and for Peter. The Saviour was teaching that it is advisable to do what government officials command us to do, even if we have the right to be exempted. We are to live in peace and to seek to avoid anything that might be used to speak against us and impede the spread of the gospel.

This leads to a challenging question. What is a believer supposed to do if the government is going to use taxes collected for a nefarious purpose that is against the Word of God? The temple tax Peter paid would go into the same coffers as the little coins that the poor widow dropped in the temple collection box (Mark 12:41). And yet, in a very short time, wicked Jewish leaders would take 30 silver coins from the temple account for taxes and offerings and use them to bribe Judas into betraying the Lord Jesus. The fact that Jesus, knowing how the Jewish leaders would use the funds, commanded Peter to pay the temple tax and commended the widow for her temple offering demonstrates that we are not responsible for how government uses or misuses our taxes. So, even if the money is going to be used for immoral purposes, that is never an excuse not to pay our taxes. Paul agreed as he said, "Render therefore to all their due: taxes to whom taxes are due, customs to whom customs" (Rom 13:7). It is not in our purview to judge their use of tax revenue. Government officials will be held accountable by God as to how they have administered money entrusted to them.

We all know that governments fail often in their decisions and edicts. We are not sure if Peter physically saw it or not, but he certainly heard about the scene where Roman soldiers erected three crosses on the side of the road leading into Jerusalem. In two of the cases of crucifixion, the thieves deserved capital punishment and the government carried out justice. However, the cross in the middle was the grossest injustice ever committed in the history of mankind. Peter explained it when he boldly declared to the Jewish leadership, "Ye denied the Holy One and the Just, and desired a murderer [Barabbas] to be granted unto you; And killed the Prince of life" (Acts 3:14-15). Peter himself would eventually experience government injustice as the Jews would imprison him twice and beat him once without reason, and then Herod would have him arrested without just cause as well. However, neither the apostles nor the believers in Jerusalem endeavoured to stop these types of injustice through political involvement or social action. Instead, they submissively practiced what Peter taught: "Fear God. Honour the king" (1 Peter 2:17).

But what if there is conflict between what God wants and what the king requires? Peter and John faced that very dilemma in Jerusalem. The Jewish authorities had "commanded them not to speak at all nor teach in the name of Jesus" (Acts 4:18). The apostles' first response was to put the ball back in their court by saying, "Whether it is right in the sight of God to listen to you more than to God, you judge" (Acts 4:19). Later, the Jewish leaders tried again to stop the apostles from preaching the Gospel. This time, "Peter and the other apostles answered and said, 'We ought to obey God rather than men'" (Acts 5:29). While the dilemma they faced was over the spiritual work of preaching the gospel, the general principle is that we are required by God to submit to government edicts unless they violate Scripture. That applies to God's moral law as well. For example, suppose a government were to limit families to one child and require an abortion of any child conceived thereafter. Thus, if a Christian woman were to become pregnant, because of God's command not to kill she would have to proceed with the birth and obey God regardless of the consequences.

As they did with the Lord Jesus, the Jewish leaders found "nothing how they might punish them [the apostles]" (Acts 4:21). Despite their finding, they broke their own laws by beating Peter and the other apostles and imprisoning them (Acts 5:40). Amazingly, the apostles responded like their Saviour by keeping silent. Their practice was not to defend themselves against personal attacks, but to speak up only when the gospel, the person and work of Christ, or the character of God was being assaulted. They did as the Lord Jesus did - "Who, when he was reviled, reviled not again; when he suffered, he threatened not; but committed himself to him that judgeth righteously" (1 Peter 2:23).

At times, though, Christians can sense a temptation to justify civil disobedience because we are citizens of Heaven. Yes, Peter did teach that we should live "As free" (1 Peter 2:16). However, biblical freedom is never the idea of a person having the liberty to do whatever they want. Rather, it is the freedom to do what God wants. Peter went on to exhort that we should not use our liberty "for a cloke of maliciousness, but as the servants of God" (1 Peter 2:16). Dressing civil disobedience in the religious garb of Biblical language is both wrong and hurtful to the gospel.

If we are honest with ourselves, sometimes we can lack motivation to complete government requirements especially if we know that a government is corrupt, inefficient, and anti-God. However, according to Peter, we are to submit to government "for the Lord's sake" (1 Peter 2:13) and as "the servants of God" (1 Peter 2:16). Appreciating that human government is a divine institution and that it is God who commands us to submit, allows us to see these obligations as opportunities to serve and please our God rather than just our civil duties.

The Jews employed stoning as a death penalty in the case of Stephen. The Romans preferred crucifixion, but it was only to be applied to foreigners, criminals, and slaves. Thus, Roman citizenship provided freedoms, rights and protections that were worth having. Paul said about himself, "I was born a citizen" (Acts 22:28), so he would not die by crucifixion. On the other hand, the Roman commander of the troops who had arrested Paul said, "With a large sum I obtained this citizenship" (Acts 22:28). He had probably paid a bribe under the table to acquire it. But Peter was not born a Roman citizen, nor would he participate in fraud, bribery, or corruption as that would be dishonouring to his Lord. Thus, although it was carried out unjustly, in the end, the Romans crucified Peter. He died at the hands of human government, but with "a blameless conscience both before God and before men" (Acts 24:16). And that is a goal worth pursuing!

CHAPTER 16

Peter the Target

Significance in Satan's attacks

No intelligent thief would ever break into a home to steal paper plates or disposable cups. Thieves target homes where they hope they can find electronics, jewellery, or cash. Likewise, no military general launches a campaign to infiltrate enemy territory with the mission to destroy a rubbish dump or capture a basic restaurant. In any conflict, high-value targets are identified and then carefully pursued.

Peter was a high-value target and so are you. Satan is too smart to waste his time on someone who is not important. One day, the Lord Jesus told Peter, "Simon, Simon, Satan hath desired to have you [the 12 disciples]" (Luke 22:31). Of all the people in Israel at that time, Satan had selected the 12 disciples as particular targets and he was planning an all-out attack. Why them? Satan set his sights on them because they were extremely important to the Lord.

Satan can make his presence felt, but he is not omnipresent. He has great power, but he can only be in once place at a time, and there is a limit as to how many tasks he can take on with the resources he has available. Yes, he does have plenty of soldiers (demons) whom he commands and coordinates in his battles against Christians. Truthfully, few of us would be important enough to be attacked by Satan himself. However, we should take no comfort that we may only be attacked by demons. The "god of this world" directs them masterfully and they have plenty of ability in themselves. Their goal is always to inhibit or ruin believers because they recognize that believers are of great value to God.

Strategy in Satan's Attacks

His Tricks

Peter described him "as a roaring lion" (1 Peter 5:8). *Oruomai*, like *roar* in English, is a Greek word formed by onomatopoeia - using the very sound the subject (i.e. a lion) makes. It speaks of his attempts to boast of power and infuse fear in his targets. Satan has innumerable disguises and is more adaptable than a chameleon. In Genesis 3, he appeared as a snake and yet Paul wrote, "Satan himself is transformed into an angel of light" (2 Cor 11:14). Peter's experience gave him insight as to the devil's lethal combination of craftiness and cruelty.

His Cruelty

Peter's description of the devil "as a roaring lion" indicates Satan's fearlessness. He would dispute with Michael the archangel over Moses' body (Jude v.9) and even try to tempt the Son of God in the wilderness. His cohorts, the demons, are not easily spooked or made to cower either. But, being "as a roaring lion" primarily reminds of us of Satan's viciousness. When Samson travelled to Timnath, "a young lion roared against him" (Judges 14:5) and would have consumed him for lunch if God had not given Samson special strength to destroy him. Likewise, David and Benaiah both faced lions that were aggressively on the attack. David killed one with his hands and Benaiah killed one with a sword. But Scripture also relates to us the story of a young prophet who did not have such success. When traveling, "a lion met him by the way, and slew him" (1 Kings 13:24). That is why King Darius was amazed that Daniel had not become a saintly snack during his night in a den of lions (Dan 6:20-22).

Satan is the cruellest creature in the universe. He has no conscience and is blood-thirsty, eager to see God's creatures with ruined lives and suffering in hell. For him, it is a supreme delight to destroy Christian testimonies, torture God's people, and defile or dismantle local churches. So, while Peter "went out and wept bitterly" (Luke 22:62), Satan was delighted.

Thank God, though, the Lord Jesus is also called "the Lion of the tribe of Judah" to emphasize His majesty and superiority. The wise man wrote of the "righteous [who] are bold as a lion" (Prov 28:1). They are fearless and courageous, willing to take on daunting enemies. Thus, it is a fitting metaphor to describe, "Jesus Christ, the righteous" (1 John 2:1), who unflinchingly took on Satan at the cross.

His Craftiness

Notice Satan's *modus operandi* is not to appear as some severely sunburnt creature with horns and an arrow-shaped tail who wears bright red clothing while carrying a pitchfork. Today, he has successfully established this cartoon image which deviously leads people to view him as an imaginary creature, fear him less, and not notice his malicious and subtle activities.

Peter spoke from personal experience when he described Satan as one who "walketh about" (1 Peter 5:8). Some versions speak of him prowling (NASB, ESV, HSCB), but the verb *peripateō* is translated as "walking" the majority of the 96 times it is found in the New Testament. It gives insight to the slow, patient, calculated actions of the devil to reach his goals. He is not flailing here and there desperately trying to find a victim. Instead, he avoids quick movements that might draw attention to himself. Peter didn't even sense that Satan was in the area. It was the omniscient Christ who had to tell him on that occasion, "Simon, Simon, behold, Satan hath desired to have you" (Luke 22:31). Again, on the other occasion, Peter was oblivious, but Jesus could see the devil trying to work through him. Jesus detected what was really happening and He "said unto Peter, 'Get thee behind me, Satan'" (Matt 16:23).

The devil frequently moves in stealth-mode waiting for the moment when his target is most vulnerable. Treating the Lord Jesus like any other man, the devil no doubt thought the Saviour would be most likely to fall "when they [the 40 days in the wilderness] were ended, [and] he afterward hungered" (Luke 4:2). It is at that point, the Scripture records that Satan began to tempt Him. Likewise, the

Lord Jesus warned Peter and two other disciples to "Watch and pray" in the Garden of Gethsemane. He knew they had been up all night and were physically and emotionally exhausted. He sensed their susceptibility and pleaded with them to lay hold on God. He knew Satan was moving in and, sure enough, within a few hours Peter would deny the Lord.

His Thinking

Peter pointed out that Satan has two primary goals. He called him "your adversary," which means he is "one who is actively and continuously hostile toward someone" (Louw-Nida). More specifically, in the New Testament the word is used to describe "one who brings a charge in a lawsuit" (BDAG). It is not that he is a nuisance who calls us names and mocks our frailty - he is our legal adversary who seeks to bring every accusation he can against God's people.

The pattern in Scripture is that as soon as Heaven identifies something that belongs to God, Satan attacks it. Peter heard the Lord Jesus present the Parable of the Sower and the Four Soils. In it, Jesus explained: "Now the parable is this: The seed is the word of God. Those by the way side are they that hear; then cometh the devil, and taketh away the word out of their hearts, lest they should believe and be saved" (Luke 8:11-12). Here, the devil immediately opposes the seed, the Word of God. The very temptation of Christ occurred after the voice from Heaven declared, "This is my beloved Son in whom I am well pleased" (Matt 3:17). Peter would never forget the day in Caesarea-Philippi when Jesus revealed something new. He said, "... upon this rock I will build my church; and the gates of hell shall not prevail against it" (Matt 16:18). Jesus knew that as soon as He introduced His plan to build His church, Satan would begin to plot ways to oppose it. His main and unwavering goal is to rob God of honour and glory which is why he attacks the Word of God, the Son of God, and the Church of Christ. And, since glorifying God is the main purpose of both a child of God and a local assembly of God, we should expect adversity and Satanic opposition as well.

Peter identified the second goal of Satan as "seeking whom he may devour" (1 Peter 5:8). He is seeking to devour (*katapinō*), which is a compound word meaning to drink down and is most often translated swallowed or swallowed up. Satan is not interested in frightening you off your spiritual mission, nipping your heals, or even maiming you. He desires the complete ruination of your spiritual life. He is a formidable foe and one who is not to be underestimated or mocked.

His Timing

While Satan is always walking around like a lion and perhaps orchestrating negative influences in our world, he seems to spring into action at specific times. Paul agreed as he instructed believers to put on "the whole armour of God, that ye may be able to withstand in the evil day" (Eph 6:13). Peter's experiences illustrate for us three typical "evil days" or occasions when the Devil tends to move into action.

At a Time of Success (Matt 16:13-23)

Peter had just made the greatest statement of his life. The Lord Jesus had taken His disciples to Caesarea Philippi which was also known as Banias or Panias (as noted in an earlier chapter), a Satanic command and control centre. Pagans celebrated and worshiped the gods there who supposedly ascended from inside the earth out of a spring of water that flowed to the surface. It was in that environment that Jesus asked His disciples, "Whom do men say that I the Son of man am?" (Matt 16:13). Then, He asked, "But whom say ye that I am?" (Matt 16:15). Immediately, Simon Peter stepped forward and boldly declared, "Thou art the Christ, the Son of the living God" (Matt 16:16). His great confession stands in contrast to the multiplicity of pagan gods. Jehovah is the one, singular God who is alive (not made of stone), and He has one single Son who is equal to Him. What a confession! The Lord Jesus then compliments him for his statement and promises to give him "the keys of the kingdom of heaven" (Matt 16:19).

It is shortly after this summit of success in Peter's life that the Lord Jesus spoke of His own rejection and death that would soon come. Peter then responded with a strong rebuke of his Lord for having spoken about the mistreatment and cross that lay ahead. It was then, right after Peter's great success, that Jesus had to say, "Get thee behind me, Satan: thou art an offence unto me: for thou savourest not the things that be of God, but those that be of men" (Matt 16:23). Therefore, success is no refuge from becoming a target of Satan. In fact, knowing the tendency toward pride in the human heart, he often introduces temptation immediately following success. When we or others put us up on a pedestal because of our successes, remember, there is only one direction we can go – down! The Lord Jesus understood this. After the tremendous success of feeding 5,000 men plus women and children (the only miracle recorded in all four gospels), Jesus "sent the multitudes away, [and] he went up into a mountain apart to pray" (Matt 14:23). While He could never have sinned or felt pride, He was teaching His followers that successes should cause us to be extra vigilant since they are often followed by attacks of the enemy.

At a Time of Strife (Luke 22:21-34)

Luke says that after the institution of the Lord's Supper in the upper room, the disciples began to wonder who the betrayer would be. Then, "there was also a strife among them, [as to] which of them should be accounted the greatest" (v.24). At that point, the Saviour intervened and taught them that greatness is accomplished through humility, not fighting for one's rights. Christ even expressed His appreciation by saying, "Ye are they which have continued with me in my temptations" (v.28), and He promised them a future in His kingdom. This should have been enough to humble them, but He had to add, "Simon, Simon, behold, Satan hath desired to have you, that he may sift you as wheat: But I have prayed for thee, that thy faith fail not" (v.31-32). What a shock to Peter and the others. While they were posturing and arguing about positions in the Kingdom, Satan was seeking to blindside them. He was presenting a legal case before the Lord (similarly to what he did with Job), as to why he should be permitted to attack them. Likely, he could see a potential inroad in their carnal interactions.

Considering the frequency of conflicts among married couples, friends, and God's people in the Old and New Testaments, strife is one time when people become especially vulnerable to spiritual falls. "Divide and conquer" has been a successful and frequently employed tactic of Satan throughout 6,500 years of human history. No wonder, then, that one of the seven things that the Lord hates is "he that soweth discord among brethren" (Prov 6:19).

At a Time of Spiritual Activity (Acts 5:1-10)

Everyone, including Ananias and Sapphira, was surely excited to see that Jerusalem had become a beehive of activity for God. "Three thousand souls" (Acts 2:41) had been saved on the day of Pentecost. Evangelism continued and shortly "the number of the men was about five thousand" (Acts 4:4). They all "continued steadfastly in the apostles' doctrine and fellowship, and in breaking of bread, and in prayers" (Acts 2:42), and they were "continuing daily with one accord in the temple, and breaking bread from house to house" (Acts 2:46). They enjoyed times of prayer when "they lifted up their voice to God with one accord" (Acts 4:24) and they enjoyed a special harmony as "the multitude of them that believed were of one heart and of one soul" (Acts 4:32). Seeing the practical needs of so many new brothers and sisters in the faith, believers began to sell property in order to have money to buy supplies for those in need. Caught in the current of activity and wanting to contribute something, Ananias and Sapphira voluntarily sold some property. You might think that since they were involved in such a powerful work of God, Satan would not be able to touch them. Wrong! Right at the peak of activity and sacrifice in the new assembly in Jerusalem, Peter had to ask, "Ananias, why has Satan filled your heart to lie to the Holy Spirit and keep back part of the price of the land for yourself?" (Acts 5:3). Spiritual sloths are of no concern to Satan. They are doing nothing for God, so he does not need to worry about them. Believers who are actively involved in spiritual service and sacrifice are the ones who need to be on guard. The most active servant and sacrificial man ever was the Lord Jesus and Satan attacked Him. It is not a cause for fear, but we must recognize the reality that spiritual activity draws the attention of the enemy.

His Tools

There are three occasions in the life of Peter where Satan was clearly active. Twice he saw it in his own life and once in the lives of Ananias and Saphira. It appears that in each circumstance, the enemy was employing a different instrument to oppose, hinder and destroy Peter and others.

The tool of trials: Matt 16:10-23

Jesus had taken His disciples part way up Mount Hermon in the north of Israel. There, in Caesarea Philippi, following Peter's great confession, the Lord introduced something that was hidden in the Old Testament – His church. It was also a key moment as "From that time forth began Jesus to shew unto his disciples, how that he must go unto Jerusalem, and suffer many things of the elders and chief priests and scribes, and be killed, and be raised again the third day" (v.21). As Jesus spoke of the horrific events on the horizon for Him, Peter knew that would imply uncertainty, discomfort, and potential persecution of the 12 disciples as well. So "Peter took him, and began to rebuke him, saying, 'Be it far from thee, Lord: this shall not be unto thee.'" (v.22). Jesus, then, had to point out to him that he was thinking on the human level of self-preservation and not on the spiritual level considering God's plans. Circumstances that looked daunting and disappointing opened up the possibility for Satan to influence him and use him. Please don't think that Satan no longer uses trials, tragedies, and disease as tools to influence us toward wrong attitudes and sin. He used them in the case of Job, and he is still using them today. When Peter later wrote about Satan, it was in the context of suffering and "cares" (1 Peter 5:7). Peter was referring primarily to circumstances that produce anxiety, even ones that are so intense that they make you feel that no one understands your pain, loss, and loneliness. (Sounds like Job's experience, doesn't it?) That is why Peter proceeds to advise those in trial to recognize "...that the same afflictions are accomplished in your brethren that are in the world" (1 Peter 5:8-9). Satan also tries to "sift us" which Thayer says he accomplishes "by inward agitation to try one's faith to the verge of overthrow". We need to be extra prepared for trials which are well-honed instruments of the accuser of the brethren to impede their obedience and faith and thus rob God of glory.

The tool of interpersonal relationships: Luke 22:21-34.

On the night of Peter's denial, who was Satan's instrument? Peter or John? Likely the answer is - both. Clearly Peter allowed his competitive nature to bring out the worst in him and he did not recognize that it put him in a very vulnerable position. Jesus had to tell him, "Simon, Simon, behold, Satan hath desired to have you, that he may sift you as wheat" (Luke 22:31-32). Satan was working in conjunction with Peter's pride to bring him to failure. Having Christian friends is a priceless treasure, but they do not provide immunity against Satanic attacks. While fellowship and labouring together are indispensable, we must always be on guard that our interactions with others do not create opportunities for Satan to launch an attack against us by appealing to our sinful nature within.

At the same time, John himself mentions how Peter stepped into a position of weakness when he denied the Lord Jesus. He tells us that "Peter stood at the door without. Then went out that other disciple ... and brought in Peter" (John 18:16). As believers, we can be a blessing and preservative to one another, or we can also lead others into positions, activities, and conversations that they cannot handle. John seems to have struggled with this memory of how he carelessly put his friend and spiritual brother at risk. As an older man, John wrote repeatedly in his Gospel and Epistles about the need to love one another. Thus, it appears that he learned from this awful experience when his choice contributed to Peter's fall.

The tool of money: Acts 5:1-11

The number of believers was growing rapidly in Jerusalem. That meant the number of hungry mouths was increasing as well. All the Christians began to give. Even "as many as were possessors of lands or houses sold them, and brought the prices of the things that were sold" (Acts 4:34). For example, a brother called Barnabas, "Having land, sold it, and brought the money, and laid it at the apostles' feet" (Acts 4:36-37). Not to be outdone, a couple called Ananias and Sapphira "sold a possession" as well, but "kept back part of the price" (Acts 5:1-2). Even though no one else seemed to notice, with apostolic wisdom Peter discerned what was really going on. He said, "Ananias, why hath Satan filled thine heart to lie to the Holy Ghost, and to keep back part of the price of the land?" (v.3). Peter had already seen Satan use money and greed as a trap in the case of Judas. Now it was happening again shortly after the formation of the first assembly. Paul warned, "For the love of money is the root of all evil: which while some coveted after, they have erred from the faith, and pierced themselves through with many sorrows" (1 Tim 6:10). Money, and even the handling of the Lord's money, can still be a tool of the tempter. When dealing with money and financial matters at any time, we must guard our hearts and realize how dangerous it can be.

His Ties

Satan is always seeking to utilize his unholy alliance with the world around us and the flesh within us. He is the "prince of the power of the air" directing the "course of this world" (Eph 2:2). Peter saw it at first-hand when the Lord spoke in Matthew 16 of how the world would reject Him. The result? Pride within Peter rose up and he dared to rebuke his Lord. In Luke 22 Satan enjoyed watching as the disciples bickered over place and prominence in the Kingdom. Satan brought out the worst in them as he is a master at activating all the works of the flesh. The disciples were responsible for their foolish choice to argue and jockey for place and pre-eminence that day. And yet, Satan, in cahoots with the flesh, was triggering the impulses within them towards self-centred and self-seeking behaviour.

Peter also saw the alliance of Satan, the world, and the flesh in Acts 5. Peter identified how Satan was using greed to cause Ananias and Sapphira to lie to the Holy Spirit when they falsely claimed to be giving all the proceeds from the sale of their property to the Lord, when they were not. Apparently, the devil had cleverly appealed to the selfish and competitive nature within them. Two millennia have passed, and he is still controlling the world around us to apply pressure on believers. At the same time, he is constantly appealing to the flesh within us to bring about failure and sin in our lives. We need to be more alert to this axis of evil which is doggedly scheming and working to rob God of pleasure from our lives.

Steadfastness against Satan's Attacks

Peter instructs us that, in order to survive and succeed, we must first "be sober, [and] be vigilant" (1 Peter 5:8). Sober (*nephō*) means "to be free from the influence of intoxicants" (Vine). Alcohol and drugs subtly impact a person's rationality and judgment. But, beyond beer and brandy, we should analyse everything in life that we assimilate whether teaching, entertainment, examples, images, etc. as to how it will impact on our sensitivity toward temptation.

According to BDAG, vigilant means "to be in constant readiness; be on the alert". Mounce gives the definition "to be awake, to watch". The idea is to combat the internal urge to drop your guard and give priority to a basic need like sleep. Combining the two words, we must be careful about external influences that might distract us or impede us from making wise, Biblical decisions (sober). We also must be on guard as to internal tendencies or traits that might equally dull our sensitivities toward temptation and leave us prone to fall.

Then, Peter adds, "Resist him [and be] firm in the faith" (1 Peter 5:9, HSCB). James, the half-brother of Jesus agreed as he wrote, "Resist the devil, and he will flee from you" (James 4:7). Paul said, "Put on the whole armour of God, that ye may be able to stand against the wiles of the devil" (Eph 6:11). Therefore, success is achievable, but it will require intentional and even radical action on our part.

Resist (*anthistemi*) means to "set against" (Vine) or to oppose and stand against him. But how? Peter said we can do so by being "firm in the faith". Firm is an adjective, not a verb. Therefore, in many versions the verb "to be" is implied or supplied. Firm (*stereos*) is used to describe something stable and resistant to change such as "the firm foundation of God stands" (2 Tim 2:19, J N Darby). Debate arises over whether Peter is saying we must remain in the subjective faith of reliance upon God, or the objective faith of the body of truth. In favour of the objective faith is the example of the Lord Jesus who parried every blow of Satan in the Temptation by quoting the Word of God. Paul said we need all the armour of God including "the sword of the Spirit, which is the word of God" (Eph 6:17). What will preserve us in times of temptation and attack is not just a general knowledge or memorisation of Scripture as valuable as that is. Like Christ, we require a specific word from God (using Scripture) to defend ourselves in each particular temptation. Often it is even necessary to read or quote applicable Scripture out loud just as Christ did in order to parry the blows of the enemy.

The need for faith and reliance on God is also true. No amount of white-knuckle, self-determination will suffice nor will shouts of rebuke. Trying to fight Satan with the flesh is hopelessly ineffective. Our enemies are greater than our abilities and we must turn to God for help. Paul warned Christians about the "wiles of the devil" (Eph 6:11) and our wrestling "against principalities, against powers, against the rulers of the darkness of this world, against spiritual wickedness in high places" (Eph 6:12). He begins the section by saying, "Finally, my brethren, be strong in the Lord, and in the power of his might" (Eph 6:10). He ends the section by coming full circle on the issue of dependence on God by saying, "Praying always with all prayer and supplication in the Spirit, and watching thereunto with all perseverance and supplication for all saints" (Eph 6:18).

Perhaps the ambiguity in the text in 1 Peter 5 is intentional as to what "the faith" refers and it is best to consider both truths. Our only hope of survival is to discern when and how Satan is working, and then we must cry to God in dependent prayer and use His Word as our defence.

Superiority over Satan's Attacks

Satan or demons are mentioned in 22 of the 27 books of the New Testament. Satan is the antagonist from Genesis to Revelation and his goals and attacks against individuals, couples, churches, governments, and even the person of Christ are interwoven throughout Scripture. At times, he appears to achieve victory. The Garden of Eden was his first attack on a human being and on a married couple and he achieved success. But even then, God reminded Satan of his sin and ultimate doom when He spoke of the Lord Jesus, the "seed of the woman". He said to Satan, "He shall crush thy head!" (Gen 3:15, Darby).

Yes, angels rebelled, but "God spared not the angels that sinned, but cast them down to hell, and delivered them into chains of darkness, to be reserved unto judgment" (2 Peter 2:4). Those angels are still locked up and will be forever. At Caesarea Philippi, Jesus declared His power over Satan. He said, "Upon this rock I will build my church; and the gates of hell shall not prevail against it" (Matt 16:18). As the Lord Jesus anticipated His cross, Peter heard Him say, "... now shall the prince of this world be cast out" (John 12:31). With the descent of the Holy Spirit, Jesus also assured, "The prince of this world is judged" (John 16:11). Ultimately, as powerful as Satan is, his doom is guaranteed.

From his own personal experience, Peter recognized that "greater is he that is in you, than he that is in the world" (1 John 4.4). Yes, the Lord was aware and even predicted Peter's sin of denying the Saviour three times. At the same time, the Lord Jesus said, "Satan hath desired to have you, that he may sift you as wheat: But I have prayed for thee, that thy faith fail not: and when thou art converted, strengthen thy brethren" (Luke 22:31-32). The power and grace of our Lord is excelling and prevailing. There was no doubt that Peter would be restored. The Lord did not say "If thou art converted" but "When thou art converted". Satan must have been laughing and demons giving each other high-fives when, after sinning, Peter "went out, and wept bitterly" (Luke 22:62). However, what were they thinking when Peter stood up and preached the gospel on the Day of Pentecost and 3,000 souls were saved and the first assembly was formed? Wonder what they thought when Peter had the vision the sheet and the unclean animals showing the radical plan that the gospel should go out to Gentiles? Wonder what they thought when Peter stood up at the great conference in Jerusalem in Acts 15 and helped solve the crisis about the salvation of Gentiles versus Jews? Wonder what they thought when Peter penned two priceless books of the New Testament before he died a faithful martyr for Christ?

Let us never forget that with Christ, we are on the winning side. He has won the great victory at the cross and it is just a matter of time until His enemies will cease to attack. Peter even referenced a divine promise in his great sermon on the day of Pentecost. He quoted Psalm 110:1: "The Lord said unto my Lord, Sit thou on my right hand, Until I make thy foes thy footstool" (Acts 2:34-35). Thankfully, in light of eternity, it won't be long until Satan and his hosts will not be able to influence us anymore. We will no longer have the flesh, and the world will be snatched from the Devil's control forever.

So, may we never forget that, like Peter, every Christian can become a target of Satan and his agents. While it may even appear that Satan is gaining the victory in our Christian experience at times, his "apparent" success is never the end of the story. Christ has greater power and He can recover saints today just as He did with Peter. Thank God He can restore, reinstate, and remake out of the riches of His grace and by the power of His might. The overwhelming plan and power of God in our lives, despite being potential targets of Satan, should make us bow like Peter and say, "To him be glory both now and for ever. Amen" (2 Peter 3:18).

CHAPTER 17

Peter the Failure

"Let us stop the progress of sin in our soul at the first stage, for the farther it goes the faster it will increase"

Thomas Fuller

Other than the Lord Jesus, every other man and woman in the Bible failed at some point whether their error is recorded in Scripture or not. However, there is no secret about Peter's mistakes. In fact, we know more about his faults and failures than those of the other 12 apostles combined. They include sins of omission and commission that can be detected in his words, his actions, and his thoughts. Sometimes he even repeated the same sin more than once (e.g. the three denials). Perhaps the most frightening aspect is that he even failed as a mature believer (Gal 2:11).

Here is a sampling of Simon Peter's failures:

- He made a promise he did not keep (Mark 14:31).

- He rebuked the Son of God for speaking about His death on the cross (Matt 16:22).

- He put Christ on the same level as Moses and Elias on the Mount of Transfiguration (Matt 17:4).

- He coveted the first place in Christ's kingdom and argued why he deserved it (Mark 9:34).

- He forsook the Lord Jesus and fled (Mark 14:50).

- He attempted to murder a temple policeman (John 18:10).

- He denied the Lord Jesus three times (Mark 14:30).

- He espoused wrong doctrine and he refused to eat with Gentiles (Gal 2:11).

Some would also add to this list his failure to understand the teaching of the Lord Jesus (Mark 9:32), his failure to stay awake on the Mount of Transfiguration (Lk 9:32) and in the Garden of Gethsemane (Luke 22:45), and his failure in faith to keep walking on the water of the Sea of Galilee (Matt 14:30-31). And yet, most admirably, Peter never let his flaws and mistakes cause him to throw in the spiritual towel or to become stuck in a stagnant pool of self-pity. Simon Peter handled his failures in a Biblical, balanced and healthy manner as he confessed his sin, learned from it, and continued on with greater humility.

Lessons about the Flesh

Peter first heard the gospel by listening directly to the sermons of John the Baptiser or through reports by Andrew of John's preaching. John was a faithful and fiery messenger whose preaching resulted in people being "baptised of him in Jordan, confessing their sins" (Matt 3:6). John was not an "easy-believism" preacher. He warned, "O generation of vipers, who hath warned you to flee from the wrath to come? Bring forth therefore fruits meet for repentance" (Matt 3:7-8). A kind and Biblical "plowing up" over the depravity of the human heart and one's personal accountability for sin before God always serves a person well. It helps souls appreciate their need of the Saviour and it also has an impact on their Christian walk after salvation. Thus, Paul reminded the Ephesian elders that during his time in Ephesus, he preached "repentance toward God, and faith toward our Lord Jesus Christ" (Acts 20:21).

Often at conversion or at some point prior to beginning public service, God has us pass through experiences which illuminate our minds as to His holiness and our unholiness.

- Moses: God revealed his purity to Moses as he stood on holy ground at the burning bush at Horeb. Moses went away that day having learned that God is the great "I am" (Ex 3:14). At that time, God also had Moses put his hand in his tunic and it came out leprous. On that occasion, Moses witnessed God's holiness and he also saw his own sinfulness. Moses learned that "out of the abundance of the heart the mouth speaketh" (Matt 12:34). Years later, even though he was a great leader, Moses would reveal his sinful heart by employing unkind language when the people rebelled against God.

- Isaiah: As perhaps the greatest Old Testament evangelist, Isaiah saw the Lord "sitting upon a throne, high and lifted up, and his train filled the temple" (Isa 6:1). In the vision, the seraphim "cried one unto another, and said, 'Holy, holy, holy, is the LORD of hosts'" (Isa 6:3). When Isaiah saw the pristine holiness of the Almighty, he cried out, "Woe is me! for I am undone; because I am a man of unclean lips" (Isa 6:5). Later, he wrote and included himself when he said, "We are all as an unclean thing, and all our righteousnesses are as filthy rags" (Isa 64:6). In his role as a prophet, he would never forget that he was speaking on behalf of a thrice-holy God who hates sin.

- Paul: Paul saw the brilliant holiness of Christ on the road to Damascus which left him convinced that God is "dwelling in the light which no man can approach" (1 Tim 6:16). Paul, who "touching the righteousness which is in the law, [was] blameless" (Phil 3:6), suddenly realized something of the depravity of his heart. Later, as an apostle, he wrote to Roman Christians about "sin that dwelleth in me" (Rom 7:17).

- John: The "disciple whom Jesus loved" viewed the resplendent glory of Christ on the Mount of Transfiguration. He clearly grasped then what he articulated later in life: "God is light, and in him is no darkness at all" (1 John 1:5). And yet, at the same time, and in the same chapter, he wrote in the present tense and in the first-person plural (including himself): "If we say that we have no sin, we deceive ourselves, and the truth is not in us" (1 John 1:8), and

"If we say that we have not sinned, we make him a liar, and his word is not in us" (1 John 1:9). The revelation of God's holiness left John with the indelible impression of his own sinfulness even as a saved, believing apostle.

- Peter: Before Peter could become useful for God, he had to have the experience on the sea in which he had fished all night and caught nothing. When the Lord said to him, "Let down your nets for a draught" (Luke 5:4), Peter obeyed, and suddenly "they enclosed a great multitude of fishes: and their net brake" (Luke 5:6). It was at that point that Peter grasped both his own inability and Christ's ability. He also saw the truth of what Paul would later write, "For all have sinned, and come short of the glory of God" (Rom 3:23). Right there in the boat, he bowed himself before the Lord of glory and cried, "Depart from me; for I am a sinful man, O Lord" (Luke 5:8).

All of the spiritual "greats" were graciously given the opportunity to look through the window of the heart of God to see His holiness and greatness. At the same, the Lord had them peer through the window of their own hearts to see their sinfulness and weakness. Peter was also given the lesson that for the rest of his life, he would carry the potential within him to commit any type of sin any number of times. Mr. Albert Joyce, a respected preacher of the gospel in North America used to say, "The only thing a Christian cannot do is go to hell". While we have no license to sin ever again, we have the same sinful nature in us that we had before we were saved. To put it plainly, Jeremiah said, "The heart is deceitful above all things, and desperately wicked" (Jer 17:9). The heart of the most wicked unbeliever and the heart of the most devoted saint is the same, but even this knowledge would not prevent Peter from failing.

Lessons about Feebleness

Peter tried his hand at swordsmanship when he lopped off Malchus' ear. Likely he aimed for the high priest's servant`s neck, because whacking off a person's ear would accomplish little. It is almost humourous to consider how badly he failed with a sword as he tried to defend his Lord. So, to teach Peter about his own feebleness, the Lord did not take him to Sword School or Carpentry College. Instead, on two separate occasions, He put him right in his sweet spot – on a fishing boat with nets. As a fisherman, Peter could not have been more in his groove than when he was casting nets. Twice, while fishing, Peter had interaction with the Lord. The first time, Peter had to admit, "Master, we have toiled all night and have taken nothing" (Luke 5:5). The second time, when Peter and six others went fishing, "that night they caught nothing" (John 21:3). And yet, on the first occasion, at the Lord's command, "they enclosed a great multitude of fishes" (Luke 5:6). The second time, they brought in a "multitude of fishes" (John 21:6). The Lord taught and retaught Peter the lesson about the limitation of human ability and His matchless, infinite ability.

When it came to temptation, Peter thought he was the exception. When the Saviour told His disciples, "All of you will be made to stumble because of Me this night" (Matt 26:31, NKJV), Peter quickly replied, "Even if all are made to stumble because of You, I will never be made to stumble." (Matt 26:33, NKJV). Peter would have to go through the embarrassing experience of denying the Lord, before coming to admit, "Thou, Lord ... knowest the hearts of all men" (Acts 1:24). He knows how quickly and easily we can sin; we are feeble at best.

Lessons about Falls

The Issue of Satan

Peter's intention was likely sincere, and he never expected to stumble and fall the night he denied the Lord. However, he did not perceive that his "adversary the devil, as a roaring lion [was walking] about seeking whom he may devour" (1 Peter 5:8). That night, Peter would soon feel the hot breath of the "accuser of the brethren" and feel the pain as the enemy would sink his claws into a sincere disciple. Eve was the first human being to be attacked by Satan and she tried to blame him when she said, "The serpent beguiled me, and I did eat"

(Gen 3:13b). Yes, Scripture says that "the woman being deceived, fell into transgression" (1 Tim 2:14), yet she was still responsible for her choice. God said to her, "What hast thou done?" (Gen 3:13a). Likewise, without taking anything away from Peter's personal responsibility for his denial, the Lord did say, "Simon, Simon, behold, Satan hath desired to have you, that he may sift you as wheat" (Luke 22:31). Therefore, we must never forget that, while our intentions and our determination to avoid sin might be sincere, we have a powerful enemy who delights in putting us in situations where we are inclined to fail.

The Issue of Timing

The only occasion we read in the Gospels of the disciples singing was after the celebration of the Passover in the upper room. It had been such special experience that even the Lord said, "With desire I have desired to eat this passover" (Luke 22:15). In addition to the Passover, the Lord had instituted the simple and yet sublime meeting for the Breaking of Bread (Matt 26:26-29; Mark 14:22-25; Luke 22:19-20). He had also given them some exciting teaching about service, fruit bearing, and the coming of the Comforter, the Holy Spirit (John 13-16). He closed with a beautiful prayer, the longest recorded prayer of Christ (John 17). With that, "When they had sung an hymn, they went out into the mount of Olives" (Matt 26:30). At a time of great blessing, the Lord said to Peter and the disciples, "Watch ye and pray, lest ye enter into temptation" (Mark 14:38). Times of blessing, success and joy can be times when we let our guard down and then we are more prone to fall.

Besides a time of excitement, it was a time of exhaustion. Arriving at the Garden of Gethsemane, it wasn't long until Jesus "cometh, and findeth them sleeping, and saith unto Peter, Simon, sleepest thou? couldest not thou watch one hour?" (Mark 14:37). The Lord knew they were not just dozing; He came back to where they were a little later and "found them asleep again: for their eyes were heavy" (Matt 26:43). The emotional toll of the events that night and a lack of sleep were a lethal combination. Jesus had taught them that He was about to leave them for the Father's house (John 14:3) and knew the effect this teaching would have on His followers. He said, "Because I have said these things unto you, sorrow hath filled your heart" (John 16:6). While it had been a joyous experience to be with the Lord, the news He had given them sank down upon them with heaviness. Thus, in Gethsemane, the Lord "found them sleeping for sorrow" (Luke 22:45). Like Peter and the other disciples, our propensity to fall into sin is much greater at times of emotional stress and physical exhaustion.

The Issue of Location

Satan did not tempt the Lord Jesus for 40 days while He was at home in Nazareth. Instead, he tempted Him when He was alone in the wilderness. Satan knows that circumstances can increase the potency of temptation. Abraham found himself telling half-truths outside the Promised Land. Had he avoided that location and situation; he would have avoided the temptation altogether. Due to his Nazarite vow, Samson was to live devoted to God and not take of the fruit of the vine or be around death. Yet, he "came to the vineyards of Timnath" and then "he turned aside to see the carcass of the lion" (Judges 14:5, 8). He was flirting with sin by the places he was visiting and slowly desensitizing himself to temptation.

After the emotion-packed evening in the upper room and the harrowing experience for the disciples when Jesus was arrested in Gethsemane, "Peter followed him afar off, even into the palace of the high priest" (Mark 14:54). He could not have entered a more hostile environment as he was surrounded by the almost palpable hatred for Christ in the Jewish leaders. In that pressure-cooker situation, Peter would deny the Lord three times. Clearly, location and circumstances make a huge difference as to the likelihood of us giving in to sinful impulses.

The Issue of People

It was commendable that, as Jesus was being led to the palace of the high priest, "Peter followed him afar off" (Mark 14:54a). At the same time, he was trying to maintain his cover and not be noticed. Thus, "when they had kindled a fire in the midst of the hall, and were set down together, Peter sat down among them" (Luke 22:55). He was not only with them, but he was participating in their activities - "and they warmed themselves: and Peter stood with them, and warmed himself" (John 18:18). He was seeking warmth from the same source as the unsaved. When we are surrounded by unbelievers and getting involved with them, we are at greater risk to sin, especially if we keep our identity as Christians hidden.

The temptation to sin did not come from expected sources such as Caiaphas, the High Priest, Annas the former High Priest, or any of the other leaders. Instead, it came from "one of the maids of the high priest" (Mark 14:66). When she said, "Thou also wast with Jesus of Nazareth" (Mark 14:67), "he denied" (Mark 14:68). A little later, "a maid saw him again, and began to say to them that stood by, 'This is one of them.' And he denied it again" (Mark 14:69-70). Peter sinned twice by lying and denying when surrounded by the wrong people and when addressed by an unexpected person. And we are no different. We must be extra vigilant when we are in the company of the unsaved and be aware that often the people whom we least suspect are the ones who will lead us into temptation.

The Issue of Desensitisation

James gives us the slow-motion details of how sin occurs. He said, "But every man is tempted, when he is drawn away of his own lust, and enticed. Then when lust hath conceived, it bringeth forth sin: and sin, when it is finished, bringeth forth death" (James 1:14-15). When should Peter have shut down the process of temptation and sin? Liddel and Scott give the definition of lust as "desire, yearning, longing". Peter, sensing the first desire to hide his identity and not associate with Christ, should have fled the room. Instead, he remained and was challenged by:

- Matthew says: "a damsel (same word as maid)"; "another maid" [allos: another of the same sort]; "they that stood by" (Matt 26:69-74).

- Mark says: "one of the maids"; "the maid"; "they that stood by" (Mark 14:59, 66-68, 70-71).

- Luke says: "A certain maid"; "another [of a different sort *heteros* – a masculine adjective] " (22:56-57, 58, 59-60); "another [*allos* – another of the same sort"]).

- John says: "the damsel (same word as maid)"; "the servants and officers"; a relative of Malchus, the servant of the high priest (John 18:17, 18, 25, 26-27).

Combining the reports, there are potentially two different maids, two different men, and a group of people. Thus, one falsehood may have turned into as many as five or six lies and three denials in "about the space of one hour" (Luke 22:59). While we can deceive ourselves into thinking that we can limit sin, it can multiply very quickly on us. It is something to be feared and never to be thought of as a "one-time" event. It desensitizes and cauterizes the conscience quickly and soon can be repeated and even become an accepted activity in our lives.

Lessons about Fighting

Peter brought out all the tools he had in his inner toolbox to avoid sinning against the Lord. He maybe thought he would avoid the sin of denying Christ by doing something heroic for Him. When the soldiers arrived in Gethsemane, "Simon Peter having a sword drew it, and smote the high priest's servant, and cut off his right ear. The servant's name was Malchus" (John 18:10). Doing something heroic or great in service for our Lord will not make us immune from a fall. Peter took the sword and perhaps convinced himself that he was being noble in trying to protect Christ. However, the Lord had to tell him, "Put up thy sword into the sheath: the cup which my Father hath given me, shall I not drink it?". May God help us to learn that spiritual activity, success, and heroism will never shield us from temptation.

When Jesus said, "Assuredly, I say to you that this night, before the rooster crows, you will deny Me three times" Peter said to Him, "Even if I have to die with You, I will not deny You!" (Matt 26:34-35, NKJV). John tells us that Peter also said to the Saviour, "I will lay down my life for you" (John 13:37, NKJV). Peter's first line of defense was his good intentions. He confidently declared what he would not do ("I will not deny You") and also what he would do ("I will lay down my life for You"). However, our sincerest desires, greatest plans, and most definite proclamations are no defense against the devil and provide little protection from falling into sin.

Very often we try to fight the flesh with the flesh, and we use sin to try and stop sinning. At the second questioning about his relationship with Christ, Peter "denied with an oath" (Matt 26:72). At a further temptation, "he began to invoke a curse on himself and to swear" (Matt 26:74, RSV). Perhaps he thought that he was trying to protect himself, but it sounds like he was trying to make the tempters believe him and leave him alone (i.e. end the temptation). Peter's proclamations remind us of Eve, who, when challenged by Satan, added to the Word of God by forcefully declaring, "Ye shall not eat of it, neither shall ye touch it, lest ye die" (Gen 3:3). More emotion, passionate overstatements, and greater determination place the focus on us and they will not serve to avoid sin nor to stop sinning.

Sadly, Peter makes no comment on divine resources as a means to preserve himself from sin and failure. Perhaps, because Christ had promised that Peter would open different phases of the spread of the gospel (the keys to the kingdom, Matt 16:19), Satan was especially bent on unleashing his fury on him. Getting Peter to fail might disqualify him for divine service and stop the progress of Christ's kingdom. Thus, the Lord told Peter, "But I have prayed for thee that thy faith fail not" (Luke 22:32). Peter was tested and he failed, but due to the faithful intercession of the Lord, his faith in Christ and involvement in the service of the kingdom did not cease. Thank God that even still the Lord intercedes. Paul wrote of "Christ that died, yea rather, that is risen again, who is even at the right hand of God, who also maketh intercession for us" (Rom 8:34).

At a minimum, the Lord's concern and prayers should have made Peter realize his temptation was going to be strong and that he had limited strength in himself. The Lord confirmed this in Gethsemane when He told the disciples, "Watch and pray that you may not enter into temptation" (Mark 14:38, ESV). Since temptation is only avoided or overcome with God's help, we too, should regularly supplicate God's throne and say each day, "Do not lead us into temptation, But deliver us from the evil one" (Matt 6:13, NKJV).

Normally, Peter was in regular communication with the Lord. No disciple asked the Saviour more questions and no one interacted with Him more in the Gospels than Simon Peter. However, there was an eerie silence in Peter's experience in the Garden of Gethsemane and in Caiaphas' house. From his moments of sleep in the Garden until after his denials, Peter does not speak one word to the Lord and the Lord does not speak to him. Also, Peter often quotes Scripture in the book of the Acts revealing a mind that was saturated with the Word of God. But at that point, Peter had no word from God in the moment of temptation.

The Psalmist wrote, "Thy word have I hid in mine heart, that I might not sin against thee" (Ps 119:11). Christ proved and modeled the effectiveness of the Word of God in His own temptation in the wilderness as He deflected every blow from Satan by saying, "It is written...". Even more than the Word of God in general, the Lord Jesus had a specific and applicable word from God. He already knew a specific Scripture from Deuteronomy that related to each temptation He faced. That is what Paul meant when he exhorted believers to prepare for spiritual warfare by taking "the sword of the Spirit, which is the word of God" (Eph 6:17). There is no real definite article before "word of God" so it could be understood to mean, "the sword of the Spirit, which is a word from God."

Tragically, on that unforgettable night in the life of Peter, he had nothing from God; no relevant Scripture came to mind that he could employ in his defense. While it is easy to be hard on Peter, the reality is that most of us are grossly unprepared for temptation. We have very little of the Bible memorised and, while quoting John 3:16 in the gospel is excellent, it certainly does not fit the myriad of temptations that could come our way. Even worse, many of us have not developed the discipline of regularly getting a fresh word from God out of the Scriptures to equip us for trials and temptations.

Paul linked our dependence in supplication and our reliance on Scripture as a major part of achieving victory when under attack. He wrote to the Ephesians about the need to "take the helmet of salvation, and the sword of the Spirit, which is the word of God: Praying always with all prayer and supplication in the Spirit, and watching thereunto with all perseverance and supplication for all saints" (Eph 6:17-18). Immediately, prior to triumphing over the temptations of Satan in the wilderness, the Lord Jesus was praying (Luke 3:21). Dependence in prayer to God and receiving a word from God are our two great resources when faced with temptation. Peter did not employ them, and he fell. The Lord Jesus employed them and He was victorious.

Lessons about Failure

Recognition of Failure

No one ever plans to fail, and Peter didn't either. He actually planned to be faithful to his Lord and was even willing to die for him. Imagine the shock when he realized that he had just done what he promised he would never do. We can easily imagine a stunned look on his face mixed with confusion in his mind as he thought, "How did that just happen?" Have you ever looked in the mirror and asked that about something you said or did?

While Peter didn't know the answer, the Lord did. Before the failure took place, the Lord knew who would fail (Peter), what he was going to do (deny Christ), how many times (three), and when he would sin (between the first and second crowing of the rooster). And yet, in spite of knowing all that beforehand, Christ still let Simon be born, He saved Simon, He called him to full-time service, and He used him to preach and perform miracles. He did not bless Simon Peter with all of that because Peter would be 100% perfect and loyal. He blessed him out of divine grace – period. Isn't it both comforting and humbling to think that our Lord has blessed us even though He knows all our post-salvation failures and sin?

This is a vital fact in terms of Peter's restoration, and it is for us too. John wrote, "If we confess our sins, he is faithful and just to forgive us our sins, and to cleanse us from all unrighteousness" (1 John 1:9). Confess (*homologeo*) is a compound word combining a word meaning "the same" (*homo*) and the word, "to speak or say" (*lego*). When we sin as believers, we do not require the forgiveness from God as our judge. That was settled once and for all at the point of salvation. The forgiveness of sins we received at that moment included forgiveness for every sin in our lives from birth to death. However, sin still fractures communion and impedes communication with our heavenly Father. To have that restored, we need to confess or say what God says about our sin. Even before we commit sin, our Father is identifying our thoughts, words, or actions as particular sins. Our responsibility is to agree with our Father and confess them. At that point, "He is faithful and just to forgive us our sins, and to cleanse us from all unrighteousness".

Responsibility for Failure

Peter had many factors against him. He had been away from his home and family for periods of time as he followed the Saviour during His three years of public ministry. He was physically tired as it was very late at night. He was emotionally distraught having seen men arrest Jesus, his Saviour, Lord, and Friend. Hours before, he had tried to kill a man with a sword in the garden of Gethsemane, and the memory of that action undoubtedly replayed itself over and over in his mind. The mixed emotions of anger with himself for having forsaken his Lord in the garden and relief that he had escaped with his life would also flood over him. He was now sitting in Caiaphas' house surrounded by unsaved, wicked men who were determined to convict and kill the Son of Man.

With all of those factors, had we been in Peter's shoes, we would have played "the victim" card in an attempt to justify our sin. We might have said, "If Judas wouldn't have betrayed the Lord Jesus, this situation would never have happened". Or, "If John had not pulled some strings to get me in here, I would not have said the things I did". Or, "I was feeling stressed and worried and I am not sure what came over me to do something like that". But the Lord had made it clear beforehand, "Verily I say unto THEE, That this night, before the cock crow, THOU shalt deny me thrice" (Matt 26:34). All the factors of other people involved, the location, the time, the circumstances etc. can either facilitate or impede sin. However, in the end, Peter was responsible for each of his sins.

Peter understood that there is a big difference between character and actions. Scripture calls Judas a traitor (Luke 6:16) because that was his character. However, the Bible never calls Peter a denier or Thomas a doubter. Yes, Peter denied the Lord and Thomas doubted Him, but that was not their general character. Peter was courageous (character), but he did something cowardly (action). He was honest, but he did something dishonest. He was a unifier, but he caused division (Gal 2:11-13). So when Paul withstood Peter face to face, he focused solely on Peter's erroneous action of separating himself from Gentile Christians.

When Paul confronted him, Peter did not try to "flip things" and make the story be instead about Paul being a bully who had attacked his character. We all can employ that tactic when faced with our sin which is simply an attempt to avoid responsibility. In so doing, we misrepresent the person and message of the one who confronted us and we change the focus from what we did, to what they did. Likewise, when the Lord confronted him about his acts of denial, Peter never rewrote the narrative, never portrayed himself as an attacked victim, and never accused the Lord of a lack of love. He knew that the real reason the Lord and Paul challenged him was because they loved him. Showing a truly repentant spirit on both occasions, Peter humbly accepted his guilt and took ownership for his choices and actions. May God give us this most admirable grace as seen in Simon Peter. May we be ready to face our sin, to repent, to offer sincere apologies, and to make things right.

Reacting to Failure

Sin tends to repeat itself. Peter sat quietly by the fire but was likely tense with fear that he would be noticed. Then, "one of the servant girls of the high priest came. And when she saw Peter warming himself, she looked at him and said, 'You also were with Jesus of Nazareth'" (Mark 14:66-67, NKJV). For Peter, that which he had feared had come upon him. He could have taken time to respond thoughtfully and correctly. Instead, "He denied it...and went out on the porch, and a rooster crowed" (Mark 14:68, NKJV).

One would think that hearing the rooster would have made Peter recognize that the Lord was being merciful and reminding him that God would keep His word, even though His servant had not. But sin can cloud our discernment and impact our reasoning so that we continue further down the path of selfishness and wrong.

Peter did not sin because he was hit with a rapid-fire, shock-and-awe attack of accusations. Mark tells us that Peter received the second accusation of his association with Jesus "a little later". In other words, the Lord held back the rooster from crowing a second time to give Peter a while to reflect on his false statement. Again, Luke says that the third accusation came "about the space of one hour after" he had received the second (Lk 22:59). Again, God graciously gave him an opportunity to put the brakes on this downward slide. But, instead of being like Joseph and fleeing temptation, Peter remained in the situation.

Remember, it was likely Peter who provided much information and insight when Mark wrote his gospel. So, it is only in that gospel that we are told: "And the second time the cock crew. And Peter called to mind the word that Jesus said unto him, 'Before the cock crow twice, thou shalt deny me thrice'. And when he thought thereon, he wept" (Mark 14:72). The scene would play and replay in his mind as he would review God's gracious intervention (the first rooster crow) and how he ignored God's call in the circumstances and his own conscience within him. Have you ever reacted to sin in the same way that Peter did?

Repenting of Failure

There is an immense difference between remorse and repentance. At one point, Judas realized that whatever he had hoped was not going to happen and "when he saw that he [Jesus] was condemned, [he] repented himself" (Matt 27:3). Does that mean Judas was either saved or restored? Sadly, neither occurred. According to BDAG, this Greek word for "repented" is *metamelomai*, which means "to have regrets about something...in the sense that one wishes it could be undone". Many in prison regret that they can't go back and redo things so that the outcome would be different. They wish they could have a redo on their crime so that they would not get caught or obtain even more benefits from their action. That is remorse, not repentance.

By contrast, when Jesus said, "Except ye repent, ye shall all likewise perish" (Luke 13:3), he used the Greek word, *metanoeō*. While it literally meant to change one's mind, The Lexical Theological Workbook says, "In the NT, [it] generally refers not simply to changing one's mind but to turning back to God". That is evident in the Great Commission when the Lord Jesus said, "that repentance and remission of sins should be preached in his name among all nations, beginning at Jerusalem" (Luke 24:47). Paul also preached the same in Ephesus where he was "Testifying both to the Jews, and also to the Greeks, repentance toward God, and faith toward our Lord Jesus Christ" (Acts 20:21).

While the word repent is not specifically used of Peter after he sinned, we have enough evidence to conclude that he turned back to God to agree with Him about his sin.

Prior to failing, and even while he was denying the Lord Jesus, Peter was focused on others. Luke records this by telling us:

- "A certain maid beheld him...and earnestly looked upon him" (Luke 22:56)

- "after a little while another saw him" (Luke 22:58)

- "one hour after another confidently affirmed" (Luke 22:59)

- "I know not what thou sayest" (Luke 22:60).

Thankfully, though, Peter's focus began to change when, upon the hearing the rooster, "the Lord turned, and looked upon Peter" (Luke 22:61). Matthew says at that point, "Peter remembered the word of Jesus" (Matt 26:75). Mark testifies that "Peter called to mind the word that Jesus said unto him, Before the cock crow twice, thou shalt deny me thrice" (Mark 14:72). The work of true repentance had begun in Peter as his focus changed to the Lord's view of his sin and what the Lord had said about it. Peter quickly realised that what mattered was his relationship with the Lord. His attention quickly changed to what the Omniscient, all-seeing God had observed when he (Peter) denied knowing the Lord Jesus.

The impact of this change in his thinking (a genuine change of mind and turning to agree with God's viewpoint) is evident because Luke and Matthew tell us that Peter then "went out and wept bitterly" (Matt 26:75; Luke 22:62).The Dictionary of Biblical Languages says that the word translated "bitterly" means: "with agony... i.e. with mental suffering". Peter was aligned with heaven about his sin and thus the awfulness of his choice weighed heavily upon him, and rightly so.

This was not a surprise to the Lord, but rather a moment He had been anticipating. He had said to Peter beforehand, "When thou art converted" (Luke 22:32). Notice He did not say, "If you are converted," but, "When you are converted". The word converted is a compound word in Greek meaning to turn towards. The Lord always longs for this critical moment in the restoration of His own when, like Peter, they finally turn towards Him.

Lessons about the Future

The Lord wants Restoration

God does not have a spiritual scrap heap full of Christians who have failed. Peter had once heard the Lord Jesus tell in Matthew 18 about a shepherd who went after a wayward and misdirected sheep. Now, he had become that wayward sheep. And, true to the parable, the Good Shepherd immediately began to work to see him brought back to fellowship and usefulness.

Even before Peter's famous fall, Satan was seeking permission to launch an attack on all the disciples. Jesus said, "Behold, Satan hath desired to have you (plural), that he may sift you (plural) as wheat" (Luke 22:32). Knowing Satan's intentions and how the particular aim of his assault would be against the leader of the disciples, Jesus said, "But I have prayed for thee (singular)". He so loved Peter that He was praying for Peter's restoration even before he failed. Satan could spring a similar attack on anyone of us. What a comfort to know that the Lord, who knows all, is praying for restoration today just as much as He was then.

The parallels between salvation and restoration are noteworthy and numerous. Both an unsaved sinner and a wayward saint suffer loss, feel guilt, and sense the impact of their sin on their relationship with heaven. Both must come to repentance, appreciate they are loved by God, and receive forgiveness voluntarily. The two Shepherd Parables in Matthew 18 and Luke 15 deal with a wayward saint and a lost sinner respectively. In one, the Shepherd "seeketh that which is gone astray" (Matt 18:12) and, in the other, the Shepherd "goes after that which is lost, until he find it" (Luke 15:4). When the sheep picturing the lost soul is found, the Shepherd is "rejoicing" (Luke 15:5). And when the Shepherd finds the sheep picturing a believer who has failed, "he rejoiceth" (Matt 18:13). So, which does the Lord enjoy more, the salvation of souls or the restoration of saints? The correct answer is, "Yes!" He equally loves and longs for both. Do we?

The Lord's burden was not so much the impact of Peter's sin on him emotionally or even that his physical life might be at risk. He said that He prayed, "that thy faith fail not" (Luke 22:32). His deep concern was for the spiritual welfare of His servant, Peter. The Lord could see how a fall like Peter's could lead to a failure or cessation of faith. It was not that Peter would lose his salvation as that would be impossible according to all the teaching in the New Testament. However, sin and failure can leave believers dry and devastated. Even worse, sin can desensitize a believer so that he is unaware of his decline in communion with God. That should frighten every believer!

Often when a believer sins, other Christians focus on the feelings of the one who has sinned (eg. embarrassment), his return to church fellowship, his return to service, his acceptance by others in spite of sin. However, the Saviour made the most important thing the most important thing. Even before Peter sinned, the Lord was concerned that it might lead to long-term spiritual distance, dryness, and dullness. He was burdened because Peter's enjoyment of fellowship with his heavenly father could go dormant. May God help us to have a clear focus when we or someone fall into sin. Before everything else, may our burden, prayer and efforts be concentrated on restoration to fellowship with God. That was the response of Christ to Peter's sin and it should our response as well.

The Lord waits for Restoration

The Lord did not consider rushing Peter's restoration to save him from further embarrassment. The re-establishment of fellowship was far more important than Peter's ego and pride. Thus, beforehand, the Saviour stated in prayer, "When thou art converted..." (Luke 22:32). He did not lay out a timeline for restoration to be completed. He just said, "When...". As difficult as it would be, He would let Peter feel the weight of guilt flooding his heart and permit him to weep bitter tears of regret. The Lord patiently waited for the Word of God and the work of God to bring about Peter's restoration. He would not take any short-cuts or apply undue pressure. Without any doubt, we all need more of both the Saviour's love for restoration as well as His patience for His divine work to be accomplished. It is impressive that He did not wait too long or rush too quickly. He prayed and had discernment to see God's perfect timing in the restoration of this beloved disciple. He understood that, if pressuring and rushing a soul to salvation is unbiblical and potentially damaging, pushing and hurrying a saint to restoration can also have negative, long-term effects.

While the process of restoration in Peter began the minute he sinned, the Lord waited for days and perhaps weeks before returning Peter to his leadership role among the disciples. Three days passed during which "Christ died for our sins according to the scriptures; And that he was buried, and that he rose again the third day according to the scriptures" (1 Cor 15:3-4). Then, He waited at least two weeks, until He met Peter and six other disciples on the beach at the Sea of Galilee. There, He recommissioned him to care for his sheep. While the timing of Peter's restoration may have seemed like seven eternities to Peter and others, not one minute was wasted. It was all part of the wise, divine plan to bring Peter back and to prepare him for usefulness for God.

The Lord works for Restoration

The Lord's focus and desire for Peter's restoration is evident in that, when Peter denied him and the rooster crowed the second time, "The Lord turned, and looked upon Peter. And Peter remembered the word of the Lord" (Luke 22:61). His eye immediately turns to every wayward believer as does His heart with longing for sinning saints to return to fellowship and communion with Him.

Before Peter is recorded as having met with all the disciples, he and John were informed first by Mary Magdalene that the Lord had risen. This led to the foot race to the tomb which John, likely the younger of the two, won. John arrived first, but Peter ducked into the tomb first. Before anything else, Peter was brought to meditate on the person, death, burial, resurrection and promises of Christ. The Lord he once denied was the Lord he was now appreciating. The Lord was turning Peter's attention from his failure on to the Lord Jesus himself. Instead of being occupied with his own failure, he was to be occupied with his Lord's successful death, burial and resurrection.

There was one indispensable step in Peter's restoration which Peter would never forget. After he came out of the tomb, the Lord Jesus appeared first to Mary Magdalene (Mark 16:9). Then, he appeared to a group of women traveling back home from the tomb (Matt 28:9). Following that, He likely appeared to the couple on the road to Emmaus (Luke 24:13-30). Either before or right after that, "he was seen of Cephas" (1 Cor 15:5). As the couple returned to Jerusalem from Emmaus, they must have heard the news. When they arrived, they told the disciples, "The Lord is risen indeed, and hath appeared to Simon" (Luke 24:34). The first was a miracle of power, the second was a miracle of grace. On that memorable, but private occasion, the Lord had dealings with Peter of which no details are given in Scripture. Every restored saint can reflect on how the Lord worked to bring them back into fellowship with Himself which includes private time alone with Him.

Upon Christ's resurrection, an angel was stationed at the tomb to wait and inform the group of women that the Lord Jesus had risen. He also instructed them, "But go your way, tell his disciples and Peter that he goeth before you into Galilee" (Mark 16:7). From their statement, we can conclude that Peter was likely not with the disciples at that point. Sin does that, doesn't it? It not only distances us from the Lord, it also impacts on our relationships with one another. Sin always diminishes our exercise to meet with others. So, upon Peter's return to communion with the Lord, the Saviour then sought to draw him back into fellowship and confidence with the disciples as well. Later that Sunday, Peter was back meeting with the disciples in the upper room and only Thomas missed that occasion when the Lord appeared to all who were present (John 20:19-24). Peter continued to meet with them all as "after eight days again his disciples were within, and Thomas with them" (John 20:26). From then on, Peter continued to gather with other believers with whom he shared the same convictions and doctrine.

Restoration to personal communion with the Lord was first followed a by return to the collective communion with the disciples. But the Lord still had to work out Peter's reintegration into public service. The next step, then, in the restoration process was to re-establish commitment and submission to the Lord's will in Peter's life.

The eleven disciples of Christ had all been disloyal as they had all forsaken Him and fled in the Garden of Gethsemane. Additionally, Peter had denied his Lord three times. And yet, the Lord had told them beforehand, "But after I am risen again, I will go before you into Galilee" (Matt 26:32). As already noted, the angel at his tomb reminded the women who arrived first, "...that he goeth before you into Galilee" (Mark 16:7). A very short while later, the Lord appeared to those same women and told them, "...go tell my brethren that they go into Galilee, and there shall they see me" (Matt 28:10). The Lord had prayed that Peter's life of faith would not cease, and it did not because, "The effective, fervent prayer of a righteous man avails much" (James 5:16, NKJV). We are not surprised, then, when we read that "Jesus shewed himself again to the disciples at the sea of Tiberias" (John 21:1). Peter and the others had obeyed their master and traveled 60 miles north to Galilee. The fruit of Peter's repentance was now evident in his decision to obey his Lord.

The process of reconnecting communication and communion with Christ in Peter's life continued. John tells us, "Jesus revealed himself again to the disciples by the Sea of Tiberias". Peter´s spiritual-growth trajectory and his continuing appreciation of Christ were back on track. Peter had just led six other disciples in a fishing expedition, perhaps because his faith in Christ to provide for his daily needs was diminished. That also happens when we sin. The Lord did not rebuke him, as it was responsible and commendable that he sought employment to provide for his wife and family rather than begging or dropping hints so that others would give to him. However, the Lord Jesus did give him another training seminar using the boat, nets, and 153 fish on the shore of the Sea of Galilee.

Peter's awe for the Lord was definitely returning. When John identified that it was the Lord Jesus speaking to them from the shore, "Simon Peter heard that it was the Lord, [so] he girt his fisher's coat unto him, (for he was naked,) and did cast himself into the sea" (John 21:7). Before, he moved away from the presence of Christ when he forsook Him, but now he moved closer to the Saviour. His quick adjustment to put on his coat perhaps indicates the respect he had for the Lord. One of the clear indications of divinely wrought restoration in a wayward believer is an increasing desire to be with the Lord and to show Him reverence.

When Jesus was led to Caiaphas' house prior to his crucifixion, "Peter followed him afar off unto the high priest's palace, and went in, and sat with the servants, to see the end" (Matt 26:58). He could see the Lord Jesus, but he had no communication with Him. Thankfully, things changed as now on the beach he was close to the Lord and "Jesus saith unto them, 'Come and dine.'" (John 21:12). This was parallel to the invitation the Lord would give to believers in Laodicea when he would say, "If anyone hears My voice and opens the door, I will come in to him and dine with him, and he with Me" (Rev 3:20 NKJV). Peter had last dined with the Saviour at the Passover in the upper room. In grace, the Lord worked to bring about full restoration of Peter's communion. He did it for Peter and He is still doing it today!

Again, the Lord 's Prayer for Peter had been that his confidence in God might not fail. Perhaps Peter was not just going on a fishing trip to fill the time or to find some supper. Peter's words were *"hupago halieuein."* which Darby translates literally as: "I go to fish". Peter was seemingly returning to reliance on himself and his own abilities to meet his need. He was going back to his old job. However, as Peter saw the net fill with 153 large fish, he was quickly reminded that the Lord still had power to provide for his needs. Once again, "Jesus then cometh, and taketh bread, and giveth them, and fish likewise" (John 21:13). At critical times in our lives and especially when we fail, our confidence in God can slip. So often, though, our gracious Lord works to rebuild our faith so that we learn to trust God again.

Another key consideration in the restoration of a believer who has failed is the need to return to the point of departure. When Joseph and Mary lost sight of Jesus at the temple and headed home to Nazareth, the Lord waited for them to return to that same temple three days later. The same was true for Naomi who "went from Bethlehem-Judah" (Ruth 1:1) to Moab. Ten years later, as part of her restoration to the Lord, she "came to Bethlehem" (Ruth 1:19). And for Peter, his three denials of the Lord, began when he "warmed himself at the fire" (Mark 14:54) in Caiaphas' house. Thus, the Lord arranged it so that when Peter stepped on the beach, he "saw a fire of coals there" (John 21:9). As he stared into the embers and felt the heat, he would undoubtedly recall the very point of his departure and where his thinking and speech went off track. It is important, therefore, that we as believers reflect and understand what went wrong in our own lives and that we learn from our mistakes.

Finally, before reinstituting Peter into a position of public service, the Lord Jesus addressed the heart of the matter which was the matter of the heart. Three times, Peter had coldly and clearly denied the Lord. Thus, three times, the Lord would ask Peter, "Lovest thou me?" (John 21:15, 16, 17). Peter had not lost any of his abilities nor had he lost any knowledge of God that he had already obtained. What he had experienced was a drop in his love for Christ. So, the Lord drilled down deeper by asking him, "Lovest thou ME?". Did he love any other person, any other activity, any other idea more than Christ? The first time Jesus posed the question, He asked, "Simon, son of Jonas, lovest thou me more than these?" (John 21:15). Peter had previously claimed greater love and loyalty than the other disciples when he had said, "Though they all fall away because of you, I will never fall away" (Matt 26:33, ESV). Now, the Lord was testing to see if Peter was viewing devotion as a competitive exercise and a means to achieve prominence and praise, or was he solely full of appreciation and devotion to Christ? Did Peter love the Lord because of what he might get out of their relationship for himself, or did he love the Lord Jesus just because of who He is? Most of us have no room to be hard on Peter as this story is as much a mirror into our own hearts as it is a window into Peter's. We are all sadly capable of turning spiritual things into selfish pursuits. We can worship at every Breaking of Bread because it makes us feel good. We can preach because we like a sense of public recognition. We can share the gospel because it makes us feel useful. Really, the list is endless as we are capable of having selfish motives in every activity and conversation (even spiritual ones). The Lord Jesus was making it abundantly clear that day, that Peter's reintegration into God's service was because of His grace and that His servant should be motivated only by love. As Paul said, "Though I...have not love...it profits me nothing" (1 Cor 13:1-3).

Before Peter's denial, Jesus had said, "...when thou art converted, strengthen thy brethren" (Luke 22.32). The Lord envisioned that, upon restoration, Peter would still be very useful to Him. Do we share that vision for believers that have fallen? Peter was commanded by the Lord to strengthen, which means, according to Strong, "to set fast, i.e. (lit.) to turn resolutely in a certain direction". His recommission would include the preaching of the gospel, but in a special way he was to feed and care for the Lord's sheep and the Lord's lambs. When a person falls, part of what can make their faith decline is that they quickly lose a sense of spiritual purpose and usefulness. Did John Mark feel that when he abandoned Paul and Barnabas in the middle of a missionary trip? Did David feel that when he sinned with Bathsheba? While one danger is to jump to reintegration before a fallen believer is ready, the other extreme is to avoid giving any hope of future usefulness for God. Sin can alter the possibilities of how we serve the Lord, but as long as He has us here, He always has plans and purposes for us.

Therefore, when Peter writes his final letter, he does not say "Peter the Failure who is now an apostle." Instead, he begins, "Simon Peter, a servant" (2 Peter 1:1). By God's grace, Peter had become useful to God as he laboured with a heart full of love. One other notable and commendable feature about Peter was that he did not let poor decisions in the past limit his usefulness for God. The devil loves it when believers are paralysed by guilt and shame, but Peter would not let that happen. He wisely focused on the forgiveness he had received rather than the failure he had committed. His goal was to handle this blot in his past in a balanced manner by neither explicitly bringing it up, nor by acting as if it had never happened. So, as you read through Peter's two epistles, look for the implied references to his failures and the lessons he learned from them. Without question, the whole experience left him in awe of the grace of God which had both saved him and restored him. Perhaps with tears in his eyes and appreciation in his heart, the big fisherman would declare about his God, "He restoreth my soul!" (Ps 23:3). May this consideration of Peter the Failure give us wisdom to avoid spiritual falls, and may it give us hope as our God is still moulding futures for failures just as He did for Simon Peter.

CHAPTER 18

Peter the Decision Maker

"When you come to a fork in the road, take it."
Yogi Berra, American baseball catcher, coach, and manager.

Yogi Berra developed his own combination of malapropisms and witticisms which came to be known as "Yogiisms". These pithy statements leave people confused and yet understanding a clear point. In this case, he is not talking about literally finding a silver fork lying on the street and taking it home with you. His point, as Yogi himself explained, was that instead of falling into a paralysis of analysis when facing a decision, "Make the best choice you can, and go with it". But, as a Christian, how will you know what is the best choice?

After seeing the resurrected Christ ascend into heaven, eleven disciples walked down the slopes of the Mount of Olives, crossed the Kedron Brook and entered the city of Jerusalem. While they were unsure of many things, they simply obeyed the Lord who "commanded them that they should not depart from Jerusalem, but wait for the promise of the Father" (Acts 1:4). And now, what? They had been told to go into all the world in the Great Commission (Matt 28:19), and yet the Master also told them to wait.

In the meantime, it was "in those days [that] Peter stood up in the midst of the disciples" (Acts 1:15). Those days? They were days of uncertainty, high emotion, and impending change. So, when suddenly "Peter stood up in the midst of the disciples" no one perceived his action as an opportunist making a power-grab in the Saviour´s absence or an attempt by Peter to foist his will on everyone else. He had a track record of leadership and was well-respected by everyone. Once before, in the same upper room, Peter had missed an opportunity to serve in the washing of the disciples' feet (John 13). This time, he would be careful not to miss the chance to serve in the selection of a replacement for Judas.

When Peter guided the group of "about an hundred and twenty" (Acts 1:15) that day (a group that was 10 times the size of the small group that Jesus had selected during his ministry), he operated upon principles that can also guide us towards Biblical choices.

Step 1: Establish the proper environment: vv 12-14

The best choices are made for a group in an atmosphere of harmony. Luke tells us that Peter, the 10 other apostles, the half-brothers of Jesus who had just been saved, Jesus' mother, and all the women "continued with one accord" (Acts 1:14). It was not just a lull in their previous bickering over their "greatness" rankings in the kingdom. True peace is not just the absence of problems, but also the enjoyment of what is shared in common. In a family, a marriage, or an assembly, unity should be valued and protected and become an immediate concern when it is in jeopardy. Regular and intentional acts and words to promote and maintain peaceful relationships are essential to providing the best atmosphere for when a major decision is to be made.

On that occasion, even more important than the horizontal harmony the believers enjoyed with one another, was their vertical fellowship with the Lord. Luke notes that the collective group continued "with one accord in prayer and supplication" (Acts 1:14). After three years with the Saviour, they were all accustomed to speaking directly to the Lord Jesus. Although He was gone, they would still keep up regular and genuine communication with Heaven. Whether personally or collectively applied, there is nothing that leads to good decision-making like an authentic and vibrant relationship with God. The wise king once taught his son about how to make correct decisions. His advice was, "Trust in the Lord with all thine heart; and lean not unto thine own understanding. In all thy ways acknowledge him, and he shall direct thy paths" (Prov 3:5-6). The number one requisite for good decisions is to establish and maintain spiritual fellowship with God first. Thus, no one has ever made better decisions than the Lord Jesus and no one has ever had better communication with the Father than Him.

Step 2: Sense the needs and decisions that must be faced: v 15

Scripture does not provide a record of the Lord specifically asking them to find another apostle to replace Judas. Perhaps Peter simply remembered that Jesus had said to them, "Verily I say unto you, that ye which have followed me, in the regeneration when the Son of man shall sit in the throne of his glory, ye also shall sit upon twelve thrones, judging the twelve tribes of Israel" (Matt 19:28). Thirty times in the Gospels the special group of his disciples are referred to as "the twelve", "these twelve" or "his twelve." Eight times, Judas is specifically called "one of the twelve" (John 6:71). So, with the clear designation and significance of the number 12 (authority), the promise of 12 specific thrones in the coming Kingdom, it only seemed Biblical and rational to appoint a replacement for Judas. Many times, we are inclined to avoid or postpone decisions as the process of decision-making can be stressful and the responsibility for the decision great. However, good decision-makers are never fearful that God might not direct them. Instead, they recognize needs and view times of decision-making as opportunities to seek God's guidance.

Step 3: Search the Scriptures for applicable commands, principles and examples vv 16-17

Peter always seems to have the Word of God filtering through his mind. Remember that at Christ's first command to launch his boat out into the deep waters and let down his net, Peter's response was, "At thy word, I will let down the net" (Luke 5:5). He was the disciple who told the Saviour, "thou hast the words of eternal life" (John 6:68). Even when he wandered, what generated Peter's restoration was when he "remembered the word of the Lord" (Luke 22:61). Upon Christ's ascension, Peter heard from the angelic messengers the thrilling promise of Christ's return (Acts 1:11). In spite of a cascade of mixed emotions that were likely flooding over him that day, again his mind turned to Scripture.

First, Peter reviewed the tragic history of Judas Iscariot in light of Old Testament Scriptures. Judas, who had been the treasurer for Jesus and His disciples, had turned traitor and became an accomplice in the Jewish scheme to put Jesus to death. As Peter considered this in prayer, two Scriptures linked themselves in his mind which emboldened him to address the matter with the 10 apostles and the rest of the 119 believers present in the upper room. First, he appreciated divine inspiration as he was about to quote words "which the Holy Ghost by the mouth of David spake before concerning Judas" (Acts 1:16). A good Christian decision-maker must have an awe for the authority and relevance of the Bible as the inspired Word of God. Specifically, Peter cites Psalm 69:25 which commands, "Let his habitation be desolate and let no man dwell therein". Additionally, he quotes Psalm 109:8, "... let another take his office". Before potential candidates were selected, Peter established the Biblical basis on which to make a decision about a replacement. In so doing, he was just imitating his Master. The Psalmist explained that Christ made wise and excellent choices because, "...his delight is in the law of the LORD; and in his law doth he meditate day and night" (Ps 1:2).

The need to know and review Biblical commands, principles and examples is vital for successful decision-making today. That is why New Testament church leaders are required to be "apt to teach" (1 Tim 3:2). Husbands, as leaders in family decisions, are to imitate Christ whose goal with His bride, the church, is to "sanctify and cleanse it with the washing of water by the word" (Eph 5:26). The same is seen when the wise king told the prince, "Where there is no revelation, the people cast off restraint; But happy is he who keeps the law" (Prov 29:18, NKJV). Making an honest inventory of applicable Scripture will be the best starting point for any decision we face.

Step 4: Focus on the facts of the situation vv 17-19

In times of decision, it is very easy to get side-tracked and focus on other issues, personal feelings, or conjecture. Peter, though, concentrated on the facts that "Judas...was guide to them that took

Jesus" and that "he was numbered with us, and had obtained part of this ministry" (Acts 1:16-17). Luke provides additional information in parenthesis (NKJV, NASB, ESV) to explain what the others would have already known. He says, "Now this man [Judas] purchased a field with the reward of iniquity; and falling headlong, he burst asunder in the midst, and all his bowels gushed out. And it was known unto all the dwellers at Jerusalem; insomuch as that field is called in their proper tongue, Aceldama, that is to say, The field of blood" (Acts 1:18-19). Under Peter's direction everyone in the room focused on known information as to what happened when Judas "by transgression fell, that he might go to his own place" (Acts 1:25). Thus, the solution would become evident when the problem or need was clear. It is noteworthy that Peter's concise presentation and analysis of facts is not questioned or corrected by anyone there. It takes discernment and discipline to keep a discussion focused just on the issue at hand when major decisions must be made in an assembly, a marriage, a family, or a job.

Step 5: Consider potential and viable options vv 21-23

Peter then reviewed with them the Biblical qualifications and guidelines for an apostle. A major decision like this must be made upon an objective basis. Therefore, we do not read of the emotions of Mary or Jesus' half-brothers nor of any "gut-feelings" in the apostles. In a vital selection like this, there would be no room for bias due to family connections, the pursuit of gender equity, a commitment to affirmative action, or a consideration of seniority. God's guidance must agree with His Word - period. Thus, Peter considers the teachings and practices of the Lord Jesus. Based on that, he points out that the candidate must:

- "have companied with us all the time that the Lord Jesus went in and out among us, Beginning from the baptism of John, unto that same day that he was taken up from us".

- "[be] one...ordained to be a witness with us of his resurrection".

Applying these filters greatly reduced the possibilities and disqualified family members, friends, women, and likely some men with great ability like James and Jude, who eventually wrote New Testament Epistles. Based on these Biblical guidelines, "they appointed two, Joseph called Barsabbas, who was surnamed Justus, and Matthias" (Acts 1:23). It can be a struggle to avoid making quick decisions based on emotions, decisions based on pressure from others, or decisions based on what initially appears logical. Instead, we need to discipline ourselves to consider only possibilities that agree with God's Word.

Step 6: Seek input and counsel from others who are spiritual

Peter could have made the decision himself. After all, it was to him the Lord gave a leadership role when He said, "I will give unto thee the keys of the kingdom of heaven: and whatsoever thou shalt bind on earth shall be bound in heaven: and whatsoever thou shalt loose on earth shall be loosed in heaven" (Matt 16:19). Yet, Peter recognized that "Where no counsel is, the people fall: but in the multitude of counsellors there is safety" (Prov 11:14). So, he sought the input of others and involved them in the decision-making process. Luke writes that, rather than Peter alone, "*they* appointed two" (Acts 1:23), "*they* prayed" (Acts 1:24), and "*they* gave forth their lots" (Acts 1:26). If we are honest, often we make decisions without seeking input so we can avoid anyone challenging or delaying us. Or, so that we can claim we sought advice, we only seek the opinions of those who are emotionally involved or the opinions of those we know will agree with us. Neutral and spiritual counsel in major decisions is absolutely essential. As the wise king taught his son "Without counsel, plans go awry" (Prov 15:22, NKJV).

Step 7: Commit the matter to God in prayer and trust Him as you move forward vv 24-25

Jesus had taught the disciples to pray, "Our Father which art in heaven, Hallowed be thy name. Thy kingdom come. Thy will be done in earth, as it is in heaven" (Matt 6:9-10). Following the model He gave them, they would speak to God first about His person and plans before they would pray about the issue at hand. Thus, they mention the Lord's omniscience ("Thou...knowest the hearts of all men") and His sovereignty ("whether of these two thou hast chosen"). After focusing and enjoying God first, they turned to their specific concern - the "part of this ministry and apostleship, from which Judas by transgression fell, that he might go to his own place" (Acts 1:24-25). So often, we rush to focus on our needs, and we forget about God. Before making any major decision, it would be good to consider the relevant traits and attributes of God and worship Him. This will lead us to ask, "Will our decision be consistent with His character?" Can we speak to God in prayer and have peace as we discuss the options with Him, or do they clash with His character, bringing conflict to our minds and uncertainty in our hearts?

Step 8: Consider the circumstances v 26

Casting lots was common in ancient times. The high priest usually carried with him the Urim and the Thummim, two stones he used to choose between the two goats on the Day of Atonement and to decide other matters as well. The wise man said, "The lot is cast into the lap; but the whole disposing thereof is of the LORD" (Prov 16:33). "According to biblical usage lots seem to have been used only when the decision was important and where wisdom or biblical injunctions did not give sufficient guidance" (Baker: Encyclopaedia of the Bible).

The order of the steps they made before arriving at a decision is significant. Casting lots was a circumstance in which perhaps sticks, stones, coins, or a type of dice were tossed randomly in the air only to fall in the folds of the tunic of a seated man. After assuring that all the options under consideration matched Biblical precepts and principles, this neutral, unbiased event would give guidance.

"The word 'lots' occurs 70 times in the Old Testament and seven in the New Testament. Most of the occurrences were in the early period when little of the Bible was available and when God approved of this means for determining His will (Prov 16:33)" (Nelson's New Illustrated Bible Dictionary). The practice of lots was never condemned by the

Lord, but it did fall into disuse after the descent of the Holy Spirit on the Day of Pentecost. Never are we told in any of the epistles to resort to "lot-casting" in order to make decisions. In part, this is because we now have the complete Scriptures to guide us and the Holy Spirit residing within us.

Therefore, while the tendency can be to focus on circumstances (perhaps a modern equivalent to lots), we need to develop the default process of first reviewing all relevant Scriptures, considering the character of God, seeking the input of spiritual and neutral believers, and waiting on Him in prayer. Then, we can look to unbiased circumstances (not engineered to confirm our preferences and plans). Above all, we must emphasize that the lot they cast that day indicated the choice of Matthias and that the choice was in complete agreement with the revealed Word of God. Today, it is still true that circumstances are only valid as guides for believers in the measure in which they agree with Scripture.

Because the proper spiritual steps were taken to make the decision, Matthias "was numbered with the eleven apostles" (Acts 1:26). Shortly thereafter, we are told that "the twelve called the multitude of the disciples unto them" (Acts 6:2). What peace and joy when everyone can clearly see that care and diligence have been shown in the making of a decision!

Making decisions is intimidating because we are responsible for our choices. And yet, God has given us the opportunity to make choices (free will) and the resources to guide us in the process. The uncertainty and difficulty of making decisions is also part of God's design to keep us humbly dependent on Him. A quick review of Scripture will demonstrate that all the great men and women of the Bible learned to make decisions in a Biblical way with the help of God. Peter learned, and with the grace and help of God, we can too.

CHAPTER 19

Peter the Worshiper

"A private relationship of worshiping God is the greatest essential element of spiritual fitness."

Oswald Chambers

Peter was not there when the Saviour said to the Samaritan woman, "But the hour cometh, and now is, when the true worshippers shall worship the Father in spirit and in truth: for the Father seeketh such to worship him" (John 4:23). And yet, Peter clearly responded to that call as he became a worshiper for the rest of his life.

But, first, what is worship? According to the Merriam-Webster Dictionary, our English word *worship* comes from the old English word, *weorthscipe*. It means to respect or acknowledge worth in someone or something. The most common Greek word for worship (*proskuneō*) is the word the Lord Jesus used in John 4 when He introduced a new manner of worship that was soon to be initiated. W.E. Vine says it means "to make obeisance [or] do reverence to". Therefore, worship is not a mere ritual or activity. True worship involves the mind and heart in a genuine response to the object of worship. So, when the wise men from the east were guided toward Bethlehem by seeing "the star, they rejoiced with exceeding great joy. And when they were come into the house, they saw the young child with Mary his mother, and fell down, and worshipped him" (Matt 2:10-11). As the wise men saw Christ, learned about Him, and understood the purpose of His coming, this generated a most appropriate response – worship.

Surprisingly, though, Peter never employed this word, perhaps because it had been so misused in veneration of pagan gods and in homage to Roman emperors who claimed deity. Nevertheless, reading his Biblical Biography and the epistles he penned, Peter's worshipful spirit is very evident. The first recorded word he directed to the Lord Jesus was, "Master…" in Luke 5:5. However, just three verses later, as he witnessed the Saviour fill the nets, Peter dropped to his knees calling Him, "…O Lord" (Luke 5:8). That was the beginning of a Christian life filled with increasing appreciation and worship.

To complete Peter's restoration after he sinned, the Lord met him on the beach by the Sea of Galilee and asked him three times, "Lovest thou me?" (John 21:15-17). Each time Peter answered, "Lord, thou knowest that I love thee". While the Lord used the word (*agapao*) the first two times He inquired about Peter's love, He used a synonym (*phileo*) the third time. While an honest study shows the two words often overlap in their meanings, there are some notable distinctions. *Agapao* is never used as a compound word, but *phileo* is compounded with at least 12 other words: e.g. *philosophia* (love of wisdom), *philoxenos* (love of hospitality), and *philotheos* (love of God). The word involves an appreciation for something in the object that is receiving the love.

Peter spent the rest of his life with the repeated question of the Saviour echoing in his ears which only propelled him to get to know his Lord more and more. More knowledge of Christ would result in greater understanding of His character and work. This would then produce the response of worship in Peter. If he settled for a superficial knowledge of Christ, he would be settling for a superficial worship of Christ. But if he gave himself to get to know Christ profoundly, he would learn to worship in a deeper and fuller way to the honour and glory of his Lord.

This is the evident cycle in the life of Abraham – the man of the altars. After the Lord intervened so that Abimelech of Gerar would not touch Sarah and so that Abraham's life would be preserved, "Abraham planted a grove in Beer-sheba, and called there on the name of the Lord, the everlasting God" (Gen 21:33). He learned (knowledge and comprehension) that God is not limited or impacted by time or events on earth. This touched his heart so that when the Holy Spirit says, "Now it came to pass after these things that God tested Abraham" (Gen 22:1, NKJV), he responded not to the tremendously costly trial on Moriah, but to the person he was enjoying. Thus, he told the servants, "I and the lad will go yonder and worship" (Gen 22:5). Arriving at the correct location, he built an altar and prepared to worship God by offering up the son he loved. After God intervened and provided the ram caught in the thicket, "Abraham called the name of that place Jehovah-jireh: as it is said to this day, In the mount of the Lord it shall be seen" (Gen 22:14). Appreciation of God led to the worship of God which then led to greater appreciation of God. Because this circle of worship characterized the life of Abraham, we are not surprised then when James writes that Abraham "was called the Friend of God" (James 2:23). A true friend gets to know and appreciate the good in others. That was Abraham's great longing - to get to know God better. That knowledge would lead to greater understanding and appreciation of God which would then lead Abraham to build altars and worship God.

Peter also enjoyed that same cycle for over 30 years. As noted, the first time he spoke to the Lord he used the word, "Master" which means "a person of high status" (Dictionary of Biblical Languages). It was a respectful address to one who was superior, and a good starting point. From there, Peter would enjoy a constantly increasing knowledge and appreciation of Christ.

Peter and his Appreciation of Christ

Consider the list of names, titles and figures Peter uses for his Lord throughout the rest of the New Testament:

• Master	Luke 5:5; 8:24, 45
• the Christ	Acts 2:31; 3:20; 5:42
• His Christ	Acts Acts 4:26
• The Holy one and the Just	Acts 3:14
• His Son Jesus	Acts 3:13, 26
• Jesus Christ of Nazareth	Acts 3:6; 4:10
• Lord and Christ	Acts 2:36

- This Jesus   Acts 2:23, 32, 36; 4:11
- Holy One   Acts 2:27
- Jesus of Nazareth   Acts 2:22, 38
- Prince and a Saviour   Acts 5:28
- The Holy Child Jesus   Acts 4:30
- His Servant   Acts 3:26
- Prince of Life   Acts 3:15
- Judge of the quick and the dead   Acts 10:42
- Lord and Saviour Jesus Christ   2 Peter 1:11; 2:20; 3:18
- Christ   1 Peter 1:11, 19; 2:21; 3:16, 18; 4:1, 14; 5:1
- Jesus   Acts 1:16; 3:16; 4:2; 5:30
- Jesus Christ   Acts 2:38; 3:6; 4:10; 9:36; 10:36, 48; 1 Peter 1:1, 2, 3, 7, 13; 2:5; 3:21; 4:11; 2 Peter 1:1
- Lord Jesus   Acts 1:21; 4:33; 15:11
- Lord Jesus Christ   1 Peter 1:3, 8; 2 Peter 1:14, 16
- Lord and Saviour   2 Peter 3:2
- Christ the Lord   1 Peter 3:15
- Creator   1 Peter 4:19
- Morning Star   2 Peter 1:19
- The Stone   1 Peter 2:7
- the Lord our God   Acts 2:39
- the Spirit of the Lord   Acts 5:9
- a Cornerstone chosen and precious   1 Peter 2:6
- the Cornerstone   Acts 4:11; 1 Peter 2:7
- that Prophet   Acts 3:23
- a Lamb without blemish or spot   1 Peter 1:19
- the Shepherd and Overseer of your souls 1 Peter 2:25

Paul put it plainly: "If any man love not the Lord Jesus Christ, let him be Anathema" (1 Cor 16:22). The word for love is *phileo*. So, if any man does not find and cherish features in the person of Christ and enjoy the things of Christ, he is not saved and is in danger of eternal judgment. Peter demonstrated that he was an authentic believer by his growing knowledge and appreciation of his Lord and Saviour. It is interesting to notice in the lists above that in the beginning of his commission Peter spoke often of Jesus and Jesus Christ. About thirty years later he writes two letters and never once refers to Jesus. Most often, he refers to Him using: "Lord Jesus Christ". He began his Christian experience appreciating one-word names and titles of the Saviour (e.g., Master, Lord, Jesus, etc.), but he ends his Christian experience intelligently combining titles in appropriate ways to speak of his Saviour. For example, he writes of "the Shepherd and Overseer of your souls" (1 Peter 2:25) and "our Lord and Saviour Jesus Christ" (2 Peter 3:18). In addition, he often uses new names and titles for the first time (e.g. the Overseer) as he progresses and matures.

Peter also grew in his appreciation of the possessions, relationships, and activities of the Lord as well. Consider this list found in Peter's conversations, sermons, and writings:

The Things of our Lord:

- the God and Father of our Lord Jesus Christ   1 Peter 1:3
- the knowledge of our Lord Jesus Christ.   2 Peter 1:8
- the everlasting kingdom of our Lord and
  Saviour Jesus Christ.   2 Peter 1:11
- the power and coming of our Lord Jesus Christ   2 Peter 1:16
- the longsuffering of our Lord   2 Peter 3:15
- grow in grace, and in the knowledge of our
  Lord and Saviour Jesus Christ   2 Peter 3:18
- the Spirit of Christ   1 Peter 1:11
- the sufferings of Christ   1 Peter 1:11; 5:1

- the precious blood of Christ   1 Peter 1:19
- the name of Christ   1 Peter 4:14
- the name of the Lord   Acts 2:21
- the blood of Jesus Christ   1 Peter 1:2
- the resurrection of Jesus Christ   1 Peter 1:3; 3:21
- the revelation (apocalypse) of Jesus Christ   1 Peter 1:7, 13
- the righteousness of God and our Saviour
  Jesus Christ   2 Peter 1:1
- the knowledge of God, and of Jesus our Lord   2 Peter 1:2
- the word of the Lord   1 Peter 1:25
- the eyes of the Lord   1 Peter 3:12
- the face of the Lord   1 Peter 3:12
- the knowledge of the Lord and Saviour Jesus Christ 2 Peter 2:20
- the apostles of the Lord and Saviour   2 Peter 3:2
- the day of the Lord   2 Peter 3:10;
                                                                 Acts 2:20
- the longsuffering (patience) of our Lord   2 Peter 3:15
- his abundant mercy   1 Peter 1:3
- his marvelous light   1 Peter 2:9
- his steps   1 Peter 2:21
- his mouth   1 Peter 2:22
- his own body   1 Peter 2:24
- ...whose stripes...   1 Peter 2:24
- his ears   1 Peter 3:12
- his glory   1 Peter 4:13
- his eternal glory   1 Peter 5:10
- his divine power   2 Peter 1:3
- his majesty   2 Peter 1:16
- his coming   2 Peter 3:4
- his promise   2 Peter 3:9, 13.

The growing gratitude in Peter is evident in his final communications at the end of his life. Like Paul, Peter suddenly breaks out in praise to God (doxologies) while writing very practical epistles. In 1 Peter 5:10-11, Peter is thinking of "the God of all grace" who is working out eternal purposes in the lives of His people. As he considers this unmerited kindness expressed by the Almighty, he writes, "To him be glory and dominion for ever and ever. Amen" (1 Peter 4:11). The final words of Peter recorded in Scripture also express his great longing that God might receive worship. When he mentions the combination of names and titles "Lord and Saviour Jesus Christ" for the fourth time in 2 Peter, he adds: "To him be glory both now and forever. Amen" (2 Peter 3:18). Does the consideration of God bring forth spontaneous praise in our hearts as it did in the heart of Peter the worshiper?

Peter was present when the Lord Jesus imparted a model of prayer. Today, this model is often erroneously referred to as the Lord's Prayer. However, what the Lord Jesus said was: "After this manner pray ye..." (Matt 6:9). One of the impressive features of the model He gave is that before there is any mention of human need or concern, there are three statements about God: "Our Father which art in heaven, Hallowed be thy name. Thy kingdom come. Thy will be done in earth, as it is in heaven" (Matt 6:9-10). Therefore, intelligent prayer is dependent on knowing God and being interested in His things and His concerns. A selfish prayer life that consists of just a "give-me" list, will quickly turn dry and boring. If we roll our eyes (internally) and sigh when having to put up with people who only talk about themselves, what must the Lord feel listening to us sometimes? A good challenge for all of us would be: how long can we talk to God about His character and His things without mentioning ourselves? Investment in this great discipline of talking to God about His person, His Son, His Word, His assembly, His gospel, His purposes, etc. will keep our communication with God vibrant, interesting, and authentic.

It is logical, then, to assume that Peter's constantly expanding knowledge and appreciation for Christ impacted his communication with God. Was it his influence and example, at least in part, that led the believers in Jerusalem to pray together after Peter and John were released from prison? As Oswald Chambers once said, "Worship and intercession must go together; one is impossible without the other". This holy and beautiful combination was evident on that occasion when the Christians in Jerusalem, "lifted up their voice to God with one accord" (Acts 2:24). They worshiped as they spoke to God about what "thou...hast made," "[what thou] hast said", "whom thou hast anointed", and "whatsoever thy hand and thy counsel determined" (Acts 4:24-28). They expressed 93 words in five verses of worship (Acts 4:24-28) before they spent 43 words in two verses (Acts 4:29-30) requesting boldness and power for the apostles. They clearly knew the secret to effective, enjoyable, and authentic prayer meetings.

Love for his Lord would also be demonstrated in Peter's service. Why? It is a Biblical reality that worship and service are inseparably linked. Service without worship becomes a dry, mechanical duty, and worship without service may be just a passing emotion. Even worse, it may be simply trafficking in theology as a mental exercise. In the temptation, Jesus quoted Deuteronomy 6:13 to Satan when He said, "Thou shalt worship the Lord thy God, and him only shalt thou serve" (Matt 4:10). When a believer is truly in awe of his God, he will assuredly become more involved in Divine activities and interests. Thus, based on Peter's claims of love for Christ, Jesus said to him, "Feed MY lambs!" (John 21:15), "Tend MY sheep!" (John 21:16), and "Feed MY sheep!" (John 21:17). Peter seems to have understood that his devotion for Christ would not only show in his speech on Sunday mornings, but it would also display itself through the week in His service. His daily involvement with God's people, God's gospel, God's truth, God's testimony, etc. would be an offering of praise that would frequently ascend to Heaven.

As Peter neared the end of his life, he wrote about individual believers who speak for God in the gospel or in teaching, and those who serve. He said that that the correct attitude they should have is "that God in all things may be glorified through Jesus Christ" (1 Peter 4:11). He also said, "If anyone suffers as a Christian, let him not be ashamed, but let him glorify God in this matter" (1 Peter 4:16, NKJV). Suffering for the truth and what is right, is an opportunity to honour the name of our Lord with an exemplary attitude as we identify publicly with Him. Additionally, as these believers would be evil spoken against and face persecution, their good works would both silence their accusers and perhaps lead these people to conversion so that they would "glorify God in the day of visitation" (1 Peter 2:12).

After expounding the gospel of God and the programme of God for 11 chapters, Paul wrote, "I beseech you therefore, brethren, by the mercies of God, that ye present your bodies a living sacrifice, holy, acceptable unto God, which is your reasonable service" (Rom 12:1). As significant and necessary as it is to worship with our service and our speech, it is even greater worship to give our very selves to God. This was true in the highest and greatest act of worship ever performed which was when "Christ...through the eternal Spirit offered himself without spot to God" (Heb 9:14). Paul agreed as he reminded the Ephesian believers that "Christ also hath loved us, and hath given himself for us an offering and a sacrifice to God for a sweet-smelling savour" (Eph 5:2). Oh, the infinite and eternal delight the Father found in Christ, the true burnt-offering, who gave His whole person and life to God.

Peter knew that it is not easy or popular to give oneself completely in gratitude to God. At the same time, he also understood what would motivate a believer to do something so noble despite the cost. Thus, he closed his second letter passing on perhaps one of the greatest lessons he had learned in his experience: "But grow in grace, and in the knowledge of our Lord and Saviour Jesus Christ" (2 Peter 3:18). May God help us to take this exhortation to heart and learn from Peter, a man who invested his life in becoming a true worshiper in spirit and in truth.

CHAPTER 20

Peter the Healer

Modern healings and New Testament healings are as different as chalk and cheese. They may be labelled with the same term, "healings", but the differences are immense.

At the beginning of the book of the Acts, Luke looks back to the Gospel he wrote and says, "The former treatise have I made, O Theophilus, of all that Jesus began both to do and teach, Until the day in which he was taken up" (Acts 1:1-2). And yet, while he did say that Jesus "healed them that had need of healing" (Luke 9:11), he also narrated how the disciples were "healing every where" (Luke 9:6). They were not competing with the Saviour, but rather that was part of what "Jesus began both to do and teach". He performed healings by Himself, and He performed healings through human instruments – His disciples.

The Command

It is hard to imagine the jaw-drop on Peter and the other disciples when the Lord called them and commanded, "Heal the sick, cleanse the lepers, raise the dead, cast out devils" (Matt 10:8). It was one thing for the Son of God to perform miracles and healings, but how would they ever cure the sick or raise the dead?

A vital maxim in Scripture is that God will never ask us to do something without providing the ability and resources to do it. This principle is evident in the story of Gideon when God said, "...thou shalt save Israel from the hand of the Midianites: have not I sent thee?" (Judges 6:14). With just 300 men carrying lamps, trumpets, and clay pots, how would he ever triumph over the mighty Midianites who had a trained soldiers and a cavalry of camels? When God commands, God provides. So, Gideon moved out in obedience, and, in the end, the Midianites were defeated.

The Lord Jesus himself demonstrated this principle too. The Scripture says that "the Father sent the Son to be the Saviour of the world" (1 John 4:14). Since the plan of salvation would require a substitutionary death, how would the Son of God die if "God is a Spirit" (John 4:24)? We get the answer when the Lord Jesus said to His Father in prayer, "a body hast thou prepared me" (Heb 10:5). God provided so that His Son could complete the Father's will.

Luke tells us that before He commanded the 12 disciples to go and heal the sick, the Lord Jesus "called unto him his twelve disciples, [and] he gave them power against unclean spirits, to cast them out, and to heal all manner of sickness and all manner of disease" (Matt 10:1). Therefore, no matter what God calls us to do, we will never legitimately be able to say, "I could not do it". Instead, in our failure, we must recognise that we did not take advantage of the resources God had made available for us to complete His will. Our goal, then, should be to strive to emulate the disciples who, when commissioned, immediately obeyed and went out looking to God to provide what they lacked to be able to obey His commands.

Based on this principle, Peter and John stopped at the temple gate in Jerusalem called Beautiful where Peter told a lame man, "In the name of Jesus Christ of Nazareth rise up and walk" (Acts 3:6). But, on what basis could Peter say this? To most people, this sounded impossible seeing that Peter was a fisherman not a healthcare worker. If we accept the authenticity of the Great Commission in Mark's Gospel, Jesus had declared about his disciples, "they shall lay hands on the sick, and they shall recover" (Mark 16:18). His will was that the apostles perform healings and miracles. Peter obviously knew that he did not have medical training much less the ability to heal. But he also knew that if the Lord wanted him to do it, the Lord would provide the means for Peter to complete this task.

The Completeness

Peter observed that the Lord Jesus healed people without exception, without further treatment, and without fail. As Matthew tells us, "Jesus went about all the cities and villages...healing every sickness and every disease among the people" (Matt 9:35). These astonishing miracles can be appreciated in three ways: First, Christ never faced a case for which He had to do diagnostic tests, get a second opinion, take radiographic images, or consult with other physicians. And He never had to say to a patient, "I am sorry, there is nothing more I can do". No one ever returned home sick, and He never blamed a botched healing on the lack of faith in the sick person as faith-healers do today. His healing success rate was 100% with every physical, mental, and spiritual disease. Amazing!

Second, He not only healed every type of disease, but He also healed every disease every time. It would be remarkable if He healed one deaf man, but Jesus healed every deaf man with whom He came in contact. That is why Peter preached in Caesarea that "God anointed Jesus of Nazareth with the Holy Ghost and with power: who went about doing good and healing all that were oppressed of the devil" (Acts 10:38). It was one thing that He had healed "Simon the Leper" (Matt 26:6), but He also healed 10 lepers when he was on his way to Jerusalem (Luke 17:12). So, whether it was Bartimaeus on the roadside (Luke 18:35), the man who was deaf and mute, or the man blind from birth in John 9, Jesus healed them all. Unlike the charlatan faith-healers of today, He healed every type of disease not just multiple times, but every time. Thus, to assure John the Baptist of Jesus' identity as the Messiah, He told His disciples, "...tell John what things ye have seen and heard; how that the blind see, the lame walk, the lepers are cleansed" (Luke 7:22) – all of them.

Third, when He healed, people were completely healed. They did not require physical therapy, time to recover, or follow-up visits. No wonder Doctor Luke tells us of a paralytic who, upon Jesus' word, "immediately he rose up before them, and took up that whereon he lay, and departed to his own house, glorifying God" (Luke 5:25). When the woman with the personal issue touched the hem of Jesus' robe, she had been immediately healed (Luke 8:47). When He healed the woman with the curved back, "immediately, she was made straight" (Luke 13:13). And when He spoke to blind Bartimaeus, "immediately, he received his sight" (Luke 18:43).

And so it was with Peter and the disciples as the Lord continued working through them. When Jesus sent them out two by two, "They cast out many devils, and anointed with oil many that were sick, and healed them" (Mark 6:13).

The Characteristics

Places

Modern healers only perform their "miracles" in healing services and only while music is playing. Neither Jesus nor the apostles did any such thing. The Lord Jesus healed and performed miracles in the temple, in a synagogue, on the roadside, in a house, in a field, at a beach, on the sea, etc. Likewise, Peter is recorded as carrying out healings at a temple gate, on the road, in a house, etc. They knew nothing of a pre-announced "healing service" and were not limited to healings only in religious buildings. The COVID-19 pandemic of 2020-2021 clearly demonstrated the fraudulent activities of modern faith healers. Millions have died around the globe and not one "faith-healer" has set foot in the COVID unit of a hospital or gone house-to-house healing people stricken with the coronavirus.

Patients

As Jesus moved about, He was "healing every sickness and every disease among the people" (Matt 9:35). Then, He "called unto him his twelve disciples and gave them authority over unclean spirits, to cast them out, and to heal every disease and every affliction" (Matt 10:1, ESV). This was because the same divine power operating by the Holy Spirit was working through Peter and the apostles just as it had in the Lord Jesus. There was no triage to determine who was qualified or worthy. No patient was turned away and no disease was determined to be "too advanced" or "untreatable". Peter healed Aeneas, "bedridden for eight years, who was paralyzed" (Acts 9:33, NKJV). He also healed the disabled man at the temple gate who was more than forty years old (Acts 4:22). Normally, the longer a disease is present in the body, the harder it is to treat. But, with the Lord Jesus and His apostles, neither the symptoms, the type of disease, nor how long the patient had been sick limited the power of God to heal. Three times during His years of ministry, the Lord Jesus raised people from the dead. The final miracle of Peter recorded in Scripture was the raising from the dead of Dorcas (Tabitha) in the city of Joppa.

People can have physical problems, mental and emotional problems, or spiritual problems. One day, Jesus "called the twelve together and gave them power and authority over all demons, and to cure diseases" (Luke 9:1). Matthew tells how Jesus gave them authority to heal "all manner of sickness"– every physical infirmity. But then, Matthew also tells us that Jesus gave them authority to heal "all manner of disease" (Matt 10:1). Some versions translate the latter as "afflictions". The word group of which this Greek term forms a part, is sometimes translated "sorrow" (Gen 42:38, LXX). There is likely at least an implication in this word that Jesus gave them authority over mental and psychological infirmities as well.

Modern faith healers blame the failure of a healing upon the patient's lack of faith. Neither the Lord Jesus nor the apostles did any such thing. Many who were healed were not even believers. On one occasion, though, the Lord addressed the issue of the lack of faith which inhibited a healing. A man came and said to Jesus, "Lord, have mercy on my son, for he is an epileptic and suffers severely; for he often falls into the fire and often into the water. So, I brought him to Your disciples, but they could not cure him" (Matt 17:15-16, NKJV). After He healed the man's son, "the disciples [came] to Jesus apart, and said, 'Why could not we cast him out?' And Jesus said unto them, 'Because of your unbelief.'" (Matt 17:19-20). The failure was due to their lack of faith not the father's. It was a preacher problem, not a patient problem. If modern faith healers taught that their faith was what was important and that any failure to heal was their fault, they would soon disappear off televisions, abandon pulpits, and go out of business.

Procedures

Peter, like the Lord Jesus, used multiple means to bring about healings. Jesus healed through spoken words, touch, saliva, his clothes, etc. Likewise, to a paralyzed man called Aeneas and to Dorcas (Tabitha) who had died, Peter spoke, and they were healed. To the infirm man begging at the temple gate, Peter spoke and then "he took him by the right hand and lifted him up: and immediately his feet and ankle bones received strength" (Acts 3:7). Likewise, Luke tells us: "Now many signs and wonders were regularly done among the people by the hands of the apostles" (Acts 5:12). In fact, Jesus had said, "Verily, verily, I say unto you, He that believeth on me, the works that I do shall he do also; and greater works than these shall he do; because I go unto my Father" (John 14:12). By the Spirit, would they really do even greater miracles than the Lord Jesus had done? Perhaps He was referring to the preaching of the gospel by Peter and the result: "Then they that gladly received his word were baptized: and the same day there were added unto them about three thousand souls" (Acts 2:41). Or it could be referring to actual miracles that the Lord worked through the apostles of which we do not read in the ministry of the Saviour. For example, Luke tells us, "And God wrought special miracles by the hands of Paul: So that from his body were brought unto the sick handkerchiefs or aprons, and the diseases departed from them, and the evil spirits went out of them" (Acts 19:11-12). About Peter, Luke tells us that "they brought forth the sick into the streets, and laid them on beds and couches, that at the least the shadow of Peter passing by might overshadow some of them" (Acts 5:15). At a minimum, in addition to healings by word and touch, Peter also performed miracles just by his shadow.

Priorities

The order in a commission can reflect the priority of the steps. Thus,

Jesus made it clear in His own teaching and practice that miracles should take second place to the teaching of the Word of God. So, when He "saw a great crowd...he had compassion on them, because they were like sheep without a shepherd. And he began to teach them many things" (Mark 6:34). After that, He fed the crowd of 5,000 men plus women and children. And when He sent out the 12 disciples, He said, "Proclaim as you go, saying, 'The kingdom of heaven is at hand.' Heal the sick, raise the dead, cleanse lepers, cast out demons" (Matt 10:7-8, ESV). Luke puts it more succinctly when he writes, "He [Jesus] sent them out to proclaim the kingdom of God and to heal" (Luke 9:2). As commanded, "they [then] departed and went through the villages, preaching the gospel and healing everywhere" (Luke 9:6). Although there is value in both, preaching took precedence over practical provisions.

Purposes

Miracles were not intended to show off a disciple's ability or to draw attention to himself. Unlike today, they were not seen as fund-raisers dressed in spiritual clothing either. Taking Mark's account of the commission, Jesus said, "And these signs shall follow them that believe; In my name shall they cast out devils; they shall speak with new tongues; They shall take up serpents; and if they drink any deadly thing, it shall not hurt them; they shall lay hands on the sick, and they shall recover" (Mark 16:17-18). All these miracles, including healing the sick were to be signs. Thus, after the great sermon by Peter on the day of Pentecost, "Awe came upon every soul, and many wonders and signs were being done through the apostles (Acts 2:43). Luke later describes other miracles including healings by saying: "Now many signs and wonders were regularly done among the people by the hands of the apostles" (Acts 5:12).

Signs

But what were the healings signalling and to whom? When Moses' rod turned to a serpent and then back to a rod, and his hand turned leprous, and then was healed, God referred to them as, "these two signs" (Ex 4:9). They signalled to the Israelites that Moses was chosen and sent by God. Therefore, one purpose of miracles is to demonstrate God's approval of a messenger. Thus, Peter preached on the Day of Pentecost, "Men of Israel, hear these words: Jesus of Nazareth, a man attested to you by God with mighty works and wonders and signs that God did through him in your midst" (Acts 2:22). Paul appreciated the same purpose of miracles when he wrote, "Truly the signs of an apostle were wrought among you in all patience, in signs, and wonders, and mighty deeds" (2 Cor 12:12). God had ratified Paul's role and authority by working miracles and healing the sick through him just as He had done with the other apostles.

In healings, God not only confirmed the divine appointment of a messenger, but he also authenticated the message the messenger presented. The writer to the Hebrews spoke of our "great salvation; which at the first began to be spoken by the Lord, and was confirmed unto us by them that heard him; God also bearing them witness, both with signs and wonders, and with divers miracles, and gifts of the Holy Spirit, according to his own will" (Heb 2:3-4). No one should have had any doubt as to the authority of the apostles or the veracity of their message, especially the Jews. Paul clearly stressed the miracle of speaking a foreign language without having studied it previously: "Wherefore tongues are for a sign, not to them that believe, but to them that believe not" (1 Cor 14:22). More specifically, he noted, "The Jews require a sign" (1 Cor 1:22). So, to Jewish Christians especially, Paul explained that it was "Through mighty signs and wonders, by the power of the Spirit of God; so that from Jerusalem, and round about unto Illyricum, I have fully preached the gospel of Christ" (Rom 15.19). Just like Peter and the other disciples, Paul's message had the divine stamp of approval upon it as indicated by his healings and miracles.

If you were driving towards a city, you would see road signs advising you that you were approaching that destination. However, once you passed through the city, you would no longer see signs for the city.

Why? Signs would then not be needed because the city already had come and gone. That is precisely why, in the New Testament, there is a steady decline in the occurrences of healings and other miracles. By the time the Hebrew letter was written, the period of New Testament miracles had almost passed. The author explains that the gospel message that "first began to be spoken by the Lord...was confirmed unto us by them that heard him [the apostles]; God also bearing them witness, both with signs and wonders, and with divers miracles, and gifts of the Holy Ghost, according to his own will" (Heb 2:3-4). Notice that he uses the past tense to describe the confirming witness of God through the miracles and healings of the apostles. The ending of the apostolic period of miracles coincides with the writing of the New Testament Scriptures. Like a traveller who had passed through a major city, there is no longer a need for signs. Now that we have the complete canon of God's Word, healings are unnecessary and are an insult to the adequacy and authority of Scripture. God's intent is that His Word be sufficient to confirm the validity of a messenger and his message. Nearly 2,000 years later, when we hear a man from a pulpit communicating a spiritual message, we should be like the Bereans, who "with all readiness of mind...searched the scriptures daily, whether those things were so" (Acts 17:11). Any preacher or teacher who seeks to perform signs as a way of authenticating himself and his preaching, is sending a message to God that His Word is not sufficient. How solemn!

Providence

The story of the father who sought healing for his son mentioned above (Matt 17), resulted in the Lord Jesus saying to His disciples, "If ye have faith as a grain of mustard seed, ye shall say unto this mountain, Remove hence to yonder place; and it shall remove; and nothing shall be impossible unto you. Howbeit this kind goeth not out but by prayer and fasting" (Matt 17:20-21). By linking the statement that nothing would be impossible for them with the conditions of prayer and fasting, Jesus was eliminating the idea that they could do whatever they wanted simply because they desired it to happen. As the Apostle John explained, "And this is the confidence that we have in him, that, if we ask any thing according to his will, he heareth us: And if we know that he hear us, whatsoever we ask, we know that we have the petitions that we desired of him" (1 John 5:14-15). Healings by the Lord himself and by the disciples would only come to pass if they were God's will.

The man Peter healed at the temple gate had been sick for 40 years. Just a short time before, Jesus went to Jerusalem with full power to heal. In fact, He healed a man by the Sheep Market who "had an infirmity thirty and eight years" (John 5:5). However, in His sovereign will on that occasion, Jesus would heal the man sick for 38 years but not the man sick for 40 years at the nearby Sheep Gate. As in all matters, God's timing and will are not always understood, but they are always best.

The Credit

One great promise by the Saviour was that, "when the Comforter is come, whom I will send unto you from the Father, even the Spirit of truth, which proceedeth from the Father, he shall testify of me" (John 15:26). He would work in and through the disciples and their miracles, not to draw attention to himself, but to Christ. One quickly notices the exact opposite in modern healing services. The focus is placed on the Spirit: praying to the Spirit, laughing in the Spirit, crying in the Spirit, slaying in the Spirit, etc. But, when Peter took the man's hand who was begging at the temple gate, he said, "In the name of Jesus Christ of Nazareth rise up and walk" (Acts 3:6). When asked to explain how he had healed the man, Peter doubled down on the means by what person and power the miracle had been performed. His words were, "Let it be known to all of you and to all the people of Israel that by the name of Jesus Christ of Nazareth, whom you crucified, whom God raised from the dead — by him this man is standing before you well" (Acts 4:10, ESV). Likewise, with the man paralyzed for eight years, Peter said, "Aeneas, Jesus Christ heals you; rise and make your bed" (Acts 9:34, ESV). Peter always gave full credit to the true source of healings – the Lord Jesus. By contrast, modern healers fraudulently operate by mind control or darker powers. It is evident even in the attention they draw to themselves and their ministries. They are more like Simon Magus in Samaria, who "used sorcery, and bewitched the people of Samaria, giving out that himself was some great one" (Acts 8:9). True healings like those performed by Peter the Apostle are by God's power and solely for God's glory.

CHAPTER 21

Peter the Apostle

Recently, I was in our bank when a woman came up to a teller near me and asked to deposit a wad of $100.00 bills. As the teller sorted through them, she pulled one out and passed it through a machine. It was a counterfeit bill. Shocked, the customer asked her to hold the bill up to the light. When she did, neither the customer nor I, being nosey in a polite kind of a way, could identify it as false currency. The teller then held up a real $100.00 bill beside the fake one. The counterfeit one had many similarities, but it was missing a security thread running through the left side of the bill with the letters USA and the number 100 printed in an alternating pattern. It reminded me of a spiritual maxim: the more we get to know the truth, the more we will be able to identify what is false. In the beginning of his Christian experience, Peter was clueless that Judas was a fraud. However, as he grew spiritually, his knowledge of God and truth increased so that, eventually, he would be able to identify a false believer in Samaria (Acts 8:20-24) and false teachers in general (2 Peter 2:1).

Speaking of counterfeit currency, suppose that customer had tried to deposit a handful of $13.00 bills. Even with my glasses off, I could have identified them as bogus. Nobody makes counterfeit $13.00 American bills; only imitations of what is real and valuable. Thus, we should not be surprised that the New Testament speaks about false christs (Mark 13:22), false brothers (Gal 2:4), false witnesses (Matt 26:60), false prophets (2 Peter 2:1), false teachers (2 Peter 2:1), and false apostles (2 Cor 11:13). Satan clearly understands the reality and the importance to God of the true Christ, true brothers, true witnesses, true prophets, true teachers, and true apostles. Satan has about 6,500 years of experience in spiritual forgery. As a master counterfeiter in the religious realm, he labours with a lethal combination of boldness and deceptiveness to produce spiritual knockoffs. Peter heard the Saviour warn of such men when He said, "Many will say to me in that day, 'Lord, Lord, have we not prophesied in thy name? and in thy name have cast out devils? and in thy name done many wonderful works?' And then will I profess unto them, 'I never knew you: depart from me, ye that work iniquity'" (Matt 7:22-23). The Lord does not deny that they prophesied, that they did miracles, or that they cast out demons. They likely did, although we are not told by what power. Just like the wizards in Egypt who imitated God's true servant Moses, these men appear as facsimiles of the true apostles, but are secretly workers of evil.

The Registry of Apostles

In the letters Peter wrote that are part of the New Testament Scriptures, he refers to himself as "Peter, an apostle of Jesus Christ" (1 Peter 1:1), and "Simon Peter, a servant and an apostle of Jesus Christ" (2 Peter 1:1). His claim of apostleship is indisputable because the first time we come across the Greek word *apostolos* is when Jesus "called unto him his twelve disciples" (Matt 10:1). The gospel writer goes on to say, "Now the names of the twelve apostles are these; The first, Simon, who is called Peter..." (Matt 10:2). Luke explains how Peter and the other disciples received that designation: Jesus "chose twelve, whom also he named apostles" (Luke 6:13). Like the rest, Peter was an apostle by divine appointment. Of the 81 times this word is used in the New Testament, *apostolos* is generally transliterated into the English word "apostle". In the KJV, on two occasions it is translated as "messenger" (2 Cor 8:23, Phil 2:25) and once as "he that is sent" (John 13:16). Of the 133 occurrences of the verbal form *apostelō*, all but once it is translated as "send" or "send forth". An apostle, then, is a person who is sent or commissioned for a specific purpose. Liddle and Scott give the definition as "a messenger, ambassador, [or] envoy". Similarly, Thayer defines it as "a delegate, messenger, [or] one sent forth with orders".

The consummate example of "one who is sent" is the Lord Jesus. The writer to the Hebrews calls his readers to "consider the Apostle and High Priest of our profession, Christ Jesus" (Heb 3:1). Moses was a man sent by God to represent Him to the people. Aaron, the high priest, functioned on behalf of the people before God. Both men unequivocally failed in their ministries. So, as valuable and as influential as those two men were in Hebrew history, the writer calls his audience to consider THE Apostle and High Priest who stands unique in the mission He was given and in the perfection with which He completed it.

The word *apostolos* is used frequently to refer to the 12 disciples whom Jesus personally selected and sent. In fact, that special group of men is often referred to simply as "the twelve" (Matt 26:14, 20, 47: Mark 4:10; 6:7; 9:35; 10:32; 11:11; 14:10, 17, 20, 43; Luke 8:1; 9:12; 18:31; 22:3, 47; John 6:67, 71; 20:24; Acts 6:2; 1 Cor 15:5). The Lord chose and commissioned them to preach the gospel, represent His authority, and reveal truth by the Holy Spirit (Eph 3:5). God would confirm their authenticity by doing miracles through them which were called signs (Acts 2:43; 5:12). These men and their teaching were unique and vital to God's programme because all believers in the Body of Christ, both Jews and Gentiles, are being "built upon the foundation of the apostles and prophets, Jesus Christ himself being the chief corner stone" (Eph 2:20).

Peter was very clear on his commission. Paul put it best when he said that, "the gospel of the uncircumcision was committed unto me, as the gospel of the circumcision was unto Peter; (For he that wrought effectually in Peter to the apostleship of the circumcision, the same was mighty in me toward the Gentiles)" (Gal 2:7-8). While Paul was specifically sent to preach the gospel to Gentiles, Peter was given the primary focus of taking the gospel to Jews. Thus, while we read of at least three missionary journeys by Paul to reach Gentiles in other parts of the world, we do not read of Peter traveling much outside of Israel. He kept his focus as delineated by his Lord as he completed his mission with excellence.

Like many words employed by the Holy Spirit in the New Testament, the word *apostolos* has other nuances and references as well. As mentioned, Jesus used it when He said, "The servant is not greater than his lord; neither he that is sent greater than he that sent him" (John 13:16). Obviously, on that occasion He was not referring specifically to "the twelve". Instead, He was teaching them a general principle about service. At times, the word is also used to refer to others who participated in and supported the spread of the gospel apart from, but in conjunction with, "the twelve". Paul makes this distinction when he refers to Jesus' post-resurrection appearances. He explained that upon rising from the dead the third day, "he was seen...of the twelve" (1 Cor 15:5). Two verses later, he adds that "he was seen...then of all the apostles" (1 Cor 15:7). Others who are referred to as apostles in the New Testament include:

- Paul (Saul of Tarsus) (Rom 11:13; 1 Cor 1:1)
- James, the half-brother of Jesus (Gal 1:19)
- Apollos (1 Cor 4:6-9)
- Timothy and Silvanus (1 Thess 1:1; 2:6)
- Epaphroditus (Phil 2:25)
- Barnabas (Acts 14:14)
- Two unnamed men (2 Cor 8:23)
- Andronicus and Junia (Rom 16:7).

Counting "the twelve", Judas Iscariot, and this list, there are 24 specific people referred to as apostles in the New Testament and perhaps there were more. The term grew in usage and came to broadly refer to a believer who was sent by the Lord or given some task related to the spread of the gospel. The general use becomes most evident if we accept that Junia (Rom 16:7) is a feminine name and that it likely refers to the wife of Andronicus. Thayer says that Junia could be "a woman's name, which is possible". BDAG says there is "the strong probability that a woman named Junia is meant". Clearly, the term "apostle" is not a position, but a commission. Thus, while writers such as Paul and Peter referred to their apostleship, it was never used as a title. Thus, no one is said to have called Paul's fellow labourer – "Apostle Barnabas". This is emphasized by Luke in that he only refers to apostles in the plural all 28 times he uses the word in the book of the Acts. So, when Peter references his own apostleship at the beginning of his two letters, he does not refer to himself as one of the "the twelve". He emphasizes his role, mission, and accompanying authority as being given by the Lord himself, not some title he had engraved on a gold badge on his tunic. And, most certainly, neither Peter nor anyone else took on a role as "THE apostle" of the church. Thus, among other biblically errant titles, the Pope of the Roman Catholic Church takes on the title of "Successor of THE prince of the apostles". Without any doubt, Peter would have vehemently opposed any such notion.

Considering the historical existence and the invaluable contributions of genuine apostles in Scripture, we should not be astonished that Satan soon produced *pseudoapostolos* (2 Cor 11:13). The first false apostle was Judas, and the devil continues to raise up counterfeit apostles today. This is in spite of the fact that the New Testament clearly teaches that true apostles, in the sense that Peter and John were apostles, do not exist today nor could they. This becomes evident when we consider what was necessary for this role.

Requirements to be an Apostle

a. A disciple had to spend time with the Lord Jesus during His years of ministry in order to qualify to be one of "the twelve". Thus, when the Lord Jesus "called his disciples and chose from them twelve, whom he named apostles" (Luke 6:13, ESV), Matthew specifically tells us that first, "he called to him his twelve disciples" (Matt 10:1, ESV). They physically spent time with Him before He named them apostles. They spent time in His presence on many other occasions as well. For example, on the night of His betrayal "when the hour was come, he [Jesus] sat down, and the twelve apostles with him" (Luke 22:14). Thus, when the group of believers gathered in the upper room after Jesus' ascension, Peter pointed out the need for another apostle to be recognized who would take the place of Judas Iscariot. His words were, "Wherefore of these men which have companied with us all the time that the Lord Jesus went in and out among us, Beginning from the baptism of John, unto that same day that he was taken up from us, must one be ordained to be a witness with us of his resurrection" (Acts 1:21-22). Peter appreciated the grace of God in giving him the honour of having physically been in the presence of the Lord Jesus. He said about his time with Christ on the Mount of Transfiguration, "We...were eyewitnesses of his majesty" (2 Peter 1:16). To be one of "the twelve", a candidate clearly had to have spent time with the Saviour during His years of ministry. Therefore, no one today could be an apostle like "the twelve".

b. The second group of people called apostles in the New Testament are those who saw the Lord Jesus after His resurrection. Of course "the twelve" met that requirement as well. Luke makes it clear that "with great power gave the apostles witness of the resurrection of the Lord Jesus" (Acts 4:33). Peter, like the rest of "the twelve" was therefore doubly qualified as an Apostle, and Paul recognised it when he said that after Jesus "was raised on the third day in accordance with the Scriptures...he appeared to Cephas" (1 Cor 15:4-5). While Saul of Tarsus did not spend time with the Lord Jesus during his three years of ministry, he did see the Saviour on the day of his conversion as he travelled to Damascus (Acts 9:3-6). That is why he wrote, "Am I not free? Am I not an apostle? Have I not seen Jesus our Lord?" (1 Cor 9:1, ESV). Based on this distinctive feature alone, Paul understood that there would be no more apostles. When he listed some of the post-resurrection appearances of Christ, he wrote, "And last of all he was seen of me" (1 Cor 15:8). No one since that day on the road to Damascus has physically seen the Lord Jesus. Therefore, anyone claiming to be a New Testament apostle today is ignorant of the New Testament requirements, or blatantly fraudulent.

c. Biblical apostles communicated divinely inspired truth known as "the apostles' doctrine" (Acts 2:42). They then wrote down the truth in the books that now form our New Testament. Jude wrote, "But, beloved, remember ye the words which were spoken before of the apostles of our Lord Jesus Christ" (Jude 17). Peter included himself when he wrote to believers, "be mindful of the words which were spoken before by the holy prophets, and of the commandment of us the apostles of the Lord and Saviour" (2 Peter 3:2). Paul wrote about mysteries, truth previously unrevealed in the Old Testament. He said it was truth "Which in other ages was not made known unto the sons of men, as it is now revealed unto his holy apostles and prophets by the Spirit" (Eph 3:5). He also referred to their work and teaching as "the foundation of the apostles and prophets, Jesus Christ himself being the chief corner stone" (Eph 2:20). They were men that the Lord specifically provided for the introduction of this church age. Speaking of Peter and the others, Paul recognized that Christ "gave some, apostles; and some, prophets; and some, evangelists; and some, pastors and teachers; For the perfecting of the saints, for the work of the ministry, for the edifying of the body of Christ" (Eph 4:11-12). In confirmation of the completion of their commission, Jude writes of "the faith which was once for all delivered to the saints" (Jude 3, NKJV). The cannon of Scripture was completed in the first century by the Holy Spirit working through the pens of the apostles. Therefore, the "revelation role" of the apostles was completed over 1,900 years ago and there are no new revelations today. Therefore, if any man or women claims to have received something from God outside of what is in Scripture already, he or she is clearly marking themselves out as a pseudo-apostle who is not from God.

d. True apostles performed miracles as signs to validate their authority and the gospel message they preached, particularly for the benefit of unsaved Jewish people (1 Cor 1:22; 14:22). Paul emphasized this requirement when he wrote to the Corinthian

Christians by saying, "Truly the signs of an apostle were wrought among you in all patience, in signs, and wonders, and mighty deeds" (2 Cor 12:12). Paul likely knew that Peter had healed a lame man at a gate of the temple. Later, when the Jerusalem believers prayed, they requested that God would work "By stretching forth thine hand to heal; and that signs and wonders may be done by the name of thy holy child Jesus" (Acts 4:30). Luke tells us that at that time "many wonders and signs were done by the apostles" (Acts 2:43). These miracles were intended to signal the authority of these men before God, and the veracity of their message. The writer to the Hebrews looked back on the role of apostles and treated it as a completed phase of history. He wrote about the gospel that "was declared at first by the Lord, and it was attested to us by those who heard, while God also bore witness by signs and wonders and various miracles and by gifts of the Holy Spirit distributed according to his will" (Heb 2:3-4, ESV). Peter must have viewed the ability to do miracles as something of the past as well. He does not mention the miracles he did, he does not speak about the miracles produced by other apostles, nor does he teach other believers to perform them.

e. Genuine apostles were given abilities and authority by God to lead the first New Testament churches. This is evident in the following examples:

1. About 10 years after the formation of the assembly in Jerusalem, a plurality of elders is mentioned whom God raised up to lead that local church. After that, when the church in Antioch wanted to send a financial offering to help the Jerusalem believers in need "they did so, sending it to the elders by the hand of Barnabas and Saul" (Acts 11:30, ESV). Prior to God raising up elders, when believers like Barnabas sold property, they took the funds and "laid them down at the apostles' feet: and distribution was made unto every man according as he had

need" (Acts 4:35). Once there were elders raised up, there was no need for Peter and the other apostles to function as part of local church leadership.

2. The apostles were also used by God to protect the first churches. When Ananias and Sapphira "sold a possession And kept back part of the price" (Acts 5:1), it was Peter who confronted them. The Lord gave him the gift of discernment and he quickly became aware of the dishonesty of this couple and he recognized that the Lord was moving in discipline as both believers soon died. Likewise, when Philip preached in Samaria and souls were saved, "the apostles which were at Jerusalem heard that Samaria had received the word of God, [and] they sent unto them Peter and John" (Acts 8:14). It was Peter who detected the fraudulent profession of Simon Magus and said to him, "Thou hast neither part nor lot in this matter: for thy heart is not right in the sight of God" (Acts 8:21).

3. The apostles led the local church in decision making. When dissension developed in the newly formed Jerusalem church over the distribution of funds and the care of widows, "the twelve called the multitude of the disciples unto them". They were then instructed, "Wherefore, brethren, look ye out among you seven men of honest report, full of the Holy Ghost and wisdom, whom we may appoint over this business" (Acts 6:1-3). The disciples would select, but Peter and the apostles would appoint. This was carried out and "the apostles...prayed [and] laid their hands on them" (Acts 6:6). Similarly, when Saul of Tarsus desired to "join himself to the disciples" Barnabas "took him and brought him to the apostles and declared to them how on the road he had seen the Lord, who spoke to him" (Acts 9:26, ESV). The group of apostles then led the church in receiving Saul into their fellowship as afterwards Saul "was with them coming in and going out at Jerusalem" (Acts 9:28).

4. At the beginning of the church age, the apostles represented and presented the Lord's mind. As noted, their teaching was referred to as "the Apostles' doctrine" (Acts 2:42) which they spread by word of mouth and in writing. The role of these men to speak as the authoritative voice of God was eventually replaced by the teachings codified in the 27 books of the New Testament. So, when men travelled from the assembly in Jerusalem to Antioch teaching that Gentiles had to be circumcised and keep the Law of Moses to be saved, a conference was arranged in Jerusalem to settle the matter. Representatives were there from both churches including Paul and Barnabas who were sent from Antioch. When they arrived in Jerusalem, "they were welcomed by the church and the apostles and the elders" (Acts 15:4, ESV). Later, the specific conference meeting began when "The apostles and the elders were gathered together to consider this matter" (Acts 15:6, ESV). The elders were the leadership of the church, and the apostles were the equivalent to having the New Testament in hand. Thus, after much debate, Peter the apostle spoke leading to a unanimous resolution on the matter. The two churches were mature and had their own respective leaderships. Had they had the full revelation of the New Testament, they would have had little need for the apostles to be present or to intervene as Peter did on that important day.

5. "The twelve" played an essential role specifically in Jerusalem in the beginning. After Stephen's martyrdom, "There was a great persecution against the church which was at Jerusalem; and they were all scattered abroad throughout the regions of Judaea and Samaria, except the apostles" (Acts 8:1). We never read of "the church, the elders, and the apostles" in any other local assembly. When Peter writes about local church leadership, he never mentions apostles. He just says, "I exhort the elders among you, as a fellow elder." (1 Peter 5:1, ESV).

6. The apostles were specifically involved with different stages of the

giving of the Holy Spirit. The Lord Jesus laid out His evangelism plan for the world in four stages when He told His disciples, "Ye shall be witnesses unto me both in Jerusalem, and in all Judaea, and in Samaria, and unto the uttermost part of the earth" (Acts 1:8). The book of Acts goes on to narrate the reception of the Holy Spirit in each of those stages. In so doing, Luke confirms the inclusion of all types of believers in the body of Christ. The presence of apostles at each crucial stage, and specifically Peter who was given the keys by Christ in Matthew 16, signifies divine approval for what occurred.

Jewish believers in Judea and Jerusalem: Peter preached, "Repent, and be baptized every one of you in the name of Jesus Christ for the remission of sins, and ye shall receive the gift of the Holy Ghost" (Acts 2:38).

Samaritan believers in Samaria: "Peter and John...prayed for them, that they might receive the Holy Ghost: (For as yet he was fallen upon none of them: only they were baptised in the name of the Lord Jesus.)" (Acts 8:14-16). Even Simon Magus, an unsaved man, could see that the Spirit was given through the laying on of the apostles' hands (Acts 8:18).

Gentile believers in Caesarea: "While Peter was still saying these things, the Holy Spirit fell on all who heard the word. And the believers from among the circumcised who had come with Peter were amazed, because the gift of the Holy Spirit was poured out even on the Gentiles " (Acts 10:44-45, ESV).

The laying on of hands and the involvement of Peter and the other apostles as each of these three groups (Jew, Samaritans, Gentiles) received the Holy Spirit is most significant. As God's representatives during that transition time from the Old Testament to the Dispensation of Grace, they could authoritatively confirm that all three groups would form part of the body of Christ, without difference and without exception.

Therefore, we can see that there are currently no apostles because no one today lived during Jesus' ministry or saw Him after His resurrection, the New Testament is complete and thus no apostolic signs are needed, and the Lord has already authenticated the inclusion of every type of believer in the body of Christ. In Paul's time, he described men "who would like to claim that in their boasted mission they work on the same terms as we do. For such men are false apostles, deceitful workmen, disguising themselves as apostles of Christ. And no wonder, for even Satan disguises himself as an angel of light. So, it is no surprise if his servants, also, disguise themselves as servants of righteousness" (2 Cor 11:12-15, ESV). That is why Peter's close friend, John, warned, "Beloved, believe not every spirit, but try the spirits whether they are of God: because many false prophets are gone out into the world" (1 John 4:1). May God give us a greater appreciation for the role and work of the true apostles in Scripture and may the Lord be able to say to us as He did to the church in Ephesus, "...thou hast tried them which say they are apostles, and are not, and hast found them liars" (Rev 2:2).

Rewards of an Apostle

One important spiritual principle in all Scripture can be expressed using the mathematical symbol for "proportional to" ($\propto$):

$$\text{Privilege/blessing} \propto \text{responsibility} \propto \text{reward}$$

In the life of the Lord Jesus, the divine plan was for the Son to become a man. Thus, God prepared a body for him (Heb 10:5) and "the Word was made flesh" (John 1:14). However, that great blessing came with an accompanying responsibility that He be the sin-bearer. With admiration and appreciation, Peter thus wrote of Christ: "Who his own self bare our sins in his own body on the tree" (1 Peter 2:24). Paul described heaven's response to the Son of God taking on the privilege and responsibility of humanity when he wrote, "Wherefore God also hath highly exalted him, and given him a name which is above every name" (Phil 2:9). God exalted and extolled His Son in proportion to His faithful completion of His responsibilities in the body the Father had given Him.

Likewise, the Lord Jesus recognised that it was a privilege for "the twelve" to be apostles, but He also knew they would proportionately face great difficulties as His commissioned representatives. Jesus even talked to them about how God said, "I will send them prophets and apostles, and some of them they shall slay and persecute" (Luke 11:49). However, the apostles were rewarded during their lives with front row seats to hear the Master teach and to witness His healings. They also experienced the awe of His power working through them when they performed miracles. Of course, they would never forget the tremendous honour of being able to see the Lord as "He presented himself alive to them after his suffering by many proofs, appearing to them during forty days" (Acts 1:3, ESV). And yet, the Saviour promised further rewards in the future as well.

One day Peter said to the Saviour, "Behold, we have forsaken all, and followed thee; what shall we have therefore?" (Matt 19:27). Perhaps Peter even made the statement understanding the Biblical equation above. Jesus immediately replied, "Verily I say unto you, that ye which have followed me, in the regeneration when the Son of man shall sit in the throne of his glory, ye also shall sit upon twelve thrones, judging the twelve tribes of Israel" (Matt 19:28). Those 12 men will be granted great responsibilities in the administration of the world-wide government of the King of Kings during His millennial reign.

In addition, one day, Peter and the other apostles will see the injustices they experienced on earth made right. When judgment falls on Babylon the Great at the end of the Great Tribulation in the Book of Revelation, a mighty angel loudly proclaims, "Rejoice over her, thou heaven, and ye holy apostles and prophets; For God hath avenged you on her" (Rev 18:20). In the end, they will be recognised and admired by all. At the end of our Bibles, we are told of John observing the New Jerusalem and "the wall of the city had twelve foundations, and in them the names of the twelve apostles of the Lamb" (Rev 21:14). Paul wrote about "the foundation of the apostles and prophets" in the spiritual church which is the body of Christ (Eph 2:20). Fittingly, then, God will recognise their roles and faithfulness by permanently etching their names on the physical foundations of the Holy City. God will recompense the apostles for the stability of their characters, the fundamental role they played in the beginning of the church age, and their unwavering love for Christ. Undoubtedly, Peter would be sufficiently happy just to be associated with the Lamb of God, the One he trusted to bear away his sins. However, Scripture assures us that the apostles will be eternal examples of God's promise: "...them that honour me, I will honour" (1 Sam 2:30).

CHAPTER 22

Peter the Gospel Preacher

What the Bible does not tell us about Peter is just as important as what it does tell us. There is no mention of the volume of his voice, the pleasantness of his tone, the rate of his articulation, the length of his pauses, the movements of his hands, or the notes that he prepared. All of those can contribute positively to the impact of preaching, but the spirituality, the character, and love of the truth in the preacher are far more important. The New Testament focuses on these details in Peter's experience because these are the factors that give weight and power to gospel messages.

The Attributes of the Gospel Preacher

His Devotion

After He was baptised, "Jesus being full of the Holy Spirit returned from Jordan" (Luke 4:1). From there He would face the temptation in the desert and then begin His public ministry. Likewise, as the Church Age began, the apostles were all together and Luke says, "They were all filled with the Holy Ghost" (Acts 2:4). On that Day of Pentecost, as Peter began to speak to the Jewish leaders, we read about "Peter, [being] filled with the Holy Ghost" (Acts 4:8). But what does it mean to be filled with the Holy Spirit? When Paul says to the Ephesians, "be filled with the Spirit" (Eph 5:18), he is not suggesting that they need more of the Spirit, but that the Spirit should have more of them. In so doing, they were to grant the Spirit greater control over them and allow him to bring their lives into alignment with Scripture. When Luke reported that the Lord Jesus was full of the Holy Spirit, he was noting that every area of the Saviour's life was in complete accordance with the Word of God. Likewise, in the measure that we are living in obedience to the Bible, that will be the measure in which the Spirit has control of our lives. Therefore, the clear principle is that before we begin to prepare a gospel message, we need to prepare the gospel messenger first.

Peter and John's preparation involved travelling with the Lord and physically sitting under His teaching and preaching. The impact of that period of their lives was so evident that even the Jewish leaders "took knowledge of them, that they had been with Jesus" (Acts 4:13). No wonder that "with great power gave the apostles witness" (Acts 4:33). What a searching reality that the power in our preaching equally depends on our personal devotion and time spent with Christ.

His Dependence

Before He began to preach, "Jesus also [was] being baptized, and praying" (Luke 3:21). Later, before He preached His great Sermon on the Plain, "he went out into a mountain to pray, and continued all night in prayer to God" (Luke 6:12). Similarly, before we read of Peter delivering his first sermon that resulted in 3,000 souls being saved, he and the other apostles "continued with one accord in prayer and supplication, with the women, and Mary the mother of Jesus, and with his brethren" (Acts 1:14). D. L. Moody once commented on the indispensable nature of communication with God. He said, "I'd rather be able to pray than to be a great preacher; Jesus Christ never taught his disciples how to preach, but only how to pray". Very true! So, while it is very easy to focus on fancy introductions, creative illustrations, alliterated outlines, etc., prayer is the most important exercise. In His presence, we converse with God about souls, we review the subject and verses we hope to consider, and we implore Him for His help and power. Peter truly believed in relying on God in his gospel preaching. As an older believer he expressed the fundamental reality of our dependence when he said, "If any man speak, let him speak as the oracles of God; if any man minister, let him do it as of the ability which God giveth" (1 Peter 4:11).

His Duty

When preaching, Peter did not take sneak-peaks at his watch to see if he had "filled the time". Nor was he preaching "to reach the end of his notes," or "to get through his message". As for time, while we may not have the full text recorded for us, here are the word lengths of each of Peter's five sermons in the King James Version of the Bible.

• Acts 2:14-36	550 words
• Acts 3:12-26	373 words
• Acts 4:8-12	117 words
• Acts 5:28-32	68 words
• Acts 10:34-43	225 words

The efficiency and compactness of his sermons as we are given them are to be envied, and yet we are never told that Peter was marked by punctuality or economy of words. Nor are we told that he was seeking results. It is the Holy Spirit, not Peter, who tells us that the number of those who received his word were "about three thousand souls" (Acts 2:41). Peter had a much higher goal than results. When he wrote the words quoted above: "If any man speak, let him speak as the oracles of God; if any man minister, let him do it as of the ability which God giveth", he went on to give the true motive in all service including gospel preaching. He said, "...that God in all things may be glorified through Jesus Christ, to whom be praise and dominion for ever and ever" (1 Peter 4:11). His objective was to preach the gospel so that the content of the message, the manner in which it was preached, and the messenger who presented it would bring glory and honour to God.

The Audience of the Gospel Preacher

There are five sermons of Peter recorded for us in the Book of Acts.

Passage	Location	Occasion
1. Acts 2:14-36	In a house (at least at the start)	The Day of Pentecost
2. Acts 3:11-26	In the temple (Solomon's Porch)	The healing of a lame man
3. Acts 4:8-12	Jewish Supreme Court (Sanhedrin)	First arrest of Peter and John
4. Acts 5:29-32	Jewish Supreme Court (Sanhedrin)	Second arrest of Peter and apostles
5. Acts 10:34-44	Caesarea (house of Cornelius)	First message to Gentiles(Cornelius).

Luke provides details about the varied audiences who were privileged to listen to the sermons of Simon Peter. In each message, we are given some key factors that all gospel preachers should take into consideration in their preparation and presentation of the good news of salvation.

Gender

At times Peter addressed a prominently male audience or at least he knew it was culturally wise to direct his words to males primarily. At his first sermon, "there were dwelling at Jerusalem Jews, devout men, out of every nation under heaven" (Acts 2:5). So, he directed his message to them by saying, "Ye men of Judaea, and all ye that dwell at Jerusalem" (Acts 2:14). Later in the same message he addressed them as "Ye men of Israel" (Acts 2:22) and "Men and brethren" (2:29).

Race

Peter frequently mentioned the race and culture of the people to whom he was speaking. At Pentecost, he called all the men who were listening to him, "brethren", and "all the house of Israel" (Acts

2:29, 36). When he addressed the Jewish leaders, he called them "men of Israel" (Acts 3:12). Later, he addressed the Jewish leadership again calling them "elders of Israel", and from there he broadened his message out to include "all the people of Israel" (Acts 4:8, 10). But, when he spoke to Cornelius and the Gentile audience, he spoke of "persons" and "every nation" (Acts 10:34, 35).

Religious Background and Bible Knowledge

The Lord Jesus knew Nicodemus had great familiarity with the Old Testament. Thus, when He used the wind blowing as an illustration of the Holy Spirit, He knew that Nicodemus would think of the Valley of Dry Bones in Ezekiel 37. And when He referred to Himself being lifted up on the cross (John 3:14), Nicodemus would recall the account of the serpent on the pole in Numbers 21. Similarly, when Philip went to Samaria, he "preached Christ unto them" (Acts 8:5) because the Samaritans were familiar with the Old Testament concept of an Anointed One (the Messiah). But, when he met the Ethiopian treasurer who was likely new to Judaism and had just visited Jerusalem and heard of the crucifixion, "Philip opened his mouth, and began at the same scripture, and preached unto him Jesus" (Acts 8:35). He spoke of the Saviour in a way that his audience would mostly understand.

Peter demonstrated a similar sensitivity to the level of Bible knowledge in the audiences he addressed. In his first four sermons, he was communicating with "the children of the prophets, and of the covenant" (Acts 3:25), so he wisely included references to Old Testament characters such as David, Samuel and Abraham and quoted from the Old Testament. With a Jewish audience, he could freely refer to "The God of Abraham, and of Isaac, and of Jacob, the God of our fathers" (Acts 3:13). However, when he met Cornelius, a Gentile, Peter simply used the name of God seven times, and he limited his use of Old Testament illustrations and quotes. Thus, a good evangelist will adjust his vocabulary and Bible references according to the audience's knowledge level and understanding of Scripture.

Cultural and Linguistic Factors

Luke tells us that on the Day of Pentecost, "there were [also] dwelling...Parthians, and Medes, and Elamites, and the dwellers in Mesopotamia, and in Judaea, and Cappadocia, in Pontus, and Asia, Phrygia, and Pamphylia, in Egypt, and in the parts of Libya about Cyrene, and strangers of Rome, Jews and proselytes, Cretes and Arabians" (Acts 2:9-11). So, when Peter and the apostles preached that day, God gave them the miraculous ability to speak in the language and the dialects of the audience. God's desire is always that truth be communicated so that people can understand it. This is evident in that the Lord Jesus and the apostles quoted from the Septuagint, the Hebrew Old Testament that had been translated into Greek, the most universal language at that time. Likewise, the New Testament was written in *koine* (common, shared) Greek. But this goes far beyond the issue of translations and versions of the Bible. It includes the concept that missionaries, evangelists and local believers should do their best to learn the languages, dialects, regional vocabulary, accents, customs, and cultural practices of their target audience. They are tools to be used to make a connection with an audience, to win the confidence of people, and to communicate the gospel so that it can be more readily understood.

It is important also to note that Peter did not sit and wait for souls to come into his Galilean culture and comfort-zone. Instead, "when the apostles which were at Jerusalem heard that Samaria had received the word of God, they sent unto them Peter and John" (Acts 8:14). Peter was a true Jew, so he understood what the Samaritan woman mentioned to Jesus: "the Jews have no dealings with the Samaritans" (John 4:9). Yet, he was the first to support God's work among them. Similarly, when he went to Cornelius' house, he told him; "Ye know how that it is an unlawful thing for a man that is a Jew to keep company, or come unto one of another nation" (Acts 10:28). Yet, because God had spoken to him and given him the vision of the sheet with animals let down from heaven, he confidently approached a Gentile man and his Gentile family. Peter's sensitivity to the culture and language of his audience should be the aspiration of every soul-winner and preacher of the gospel.

Social Status or Recognized Positions

In Acts 4, Peter addressed "rulers, and elders, and scribes, And Annas the high priest, and Caiaphas, and John, and Alexander, and as many as were of the kindred of the high priest, [who] were gathered together at Jerusalem" (vv 5-6). Peter, along with John, addressed the 71-man Jewish Supreme Court in the next chapter when "they set them before the council" (Acts 5:27). Peter's gospel is the same, but his approach and word choice varies depending on his audience - the general public or religious authorities.

Interest in God, the Bible and Salvation

On the Day of Pentecost, Peter spoke to "Jews and proselytes" (Acts 2:10), an audience with a certain level of interest in spiritual things. Many of them were in Jerusalem because their custom was to travel to the Holy City three times each year for the Feasts of Passover, Pentecost, and Tabernacles (Ex 23:17; 34:23; Deut 16:16). Their devotion would require financial sacrifice and their time away from home would impact their businesses, families, and marriages. In Acts 3, "all the people ran together" in the temple. The fact that they met in the temple indicates that they had some level of interest in God and the Scriptures. However, Peter and John also faced a hostile audience of Jewish leaders in Acts 4 and 5 who twice put them in prison for having declared the good news. It must have been a delight then when Peter arrived at Cornelius' house. There, he faced a preacher's dream: an audience of sincere and searching souls of which Cornelius said, "Now therefore are we all here present before God, to hear all things that are commanded thee of God" (Acts 10:33).

Places

Luke tells us about "the house where they [the apostles] were sitting (Acts 2:2) on the Day of Pentecost. In the next chapter, Peter and John preached "in the porch that is called Solomon's" (Acts 3:11), an area in the temple where the public could gather. Then, he preached to the religious leaders in the Sanhedrin counsel room on the north side of the temple, traditionally called the Hall of Hewn Stones. Later, they ended back in the same room before the council again in Acts 5 where Peter preached another message. In Acts 10, Peter discoursed in Cornelius's house. A gospel preacher will adjust his approach considering the location where the message will be heard. The same message presented in a funeral home, in the open air, on a university campus, in a home Bible study, or in "English as a Second Language" class may require adjustments in volume, vocabulary, sentence length, and gestures to convey the message clearly.

The Attention-getter of the Gospel Preacher

Nobody needed to explain to Peter the concept of using a hook. Just as he had carefully selected lures to attract fish on the Sea of Galilee, Peter used five different introductions in his sermons to capture the attention of his audience and to introduce his subject.

Sermon 1: A common belief or perception

When Peter and the apostles spoke in tongues on the day of Pentecost, some in the audience mocked, saying, "These men are full of new wine". Peter then seized that common perception and used it to launch his message by saying, "Ye men of Judaea, and all ye that dwell at Jerusalem, be this known unto you, and hearken to my words: For these are not drunken, as ye suppose, seeing it is but the third hour of the day" (Acts 2:13-15).

Sermon 2: A recent event or experience

By the power of the Lord Jesus, Peter and John had just healed a lame man at a gate of the temple in Jerusalem. The news of the miracle spread and a crowd began to gather. Luke says that "when Peter saw it, he answered unto the people, 'Ye men of Israel, why marvel ye at this? or why look ye so earnestly on us, as though by our own power or holiness we had made this man to walk?'" (Acts 3:12). The springboard he used to jump into his message was the news of the day that people were talking about.

Sermon 3: A question that your audience asks

When the Jewish leaders came together, they asked Peter and John, "By what power, or by what name, have ye done this?". Peter seized their question and began his message by saying, "Ye rulers of the people, and elders of Israel, If we this day be examined of the good deed done to the impotent man, by what means he is made whole" (Acts 4:7-9). They inquired about the way by which the healing of the lame man occurred. By starting with their inquiry, the audience was all ears for Peter to proceed.

Sermon 4: A maxim or generally held saying or principle

During their periods of captivity under foreign nations, the Jews had undoubtedly struggled with the tension between submission to God's Word and the demands of the government that ruled over them. Even now they faced the same dilemma with the demands of the Roman Empire which at times contradicted the Old Testament. Peter picked up the sentiment many Jews felt, and perhaps even a saying of the times, when he began his message with the maxim, "We ought to obey God rather than men" (Acts 5:29).

Sermon 5: A personal story, discovery, belief, or experience

After the revelation of God through the sheet being lowered down with the animals in it, Peter began his sermon to Cornelius and the other gentiles present by sharing his new belief. The statement would shock gentiles who were often referred to by Jews as dogs. Peter began, "Of a truth I perceive that God is no respecter of persons: But in every nation he that feareth him, and worketh righteousness, is accepted with him" (Acts 10:34-35). Peter had discovered that every person in the world was a candidate for the gospel, not just Jews.

The Attention-keeping of the Gospel Preacher

Questions

While questions can be used for introductions, they can also be employed to maintain attention and convey truth. In all five of his sermons, Peter addresses explicit questions that his audience asks, or he anticipates questions the audience might ask (implied questions). Peter had learned this technique from the Lord Jesus, the perfect preacher. On one occasion, the Lord provided invaluable instruction about forgiveness as an answer to Peter's explicitly expressed question: "Lord, how oft shall my brother sin against me, and I forgive him? till seven times?" (Matt 18:21). On a different occasion, the Lord addressed a question that Peter and the other disciples were mulling over but were afraid to ask. Scripture even says, "Jesus knew that they were desirous to ask him, and said unto them, 'Do ye inquire among yourselves of that I said, A little while, and ye shall not see me: and again, a little while, and ye shall see me?'" (John 16:19). Peter, the man who asked more questions of the Lord than anyone else in the New Testament, always looked to engage his audience's mind by stating a question or answering one that his audience might have asked or be contemplating.

On the day of Pentecost, in response to the audience hearing Peter and the apostles present the gospel in their native tongues and dialects, the people asked, "Behold, are not all these which speak Galileans? And how hear we every man in our own tongue wherein we were born?...What meaneth this?" (Acts 2:7-8, 12). Peter addressed these questions to engage his audience before he moved on into the gospel.

In his second address in Solomon's Porch, Peter knew that the Jewish people in the temple that day were wondering by what power the lame man had been healed. So, he verbalised the question that they had been mulling over in their heads: "Why marvel ye at this? Or why look ye so earnestly on us, as though by our own power or holiness we had made this man walk?" (Acts 3:12).

In his third sermon, when the rulers, elders, and scribes gathered at Jerusalem, they provided the question for Peter by asking directly, "By what power, or by what name, have ye done this?" (Acts 4:7). Peter took advantage of the direct question of the religious leaders to explain that through the Lord Jesus alone the man was healed and souls are saved.

In his fourth gospel message, in response to the miraculous rescue operation that freed Peter and John from prison, the Jewish leaders asked them, "Did not we straitly command you that ye should not teach in this name?" (Acts 5:28). Even though they knew the answer to their interrogation, Peter used the question to explain how the divine power that had freed them was the same power that operated in the resurrection of Christ, the One whom "God exalted with his right hand to be a Prince and a Saviour" (Acts 5:31).

In Peter's final gospel address in the book of the Acts, Cornelius received him in his house because an angel had appeared to him and told him to send for "Simon, whose surname is Peter". No one needed to state the obvious question that was looping through their minds: "What does God want to say to us?". With that, Peter started speaking to them about God, His Word and how they could "receive remission of sins" (Acts 10:43) even though they were Gentiles.

Events

People pay attention best when speakers use concrete examples. In his five sermons, Peter makes reference to real people in the past such as such as David (Acts 2:29), Moses (Acts 3:22), Samuel (Acts 3:24), and Abraham (Acts 3:25) and specific events in their lives. He also refers to more recent events such as "the baptism which John preached" (Acts 10:37) and the crucifixion of Christ (Acts 2:23). He also uses events in the present experience of his audience such as the apostles speaking in tongues (Acts 2) and the healing of the lame man in the gate of the temple (Acts 3-4). Peter also speaks of events in the future when he mentions "the last days" (Acts 2:17) and the "times of refreshing [that] shall come from the presence of the Lord" (Acts 3:19). Masterfully, Peter wove in real events from the past, the present, and the future to help maintain the attention of his audience and to explain the gospel message.

The Approach of the Gospel Preacher

In 2005, Haddon Robison and Craig Brian Larson, published a collection of articles in a book titled: *The Art and Craft of Biblical Preaching: A Comprehensive Resource for Today's Communicators.* The title alone indicates that both authors clearly understood that gospel preaching is not simply an exercise in which a man opens his mouth and shouts Bible words, stories or truths that come to mind. Gospel preaching is a specific means of communicating a message from God. As a master carpenter, Jesus would have known when and how to employ different tools for different purposes as He worked in Nazareth. As a master fisherman, Peter had different rods, nets, and hooks which he had learned to use effectively on the Sea of Galilee. Preaching is no different. If any brother wants to excel in gospel preaching, he will want to study and learn the "art and craft" of how to effectively communicate the good news of salvation.

God does not judge gospel preachers by the number of souls they see saved. (Thank the Lord!). However, if He did, Peter would be in a class by himself. Since the days of the Lord Jesus, few if any could claim to have seen 3,000 souls saved in one sermon as Peter did on the Day of Pentecost. Yet, Peter learned that to be an effective evangelist and gospel preacher he had to depend on the Lord for help and power. The first time Jesus sent out the 12 disciples to preach, He knew they would feel like Moses: worried about what they would say and how they would say it. If they had to speak in times of stress and opposition, their uncertainty and lack of experience would be an even greater concern for them. So, the Lord Jesus told them, "When they deliver you up, take no thought how or what ye shall speak: for it shall be given you in that same hour what ye shall speak. For it is not ye that speak, but the Spirit of your Father which speaketh in you" (Matt 10:19-20). And yet, while he assured them the Spirit would meet their need, Peter did not show up unprepared and he certainly would not be one to dress up his lack of preparation by declaring, "Well, the Good Book says, 'Open your mouth wide, and I will fill it'" (Ps 81:10). Thankfully, the Bible does not require us to be expert communicators before we try to preach the gospel, and God is able to meet our need when we must speak spontaneously. And yet, is not the God we represent and the message we declare worthy of the best communication we can provide? Should we not stive to constantly improve so that we can communicate this blessed message as accurately, clearly, biblically, tactfully, courageously, graciously, reverently, and powerfully as possible?

The Holy Spirit chose to employ many distinct words in Scripture to describe men communicating divine truth. Below is a list of some of the words Peter used that emphasise different aspects of the role and responsibilities of a good communicator. While some words overlap in their semantic range, these are not mere synonyms. They are terms that cover the substance of the message, the audible pronunciation of the message, the ordering of the message, the authority of the message, the motive of the messenger, the personal experience of the messenger, the passion of the messenger, the confidence of the messenger and more.

Greek Word	English Translation	Occurrences in the NT	Uses by Peter
laleo	Speak, say (emphasis on substance)	296 times	Acts 4:20, 29; 8:25; 10:44, 1 Peter 4:11
lego	Say, speak (emphasis on sentiment)	1,326 times	Acts 2:40; 10:26
apophthengomai	Said, utterance (emphasis on sound not content)	3 times	Acts 2:4,14
diamarturomai	Testify, exhort (with authority)	15 times	Acts 2:40; 8:25; 10:42

eipon	Say, answer, ask	1025 times	Acts 2:29; 5:28; 4:7,19; 20:34
parakaleo	Exhort, beseech, call upon	109 times	Acts 2:40; 1 Peter 2:11; 5:1,12
apokrinomai	Answer, reply, begin to speak	250 times	Acts 3:12; 4:19; 5:28; 10:46
katangello	Proclaim, make known in public	17 times	Acts 4:2
didasko	Teach, give instruction	97 times	Matt 11:1; Acts 4:2,18, 5:21,25,28,42
phthengomai	Utter a sound	3 times	Acts 2:18; 2 Peter 2:16,18
ektithemi	Expound, explain thoroughly	4 times	Acts 11:4
phemi	Say, state, enlighten	65 times	Acts 10:28
prostasso	Arrange, set in order, command	7 times	Acts 10:33
kerruso	To officially announce or make public declarations	61 times	Matt 10:7; 11:1; Mark 16:20; Luke 24:47; Acts 10:42
diakonia	Ministry, service	34 times	Acts 6:4; 1 Peter 4:11
euangelizō	Announce, preach good news	55 times	Acts 5:42; 8:25
apologia	Answer, make a defence	8 times	1 Peter 3:15

Even though the words in the above list direct our attention to a variety of facets of both the communication of the gospel and the communicator of the gospel, Peter was conscious that one aspect deserved special attention. He never forgot the specific words of the Lord Jesus when He said, "...that repentance and remission of sins should be preached in his name among all nations, beginning at Jerusalem" (Luke 24:47). "Preached" is the word *kerusso*, which Thayer defines as: "to proclaim after the manner of a herald; always with a suggestion of formality, gravity, and an authority which must be listened to and obeyed". One man standing on behalf of God in front of an audience and proclaiming the good news of salvation by grace through faith in Christ is different from trying to teach the gospel or share the gospel in a conversation. Peter remembered the specifics of his commission and never lowered his appreciation for public preaching. In his last gospel sermon in the Book of the Acts, he told Cornelius and those in the audience, "He [the Lord Jesus] commanded us to preach [*kerusso*] unto the people" (Acts 10:42). May God help us to understand more of the varied aspects of communicating truth, and may our commitment and appreciation grow for the public heralding of the gospel message.

The Ambitions of the Gospel Preacher

Preach a Christ-centred Message

Immediately before He ascended to Heaven, the Lord Jesus told His disciples, "Ye shall be witnesses unto me" (Acts 1:8). Based on that command, regardless of the audience present, the apostles would always be sure to present the Redeemer and His saving work at the cross. Paul put it quite succinctly when he said, "We preach Christ crucified" (1 Cor 1:23). Peter could have said, "Amen! I do too!" Notice his clear, Christ-focused presentation in each message:

Sermon 1:

"Jesus of Nazareth, a man approved of God among you by miracles and wonders and signs, which God did by him in the midst of you, as ye yourselves also know: Him, being delivered by the determinate counsel and foreknowledge of God..." (Acts 2:22-23). A bit later, he added, "God hath made that same Jesus...both Lord and Christ" (Acts 2:36).

Sermon 2:

"The God of our fathers, hath glorified his Son Jesus" (Acts 3:13). He spoke further of "the Holy One and the Just" (Acts 3:14), "the Prince of life" (Acts 3:15), and the "Christ [which] should suffer" (Acts 3:18).

Sermon 3:

Peter confidently presented "the name of Jesus Christ of Nazareth" (Acts 4:10).

Sermon 4:

This was a short message, but he still spoke of "Jesus...a Prince and a Saviour" (Acts 5:30-31).

Sermon 5:

Before Cornelius and other Gentiles, Peter proclaimed "Jesus Christ: (he is Lord of all)" (Acts 10:36), and he reminded them "How God anointed Jesus of Nazareth with the Holy Ghost and with power: who went about doing good, and healing all that were oppressed of the devil; for God was with him. And we are witnesses of all things which he did both in the land of the Jews, and in Jerusalem" (Acts 10:38-39).

Preach a Clear Message

In the great commission, Jesus granted to His followers the privilege of announcing eternal blessings to all men. Consider the following list of benefits through Christ that Peter presented in his gospel messages:

Sermon 1:

Peter assured the thousands listening to his message that everyone could receive "the remission of sins" (Acts 2:38).

Sermon 2:

He told the Jewish leaders that they and all Jews could enjoy true conversion, the "turning away...from...iniquities" (Acts 3:26). He also promised that upon repentance and faith in Christ, "sins may be blotted out" (Acts 3:19).

Sermon 3:

He then spoke to the same men about "salvation" as he specifically stated: "we must be saved" (Acts 4:12).

Sermon 4:

He had preached it already, but again he announced the "forgiveness of sins" (Acts 5:31).

Sermon 5:

Peter told Cornelius that he and the other apostles were "preaching peace" (Acts 10:34-36), which could be obtained and enjoyed upon reception of the "remission of sins" (Acts 10:43).

Preach a Convicting Message

Jesus had told the disciples about another Comforter, just like Him, who would soon descend to earth. He was referring to the Holy Spirit when He said, "and when He has come, He will convict the world of sin, and of righteousness, and of judgment" (John 16:8, NKJV). Peter had personally learned the power of the human conscience as it overwhelmed him with guilt when he denied the Lord Jesus. It left him weeping bitterly. Thus, he understood that in gospel preaching, we must also seek to reach the human conscience. In other words, we need to have courage to carefully speak to people about their sin. It is not easy or popular, but it is both biblical and Christ-like. Thus

Peter confronted his audience in every sermon addressing their transgressions and their accountability to God.

Sermon 1:

On the day of Pentecost, Peter confronted the Jews who were permanent residents in Jerusalem and those who were visiting. He faithfully and directly reminded them of their most sinful choice by declaring, "Ye have taken [Jesus], and by wicked hands [him ye] have crucified and slain" (Acts 2:23).

Sermon 2:

He did not waver when he spoke to the Jewish leaders either. To them he pointed out their violations of the 10 commandments when he said, "But ye denied the Holy One and the Just, and desired a murderer to be granted unto you; And killed the Prince of life, whom God hath raised from the dead" (Acts 3:14-15).

Sermon 3:

Again, before those same men he spoke of "Jesus Christ of Nazareth, whom ye crucified" (Acts 4:10). He was not going to receive any applause for confronting them about their sin of murder. However, Jesus had told His disciples to preach both "repentance and remission of sins" (Luke 24:47). While the second part would be much more enjoyable and much more easily accepted by his audiences, Peter clearly believed that a person could not be saved without repentance. Paul agreed and thus, while in Ephesus, he was "Testifying both to the Jews, and also to the Greeks, repentance toward God, and faith toward our Lord Jesus Christ" (Acts 20:21). If Peter and Paul did not have authority to drop repentance out of their gospel preaching, we certainly don't either. It is an unchanging requirement in every culture and in all times. To bring about repentance, Peter often preached about sin. Even in the illustration he employed, Peter reminded the Jewish leaders of their great sin of rejecting Christ. He said, "This is the stone which was set at nought of you builders" (Acts 4:11).

Sermon 4:

Again, Peter spoke directly and passionately to the Jewish leaders when he told them about "Jesus, whom ye slew and hanged on a tree" (Acts 5:30).

Sermon 5:

Peter spoke more about Christ and His sufferings than he did about coming judgment, and yet he did speak to Cornelius of Jesus, who "was ordained by God to be Judge of the living and the dead" (Acts 10:42, NKJV).

Preach a Convincing Message

Peter sought to leave his audiences without any reason to doubt the gospel. When Paul preached, he pointed out the solid foundation of the message by proclaiming, "And if Christ be not risen, then is our preaching vain, and your faith is also vain. Yea, and we are found false witnesses of God" (1 Cor 15:14-15). The certainty of our message rests on the undisputed historical event that "now is Christ risen from the dead" (1 Cor 15:20). Perhaps many of us take people's knowledge of the resurrection of Christ for granted and we do not explain how it provides confidence in the gospel and the Word of God. Look at how Peter included this vital subject in every sermon:

Sermon 1:

To the massive crowd on the Day of Pentecost, he declared, "This Jesus hath God raised up, whereof we all are witnesses" (Acts 2:32).

Sermon 2:

In front of the Jewish people, he confidently declared, "God, having raised up his Son Jesus, sent him to bless you" (Acts 3:26).

Sermon 3:

In front of religious and political leaders, he proclaimed again: "Jesus Christ...whom God raised from the dead" (Acts 4:10).

Sermon 4:

Likewise, you can sense Peter's assured and joyous tone when he spoke again to the Jewish leaders announcing that, "The God of our fathers raised up Jesus, whom ye slew and hanged on a tree. Him hath God exalted with his right hand to be a Prince and a Saviour" (Acts 5:30-31).

Sermon 5:

And to the Gentile centurion, Cornelius, he also declared about the Saviour: "Him God raised up the third day, and shewed him openly" (Acts 10:40).

The other key to confidence in the gospel is that it is based on the Word of God. Thus, Paul preached that, "Christ died for our sins according to the Scriptures; And that he was buried, and that he rose again the third day according to the Scriptures" (1 Cor 15:3-4).

Peter also preached Bible-based sermons. While John recorded the words of Christ that "Except a man be born of water and of the Spirit, he cannot enter into the kingdom of God" (John 3:5), Peter knew that the Spirit works through Scripture. So, when he wrote about the new birth, he explained that we are "born again, not of corruptible seed, but of incorruptible, by the word of God, which liveth and abideth for ever" (1 Peter 1:23). As you examine his sermons, it is readily evident that Peter believed in the power of the living Word of God.

Sermon 1:

On the day of Pentecost, Peter quoted, "that which was spoken by the prophet Joel" (Acts 2:16). He then alluded to Psalm 16 in which he explained that "David speaketh concerning him" (Acts 2:25). He quoted Psalm 110:1 as well. With full confidence in God's Word, he concluded by saying, "Therefore let all the house of Israel know assuredly, that God hath made that same Jesus, whom ye have crucified, both Lord and Christ" (Acts 2:36).

Sermon 2:

In his sermon to the Jewish people after he healed the lame man, Peter declared what "God hath spoken by the mouth of all his holy prophets since the world began" (Acts 3:21). He went on to point to two Jewish heroes who had received divine revelation: Moses (Acts 3:22) and Abraham (Acts 3:25).

Sermon 3:

When Peter delivered a sermon to the Jewish leaders, he quoted David, who wrote that "The stone which the builders refused is become the head stone of the corner" (Ps 118:22), and drew it clearly to their attention: "This is the stone which was set at nought of you builders, which is become the head of the corner" (Acts 4:11).

Sermon 4:

In his fourth public message recorded in the Book of The Acts, Peter addressed the Jewish leadership again by saying, "The God of our fathers raised up Jesus, whom ye slew and hanged on a tree" (Acts 5:30). The last phrase, "hanged on a tree", was a quote from Moses in the Pentateuch where he wrote: "And if a man have committed a sin worthy of death, and he be to be put to death, and thou hang him on a tree: His body shall not remain all night upon the tree, but thou shalt in any wise bury him that day; (for he that is hanged is accursed of God)" (Deut 21:22-23).

Sermon 5:

Even, to a gentile Centurion and to other Gentiles present, Peter spoke of the authority of Scripture when he declared about the Lord Jesus, "To him give all the prophets witness" (Acts 10:43).

When Peter and John went to Samaria, they "preached the word of the Lord" (Acts 8:25). They were like the Old Testament prophet Haggai - "the Lord's messenger in the Lord's message unto the people" (Hag 1:13). Peter took great care to make sure that both what he said and how he said it were Biblical. He employed Bible quotes, Bible illustrations, and Biblical language whenever possible. For example, Greek scholar and teacher, Bill Mounce, once pointed out the "many direct and indirect allusions to Isaiah 53 that occur throughout the speeches in Acts". For example, consider Peter's message in Acts 3:13-18.

Acts 3:13-18	Isaiah 52:13 – 53:12
v.13 "God ... glorified his servant"	52:13 "My servant ... shall be glorified"
v.13 "whom you delivered up"	53:6 "the Lord delivered him up"
v.14 "the righteous One"	53:11 "the righteous One"
v.18 "that...Christ should suffer"	53:5 "he was wounded...bruised... chastisement...stripe."

Preach a Commanding Message

Leonard Ravenhill, a friend of A. W. Tozer, once said, "If Jesus had preached the same message that ministers preach today, He would never have been crucified". Was that because men today avoid preaching directly and lovingly about sin and judgment like Jesus did? Or is it because they do not preach the claims and call of Christ? Sometimes, men "explain the gospel" or "teach gospel truth", but never address their audiences directly. Peter certainly did as he appealed to the will of each individual hearing his message. After every sermon, his audiences knew exactly what God expected of them and what choice they had to make. Like the Lord Jesus, Peter challenged men to bend their wills and respond to the claims of the gospel. In the end, though, he would respect their choice.

Sermon 1:

To the large crowd at the house on the Day of Pentecost, Peter proclaimed, "...be this known unto you, and hearken to my words!" (Acts 2:14). A bit later, he said again, "Hear these words!" In the end, he commanded his audience, "Repent, and be baptized every one of you in the name of Jesus Christ!" (Acts 2:22, 38).

Sermon 2:

To the Jewish crowd awed by the miracle of the healing of a lame man, Peter said, "Repent ye, therefore, and be converted!" (Acts 3:19).

Sermon 3:

Before the Jewish elders, rulers, scribes and the high priest, Peter said, "Be it known unto you all, and to all the people of Israel" (Acts 4:10). They were not to doubt, but to know and believe. To them he added, "we must be saved" (Acts 4:12). They were to seek the Lord while He could be found.

Sermon 4:

Peter held nothing back when he spoke to the Jewish leaders the second time either. He spoke of "repentance", and that God called them to "obey him" (Acts 5:31-32).

Sermon 5:

Peter implored Cornelius and the Gentile audience to exercise faith when he preached, "whosoever believeth in him [Christ] shall receive remission of sins" (Acts 10:43).

The Appeal of the Gospel Preacher

Peter never indicated he was on final approach in a message only to do a touch-and-go and take off preaching again. Instead, his conclusions were short, decisive, and impactful. Notice some of the ways he finished his messages:

Sermon 1: Conclude with a statement of confrontation

Peter had covered much truth in his longest sermon to the large crowd of Jews present in Jerusalem on the Day of Pentecost. He then brought his message to a close full of impact by challenging his audience with an awful reality: "...ye have crucified, both Lord and Christ" (Acts 2:36).

Sermon 2: Conclude with a statement of offer

As Peter spoke to the increasing crowd of Jewish people at the temple, he reminded them of their privileges as God's covenant people. Parallel to that privilege was the new reality that "Unto you first God, having raised up his Son Jesus, sent him to bless you, in turning away every one of you from his iniquities" (Acts 3:26). God was now able to bless them spiritually if they would repent and turn to the Lord. Closing by reminding an audience of God's great offer places the decision before them as to whether they will receive Christ.

Sermon 3: Conclude with a statement of requirement

Peter ended this gospel message to Jewish leaders after having pointed out that they were accountable for their sin and that salvation is only found in Christ. His final words left ringing in theirs ears were: "...we must be saved" (Acts 4:12).

Sermon 4: Conclude with a statement of explanation

It was a very brief sermon, but Peter wrapped it up by stating that it was God's choice to exalt the Lord Jesus to His right hand so that He could make it possible for "repentance to [come to] Israel, and forgiveness of sins" (Acts 5:31). Ending a message with a statement of explanation is an effective way to confront the audience with their responsibility.

Sermon 5: Conclude with a statement of promise

As Peter completed his message about the death and resurrection of Christ, his final statement to Cornelius and those with him was the guarantee that "through his name whosoever believeth in him shall receive remission of sins" (Acts 10:43).

The Assessment of a Gospel Preacher

When it comes to the message, God's view is, "As cold water to a thirsty soul, so is good news from a far country" (Prov 25:25). When it comes to the messenger who delivers the message, Paul quoted Isaiah when he said, "How beautiful are the feet of them that preach the gospel of peace and bring glad tidings of good things!" (Isa 52:7; Rom 10:15). God's appreciation for those who present the message and those who preserve the message is not something we can measure. Simon Peter was one of the "beautiful feet" - believers who preached the gospel of peace. As you analyse his sermons, you can see how the message he shared was the "good news" from the far country of Heaven bringing refreshment, life, forgiveness, and salvation to souls. May the Lord stir us then to love the gospel more, to keep the gospel biblical, and to preach the gospel faithfully for the glory of God and the eternal blessing of souls.

CHAPTER 23

Peter the Steward

"He is no fool who gives what he cannot keep, to gain what he cannot lose."

Jim Elliott – missionary and martyr in Ecuador.

On October 28, 1949, Jim Elliott wrote these words in his personal journal having been convicted by the Biblical concept of stewardship in Luke 16:9.

Simon Peter felt a similar burden about stewardship using the word in his writings and living it out in his life. The word group for stewards and stewardship occurs 19 times in the New Testament and we gain insight as to its meaning from Paul when he wrote of "Erastus the chamberlain of the city" (Rom 16:23). J. N. Darby rightly translates the same phrase, "Erastus, the steward of the city". When a person entrusts something to someone under them, that is called a stewardship and the person who receives it is called a steward. In the case of Erastus, Marvin Vincent thinks he "Probably...[was] the administrator of the city lands" in Corinth. A.T. Robertson and BDAG think it means he was the "public treasurer".

Luke uses the word to refer to a household manager (Luke 16:1) or administrator to whom the owner of the house gives certain roles and responsibilities. In that sense, the Lord gives stewardships to His people that include the following:

- Spiritual truth

    The apostles were "servants of Christ and stewards of the mysteries of God" (1 Cor 4:1, ESV).

- The care of the local church

  Paul told Titus to appoint leaders with good public testimony because "the overseer must be free from all charge against him as God's steward" (Titus 1:7).

- Financial and material blessings

  In Luke 16:1-13, the Lord Jesus told a parable about a household manager, a steward whose duties included dealing with people who owed his master money.

- Abilities

  "As each one has received a gift, minister it to one another, as good stewards of the manifold grace of God" (1 Peter 4:10, NKJV).

- Spiritual Roles

  Paul says, "I became a minister according to the stewardship from God which was given to me for you, to fulfill the word of God" (Col 1:25, ESV).

While the word is not mentioned specifically in them, the Lord Jesus also spoke the Parable of the Talents (Matt 25:14-30) and the Parable of the Pounds (Luke 19:11-27) to illustrate and teach principles of stewardship and administration.

The Reception of Stewardships

Peter spoke about abilities when he said, "every man hath received the gift" (1 Peter 4:10a). He went on to define the Giver of stewardships when he added that we are "stewards of the manifold grace of God".

In 1 Corinthians 12, Paul said about gifts: "For to one is given by the Spirit...to another...by the same Spirit" (1 Cor 12:8). In Romans 12, he said, "God hath dealt to every man the measure of faith" (Rom 12:3). In Ephesians 4, he said that it was the risen Christ who "gave gifts unto men" (Eph 4:8). Therefore, the Holy Trinity is interested and involved in the giving of stewardships to His people.

Thus, any ability, role, revelation, or resource we have did not originate with us and we can never claim ownership. In Luke 19, the Lord Jesus told the Parable of the Pounds in which a nobleman gave each of his 10 servants one pound which was worth about 100 days of work. Later, when the stewards reported to the nobleman how they had used the pound they had received, they all spoke of "thy pound", not "my pound". Likewise, while we have our names on bank accounts, investments, property, and vehicle titles, and we speak of our gospel works, our assemblies, and our abilities, let us never forget that we are just administering what really belongs to God. Paul even taught, "ye are not your own. For ye are bought with a price: therefore glorify God in your body, and in your spirit, which are God's" (1 Cor 6:19-20). Even our lives and our bodies belong to the One who has both made us and bought us.

The Responsibilities of Stewardships

Peter understood the bi-directional aspect of gifts. First, every steward is vertically responsible to God for the proper use of what has been placed into his hands. Second, every stewardship is to be used horizontally to bless others. Peter explained these two aspects in one statement: "As every man hath received the gift, even so minister the same one to another" (1 Peter 4:10). So, whether spiritual or material, every gift from the Lord should make us ask how I can use this to help, edify, and bless others.

In the Parable of the Talents, the giver distributes talents to his servants, each "according to his several ability" (Matt 25:15). What a vital lesson! With whatever sphere of service and responsibility the Lord gives us, He will always make sure we have the ability and resources to complete His will. Peter put that principle in these words: "if any man minister, let him do it as of the ability which God giveth" (1 Peter 4:11). So, may we be quick to recognize not just that the Lord has given us our gifts, but also that we need Him to provide grace and help to carry out our stewardships. Without divine direction, assistance, and resources, we will surely fail.

In few words, Peter succinctly set out another valuable principle for stewards when he wrote, "If any man speak, *let him speak* as the oracles of God" (1 Peter 4:11). And what is true of preaching is equally applicable to every other stewardship. Mr. Darby removes the words in italics in the KJV and he translates this sentence as: "If any one speak — as oracles of God". The implication is that whoever receives a stewardship, let him exercise it with seriousness because he will be handling what belongs to Almighty God. In addition, he is to exercise his stewardship in a manner that is consistent with God's Word.

Peter once stood beside a dead man and his dead wife. The Lord had blessed the couple with a piece of property which they sold (Acts 5). However, they then lied about the amount gained in order to attract undeserved praise. While they did not take their stewardship seriously, God did, and He moved in solemn discipline upon them. May the Lord help us both to handle our stewardships with reverence and to administer them in accordance with Holy Scripture.

Finally, Peter laid out the primary goal for every stewardship: "that God in all things may be glorified through Jesus Christ" (1 Peter 4:11). Peter once saw Simon Magus seek a stewardship of the ability to perform miracles. He had already been "giving out that himself was some great one" (Acts 8:9) such that "to him they [the people of Samaria] had regard" (Acts 8:11). The man was a fraud seeking glory for himself, not the Lord. Unlike Simon Magus, Ananias and Sapphira were believers, but they had divided hearts. Thus, while they gave some of the funds from the sale of their property to honour God, they kept the rest to please themselves. Clearly, God finds it unacceptable if we handle stewardships with selfish or divided motives. When Peter taught on the subject, he emphasised "all things", which means that every stewardship and everything within a stewardship is intended to bring honour and glory to our God.

The Review of Stewardship

In every parable Jesus related involving stewardship He always came to a key moment when servants were held accountable for what they had been given. In the Parable of the Talents, "After a long time the lord of those servants cometh, and reckoneth with them" (Matt 25:19). In the Parable of the Pounds, the nobleman "commanded [the] servants to be called unto him, to whom he had given the money, that he might know how much every man had gained by trading" (Luke 19:15). As to us, Paul taught, "So then every one of us shall give account of himself to God" (Rom 14:12). Peter agreed as he wrote about "the Father, who without respect of persons judgeth according to every man's work" (1 Peter 1:17). Therefore, although we can administer what God has given us while sadly thinking only about what others might consider about us, we need to keep a clear focus like that shown by the Apostle Paul. He said, "he that judgeth me is the Lord" (1 Cor 4:4). And at the great Day of Review, the Lord Jesus will evaluate us based on one principle: "Moreover it is required in stewards, that a man be found faithful" (1 Cor 4:2). Thus, in the measure that we have used what God has given us in Scriptural ways to bless others, the Lord will personally reward us.

The Rewarding of Stewardship

A rich young ruler had just walked away from the Lord Jesus "sorrowful: for he had great possessions" (Matt 19:22). The Lord Jesus used that occasion to explain that the distraction of money and material possessions will make it difficult for rich people to enter the kingdom of heaven. Peter, thinking about how he and the other disciples had given up their secular jobs to respond to the call of Christ, said, "Behold, we have forsaken all, and followed thee; what shall we have therefore?" (Matt 19:27).

In response, the Lord Jesus explained that His financial planning principles were out of this world – literally. He promised future reward for present faithfulness that will become evident in His kingdom. He told His disciples that "in the regeneration when the Son of man shall sit in the throne of his glory, ye also shall sit upon twelve thrones, judging the twelve tribes of Israel" (Matt 19:28). For having been faithful and devoted during their service in this life, the 12 will be granted even greater positions and opportunities to serve in the Millennial Kingdom. They will even be promoted to administrative positions (thrones). If they were faithful with the gospel and truth in this life, He would entrust them with responsibilities in His universal government in the Kingdom to come (judging the 12 tribes). Paul wrote that the church has been "built upon the foundation of the apostles and prophets, Jesus Christ himself being the chief corner stone" (Eph 2:20). Likewise, for their faithfulness, these men will also be given a foundational role in the celestial Kingdom. John provided confirmation when he saw the heavenly city which had "twelve foundations, and in them the names of the twelve apostles of the Lamb" (Rev 21:14).

Mark also records the time when "Peter began to say unto Him [Jesus], 'Lo, we have left all, and have followed thee'" (Mark 10:28). But he adds another valuable point about rewards for faithful stewardship. He tells how Jesus responded by saying, "Verily I say unto you, There is no man that hath left house, or brethren, or sisters, or father, or mother, or wife, or children, or lands, for my sake, and the gospel's, But he shall receive an hundredfold now in this time, houses, and brethren, and sisters, and mothers, and children, and lands, with persecutions; and in the world to come eternal life" (Mark 10:29-30). In this account, there is not only the promise of recompense "in the world to come", but also the promise of reward "in this time". At first this may sound like a justification for the "health and wealth gospel" which promises economic prosperity for those who have faith. But what the Lord Jesus was teaching was that, as we go through life, He will reward our faithfulness by giving us even greater opportunities for service. You can see this principle in Peter's experience. The Lord gave him boats, nets and a house in Bethsaida and Capernaum. Having been faithful with material things, the Lord then entrusted Peter with the keys to the Kingdom (Matt 16:19). Likewise, having been faithful with the revelation of truth to the Jews (Acts 2-5) and the Samaritans (Acts 8), the Lord gave him the revelation of truth for the Gentiles (Acts 10).

All through Scripture, reward is often tied to faithfulness and sacrifice. With this in mind, the Saviour broadened out the promise of future reward to every disciple, not just the apostles. He said, "And every one that hath forsaken houses, or brethren, or sisters, or father, or mother, or wife, or children, or lands, for my name's sake, shall receive an hundredfold, and shall inherit everlasting life" (Matt 19:29). And the distribution of those rewards will occur very soon. Peter focused on that event when he exhorted elders to faithfully execute their service in caring for the flock. To them he promised that, "when the chief Shepherd shall appear, ye shall receive a crown of glory that fadeth not away" (1 Peter 5:4). So, on the one hand, the fact that the rapture could occur at any moment should encourage us because very soon we will receive recognition and reward from the Lord Himself.

The Bible promises that "we shall reign with him" (2 Tim 2:12) in His Millennial Kingdom. So, based on our faithfulness now, He will assign us stewardships in that day to further serve and worship Him. That great prospect should make us want to shout, "Even so, come, Lord Jesus" (Rev 22:20). And yet, at the same time, knowing that the rapture could occur at any moment should motivate us to diligent administration of what God has given us.

We need to be reminded that stewardships here on earth are time-limited opportunities. Soon, our lives will be over and only what we have done for Christ will count. Peter's way of living was to keep in mind that "the end of all things is at hand" (1 Peter 4:7). May we likewise seek to be loyal and careful in our stewardships so that the Lord might to say to us as He most certainly will to Peter, "Well done, thou good and faithful servant" (Matt 25:21, 23).

CHAPTER 24

Peter the Prisoner

"In theory, theory and practice are the same. In practice, they are not".

Dr. Albert Einstein

Many of us were experts on marriage, until we got married and had to put our knowledge and ideas into practice. Equally, there are plenty who postulate about raising children but who have never faced one of their own passing through the "terrible twos". However, the Apostle Peter was no theorist. One day, he picked up his pen to write to Christians he called "strangers scattered throughout Pontus, Galatia, Cappadocia, Asia, and Bithynia" (1 Peter 1:1). These were groups of believers who escaped persecution in Judea and were now scattered throughout Asia Minor. Their suffering, uncertainty, and loss were simply because they were believers and followers of our Lord Jesus Christ. Many of them likely left their homeland having been rejected and mistreated even by their families.

In the New Testament, James and Peter both address suffering and trials. James wrote to "to the twelve tribes which are scattered abroad" (James 1:1) - Jewish Christians who had been displaced and travelled into exile. We have an example of this in Acts 11:19 where Luke tells us: "Now they which were scattered abroad upon the persecution that arose about Stephen travelled as far as Phenice, and Cyprus, and Antioch".

Specifically, when and why the believers that Peter addressed were dispersed into what is now southern Turkey, we do not know. However, they were not there for a holiday to enjoy the coastal beaches. They must have faced tough decisions and harsh challenges which motivated Peter to write to them about suffering. As he begins, he says to them, "ye are in heaviness through manifold temptations" (1 Peter 1:6). He then circles back to the same subject of trials and suffering when he addresses believers and their employment (1 Peter 2:18-21), believers and their interpersonal relationships (1 Peter 3:15-17), believers and their civil and their societal responsibilities (1 Peter 4:12-19), and believers and their spiritual lives (1 Peter 4:8-11). In all, Peter uses the noun and verb forms of the word for suffering 15 times in his first letter.

Clearly, though, Peter was not theorizing and pontificating about how to handle difficulties, false accusations, rejection, and painful abuse. He was writing about this very sensitive and emotionally packed subject from two perspectives. First, he says, "I exhort...as a fellow elder and a witness of the sufferings of Christ" (1 Peter 5:1, ESV). On that unforgettable night in Caiaphas' house, while Peter was desperately trying to keep himself incognito, he saw the cruel treatment of the Lord Jesus. He witnessed some of the most unjust trials in the history of humanity and the horrific brutality against God's Son. Thus, Peter would reflect on what he observed in his Saviour at various points in his letter. His perspective was: "Christ also suffered for us, leaving us an example, that ye should follow his steps" (1 Peter 2:21).

Secondly, while he preferred to focus on the sufferings of Christ to draw lessons and encouragement for his audience, Peter was writing out of personal experience. During the 10 years following the Day of Pentecost, he was arrested and imprisoned three times and faced other acute trials:

- After Peter and John had healed the lame man at the temple gate and had used the occasion to preach the gospel (Acts 3), "the priests, and the captain of the temple, and the Sadducees, came upon them...And they laid hands on them and put them in hold unto the next day" (Acts 4:1, 3). In the end they "further threatened them...finding nothing how they might punish them" (Acts 4:21).

These men were not engaging in mere verbal saber-rattling; they were serious. This is evident as, upon the release of Peter and John, the local believers prayed, "Lord, behold their threatenings" (Acts 4:29). They used a word Liddle and Scott define as: "threat of punishment". The Dictionary of Bible Languages says this word means to "declare harm to another". The word is also used in Acts 9:1 to refer to the murderous threats of Saul of Tarsus and his cohorts against believers in Christ.

• Later, "by the hands of the apostles were many signs and wonders wrought" (Acts 5:12), and the people "brought forth the sick into the streets, and laid them on beds and couches, that at the least the shadow of Peter passing by might overshadow some of them" (Acts 5:15). In response to the healing of many, "the high priest rose up, and all they that were with him, (which is the sect of the Sadducees,) and were filled with indignation, And laid their hands on the apostles, and put them in the common prison" (Acts 5:17-18). On that occasion, the angel of the Lord intervened and he "opened the prison doors, and brought them forth" (Acts 5:19). Upon realizing that Peter and the others were free, the Jewish leaders called them and confronted them again. In the end, they decided to let them go, but they "called the apostles, and [having] beaten them, they commanded that they should not speak in the name of Jesus" (Acts 5:40).

• Peter and the other apostles had great respect and appreciation for Stephen, "a man full of faith and of the Holy Spirit" (Acts 6:5, NKJV). So, it would be very difficult for Peter to observe how some men "stirred up the people" such that the Jewish leaders "came upon him [Stephen] and caught him and brought him to the council, And set up false witnesses" (Acts 6:12-13). After he faithfully declared the gospel, "they stoned Stephen" (Acts 7:59). Then, we read, "And at that time there was a great persecution against the church which was at Jerusalem; and they were all scattered abroad throughout the regions of Judaea and Samaria, except the apostles" (Acts 8:1). Peter lived through both the loss of a respected friend and the persecution that followed which resulted in the departure of many believers of which some were his spiritual children in the faith. Separations from friends, family and believers are always emotionally challenging.

• Following that, we are told how the prophet Agabus "signified by the Spirit that there should be great dearth throughout all the world" (Acts 11:28). Obviously, Peter, the apostles, and the rest of the believers in Jerusalem were impacted greatly by this famine, such that believers outside of Israel had to send "relief unto the brethren which dwelt in Judaea" (Acts 11:29). A natural or national crisis can produce anxiety, uncertainty, and need among believers. In difficult times, leaders like Peter not only suffer themselves, but they must attend to believers who are also suffering.

• Seeing believers suffer is never easy and even worse when you are close to them. Luke tells us, "Now about that time Herod the king stretched forth his hands to vex certain of the church. And he killed James the brother of John with the sword" (Acts 12:1-2). Many think Peter and James were cousins, perhaps like Jesus and John the Baptist. If that is the case, then Peter had to go through the grieving process over the martyrdom of a family member. At a minimum, James was a long-time friend, fellow fisherman on the Sea of Galilee, fellow disciple, one of the 12 apostles, and one of the special three (Peter, James, and John) who shared unique occasions with the Saviour during His ministry.

• Even worse, Luke tells us that "because he [Herod] saw it pleased the Jews, he proceeded further to take Peter also" (Acts 12:3). Upon arresting him, "he put him in prison, and delivered him to four quaternions of soldiers to keep him" (Acts 12:4). This was not some posh penitentiary. We are told, "Peter was sleeping between two soldiers, bound with two chains: and the keepers before the door kept the prison" (Acts 12:6).

Therefore, the New Testament records for us that Peter knew what it was to be deprived of liberty, to suffer physically, to experience grief and loss, to face persecution, to live under death threats, to see believers go through trials, and to feel the stress of uncertain circumstances. And yet, while he could have legitimately used his own experiences and challenges to comfort and embolden his fellow believers, he keeps his own sufferings in the background while focusing on the "author and finisher of our faith" who "endured such contradiction of sinners against himself" (Heb 12:2-3).

The Cause of Trials

Peter sifted down the reasons for which believers might suffer into two categories when he said, "For it is better, if the will of God be so, that ye suffer for well doing, than for evil doing" (1 Peter 3:17). As for doing evil, Peter says, "He who would love life and see good days, let him refrain his tongue from evil, and his lips from speaking deceit. Let him turn away from evil and do good." (1 Peter 3:10-11, NKJV). He even reminded them that "the face of the Lord is against them that do evil" (1 Peter 3:12). Some misguided believers and evangelical preachers have erroneously propagated the idea that if believers live rightly and have faith, they will never suffer. Yes, suffering can be a means by which the Lord is disciplining and correcting an errant saint. Peter even said, "For the time is come that judgment must begin at the house of God" (1 Peter 4:17). Paul wrote of wayward saints in Corinth of which he said, "many are weak and sickly among you, and many sleep" (1 Cor 11:30). However, we must never conclude that if fellow believers are suffering, that must mean they have done something wrong for which God is judging them. That thinking is blasphemous. It was bad enough that Job's friends had that mentality and spoke accusingly against him, but it was even worse that human beings expressed that sentiment at the cross against the Holy Son of God. One day soon, repentant Jews will confess, "we did esteem him stricken, smitten of God, and afflicted" (Isa 53:4).

Thankfully, Peter identified a second cause of suffering in the lives of believers when he wrote repeatedly about doing good - (2 Peter 2:14, 15, 20; 3:11, 17). He had observed these two causes of suffering at the cross. Two thieves were in intense pain because, as one of them said, "and we indeed justly; for we receive the due reward of our deeds: but this man hath done nothing amiss" (Luke 23:41). Later, Peter preached to Cornelius and those with him that Jesus of Nazareth had gone "about doing good, and healing all that were oppressed of the devil" (Acts 10:38). He went on to say, "And we are witnesses of all things which he did both in the land of the Jews, and in Jerusalem; whom they slew and hanged on a tree" (Acts 10:39). The Lord Jesus suffered for having done good things to help and bless others. The men on either side of him were suffering for the evil they had committed and the damage they had caused.

Peter also raised the related possibility: "If ye suffer for righteousness' sake" (1 Peter 3:14). Just living in our sick and sinful world can be hard for a believer wanting to live rightly. Peter informs us about Lot: "For that righteous man dwelling among them, in seeing and hearing, vexed his righteous soul from day to day with their unlawful deeds" (2 Peter 2:8). As a believer, living rightly versus wrongly is serious business. Peter borrows King David's words in Psalm 34 when he says, "For the eyes of the Lord are over the righteous, and his ears are open unto their prayers: but the face of the Lord is against them that do evil" (1 Peter 3:12). We must never seek to justify making wrong choices with such trite phrases as "The Lord understands", or "the Lord knows me". His stance against evil and His love for good applies equally to sinners and to saints. Of course, Paul taught, "...there is none righteous, no, not one" (Rom 3:10). So, in the strictest moral sense, when the searching eye of God looked upon the Lord Jesus, for the first time, he saw a righteous man whose prayers were of infinite delight. Peter indirectly reminds his audience of this in that great text, "For Christ also hath once suffered for sins, the just for the unjust, that he might bring us to God" (1 Peter 3:18). Our Saviour gave a perfect example of what it is to "suffer for righteousness' sake" while continually "Having a good conscience" (1 Peter 3:16).

Another reason we might experience opposition or persecution is simply because of our identification and loyalty to Christ. Peter wrote, "But let none of you suffer as a murderer, or as a thief, or as an evildoer, or as a busybody in other men's matters. Yet if any man suffer as a Christian, let him not be ashamed; but let him glorify God on this behalf" (1 Peter 4:15-16). When Jesus called him on the beach that day alongside the Sea of Galilee, Jesus said, "Follow me!" (Mark 1:16-17). Also, Peter heard the Lord Jesus teach that "Whosoever will come after me, let him deny himself, and take up his cross, and follow me" (Mark 8:34). After Peter denied the Lord and was restored to the enjoyment of fellowship with his Saviour, Jesus said to him again, "Follow me!" (John 21:19). John, in his gospel, narrates a few occasions when he and Peter were together. Five times he refers to himself as "the other disciple" (John 18:16; 20:2, 3, 4, 8) implying that Peter was a disciple or follower, and he was the other one like Peter. While it is a great honour to be able to claim the name of being a Christian, it is even better when a believer's life and loyalty indicate that he is truly following Christ. Peter understood that a believer who identifies with Christ and lives in obedience to His word will bring joy and a smile to heaven. At the same time, he will likely experience the frown and persecution of those who do not know our Saviour. Suffering for doing good, for living rightly, and for following our Lord, is to be expected. Peter said, "Beloved, think it not strange concerning the fiery trial which is to try you, as though some strange thing happened unto you" (1 Peter 4:12). As he wrote those words, he would remember the teaching of the Master: "If the world hate you, ye know that it hated me before it hated you. If ye were of the world, the world would love his own: but because ye are not of the world, but I have chosen you out of the world, therefore the world hateth you" (John 15:18-19).

The Control of Trials

When we are in a trial and suffering, things can seem chaotic. Very quickly we can lose control of our circumstances and face an uncertain future. Yet, Peter reminded persecuted believers that it is normal and to be expected - "if the will of God be so, that ye suffer..." (1 Peter 3:17). Peter had once preached to Jews about Jesus - "Him, being delivered by the determinate counsel and foreknowledge of God, ye have taken, and by wicked hands have crucified and slain" (Acts 2:23).

At the cross, not one insult, not one slap or punch, not one thorn, not one lash of the whip, and not one pound of the nails was a surprise to God. People mocked what they perceived as powerlessness (lack of control) on the part of the Saviour as He hung on the cross. They said, "...himself he cannot save" (Mark 15:31). And yet, while God may have been silent to their ears and still to their eyes, Peter recognised that the Lord was in full control. So, as Peter reminded suffering saints of the cross, could they not ask themselves, "Is God in any less control of our sufferings, than he was during the sufferings of his Son?" Suffering can surprise us, but they will never surprise our God. He never has to adjust His plans because we have come under attack or are facing pain and loss. Suffering is just a tool in His hand for our good and His glory.

The book of Acts informs us of the first time the Jewish leaders "laid hands on them [Peter and John], and put them in hold unto the next day: for it was now eventide" (Acts 4:3). The second time, they "put them in the common prison" (Acts 5:18) and later they beat them (Acts 5:40). The third time, rather than the Jews, it was the Gentile King Herod who arrested him. Peter would well remember that while the Jews had mistreated and falsely accused the Lord Jesus, the Gentiles (King Herod and Pilate the Governor) were the ones that had authority to impose the death penalty on the Lord Jesus. Later, to the delight of the Jewish leaders, King Herod killed the apostle James with a sword. He arrested Peter clearly intending to do the same with him. Each trial of Peter was worse than the previous one and the possibility of release seemed even more remote than before. However, on that occasion, Peter was asleep. How could he rest knowing that at any moment the edict could come from King Herod to lop off his head? While he trusted the Lord's promise that he would live until he was old, Peter also knew that his suffering was for being a Christian and for doing good (a healing). He also knew that his suffering was according to the will of God. What peace to know that the Almighty is always in control of our lives, even when we are suffering, and the future looks bleak.

In the first imprisonment, the Lord worked Peter's release using the simple logic and reasoning of men. The Jewish leaders concluded that "they could say nothing against it [the healing of the lame man]" (Acts 4:14), so they solemnly warned them not to preach the gospel anymore. On the second occasion, God granted Peter and John freedom when "the angel of the Lord by night opened the prison doors, and brought them forth" (Acts 5:19). Similarly, on the third occasion "the angel of the Lord came upon him, and a light shined in the prison: and he smote Peter on the side, and raised him up, saying, Arise up quickly. And his chains fell off from his hands" (Acts 12:7). Then, "When they were past the first and the second ward, they came unto the iron gate that leadeth unto the city; which opened to them of his own accord: and they went out" (Acts 12:10). God can work through natural and normal means, or He can work through supernatural means to accomplish His will. In the medical world today, God often works through doctors, surgeries, therapies, and medicines, but sometimes He just heals people apart from medical science altogether.

As surprising and awe-inspiring as those experiences were for Peter, he knew that sometimes God does not release people from suffering, nor does He always preserve His people from death. Peter knew that "Herod the king...[had] killed James the brother of John with the sword" (Acts 12:1-2). For some unknown reason, God did not stop Herod. Did Peter ever wonder or ask the Lord, "Why did You save me from being beheaded and not James?" He could have asked the same thing about the death of Stephen. After all, Peter had preached similar messages to those preached by Stephen. God allowed the Jews to stone Stephen and not Peter. So, Peter's experiences point us to the sovereign control of God in our lives. Paul explained it in this way to the Corinthians: "God is faithful, who will not allow you to be tempted beyond what you are able, but with the temptation will also make the way of escape, that you may be able to bear it" (1 Cor 10:13, NKJV). Therefore, believers who "suffer according to the will of God [should] commit the keeping of their souls to him in well-doing, as unto a faithful Creator" (1 Peter 4:19). Having our Almighty Creator in control, we can enjoy peace in the circumstances knowing that He has allowed them to befall us, and that He will also control the outcome of our suffering.

The Confirmation of Trials

Peter spoke of "the trial of your faith... [which is] much more precious than of gold that perisheth, though it be tried with fire" (1 Peter 1:7). Toss a piece of paper or a piece of plastic into a fire and it will quickly burn or melt. Put gold in fire, and while the dross will burn off, the pure gold will remain and become more noticeable. Peter had heard the Lord Jesus teach that trials and suffering are often a test of the reality of the faith of a person who professes to be a Christian. In the Lord's Parable of the Four Soils, the Sower went out to sow the seed and "some fell upon stony places, where they had not much earth: and forthwith they sprung up, because they had no deepness of earth: And when the sun was up, they were scorched; and because they had no root, they withered away" (Matt 13:5-6). Jesus went on to interpret this part of the parable when He said, "He that received the seed into stony places, the same is he that heareth the word, and anon with joy receiveth it; Yet hath he not root in himself, but dureth for a while: for when tribulation or persecution ariseth because of the word, by and by he is offended" (Matt 13:20-21).

Peter probably remembered the Lord's teaching as he addressed the issue of suffering and trials. He could recall the Sermon on the Mount in which Jesus taught, "Blessed are they which are persecuted for righteousness' sake: for theirs is the kingdom of heaven" (Matt 5:10). Likewise, the believers that Peter addressed were suffering for their Christianity, and those very sufferings were making them stronger in their convictions. In that sense, the trials confirmed the reality of their salvation. So, Peter went on to tell them, "If ye be reproached for the name of Christ, happy are ye; for the spirit of glory and of God resteth upon you" (1 Peter 4:14). One evidence of the genuineness of their salvation was how they handled trials and difficulties. Their joy in the Lord would indicate the reality of the Holy Spirit who had been dwelling in them since the day they had received Christ as their Saviour (Eph 1:13).

The Comparison of Trials

Pain and suffering can easily make us more self-centred so that we can even begin to think that we are the only ones passing through a trial and that no one understands what we are experiencing. Peter reminded the readers though, that "the same afflictions are accomplished in your brethren that are in the world" (1 Peter 5:9). The fact that others were experiencing the same sufferings should give these people a sense that they were not alone. There were other believers who could empathize with them in their trials. At the same time, knowing that others are experiencing the same challenges, should generate sympathy in us towards them and a desire to help.

In addition to making us more self-centred, suffering also inclines us to become focused on the here and now. Recognizing that human tendency, Peter's final appeal about suffering in his first letter was to "the God of all grace, who hath called us unto his eternal glory by Christ Jesus, after that ye have suffered a while, [may he] make you perfect, stablish, strengthen, settle you" (1 Peter 5:10). To put their suffering into proper perspective, Peter tries to have them view it from God's vantage point. He has them stand back and look at the big picture by first focusing on "the God of all grace". God, in His sovereign will, had saved them and had graciously given them the privilege to suffer for Christ. God could also provide grace for them to withstand the trial. But then, he says, "after that ye have suffered a while". Earlier he recognized that, "though now for a season, if need be, ye are in heaviness through manifold temptations" (1 Peter 1:6). Their trials were just speed bumps on the way to heaven and home as God had called them "unto his eternal glory by Christ Jesus" (1 Peter 5.10). For a true Christian, suffering is always temporary, and comparing it to our glorious future keeps it in perspective. Therefore, one great strategy to deal with trials and suffering is to look up and look ahead, instead of looking inside us and around us. Peter could remember the Lord Jesus doing that in the upper room. Instead of focusing on the betrayal that was taking place as He prayed, Jesus selflessly said to God, "Neither pray I for these alone [the 11 disciples], but for them also which shall believe on me through their word" (John 17:20). He focused on others, and He looked at things from an eternal perspective. He added, "Father, I will that they also, whom thou hast given me, be with me where I am; that they may behold my glory, which thou hast given me: for thou lovedst me before the foundation of the world" (John 17:24).

The Challenge of Trials

With great bravado and perhaps sincere intentions, Peter once proclaimed, "Lord, I am ready to go with thee, both into prison, and to death" (Luke 22:33). Little did he know that he would be tested on both those experiences – prison and death. Apart from the rapture, we will all eventually face suffering and trials. The question is how will we respond? Thankfully, Peter provides great insight on how best to handle difficulties and challenges in life.

Our Attitudes

The Lord calls us to control our attitudes rather than letting our attitudes control us. What makes this possible is that, through Scripture, we can view the challenges and problems in life from God's perspective. Thus, Peter could say to Christians in his day, "But and if ye suffer for righteousness' sake, happy are ye: and be not afraid of their terror, neither be troubled" (1 Peter 3:14). Also, he wrote, "If ye be reproached for the name of Christ, happy are ye" (1 Peter 4:14). Happy? According to BDAG, the word *makarios* means "privileged recipient of divine favour". Strong defines it as "supremely blest". If happiness depends on happenings, then the readers of Peter's letter who happened to be in hurtful and horrific happenings would find it hard to be happy. God was not expecting them to enjoy pain and loss. Peter was honest enough to call it what it was: "the fiery trial" (1 Peter 4:12). However, when Peter and John were released from prison, "they departed from the presence of the council, rejoicing that they were counted worthy to suffer shame for his name" (Acts 5:41). They knew that they were not suffering for something evil that they had done, but solely because of their association with Christ and for having proclaimed His gospel. While it was physically and mentally difficult, it was an opportunity for them "to give an answer to every man that asketh you a reason of the hope that is in you with meekness and fear" (1 Peter 3:15). Peter even told them, "ye are partakers of Christ's sufferings" (1 Peter 4:13). The same hatred and persecution that Christ experienced was now being redirected to them. What an honour that they could testify to the majesty of the person of Christ and the glory of His work. Peter said, "on their part he is evil spoken of, but on your part he is glorified." (1 Peter 4:14).

Our attitudes can be further helped by focusing not so much on what others are doing *to* us, but rather what God is doing *in* us. James said that, "the trying of your faith worketh patience. But let patience have her perfect work, that ye may be perfect and entire, wanting nothing" (James 1:3-4). He taught that trials are tools in the hand of our God to increase our faith (patience), to bring us to maturity (be perfect), and to equip us for future service (entire, wanting nothing). Peter taught that "the trial of your faith, being much more precious than of gold that perisheth, though it be tried with fire, might be found unto praise and honour and glory at the appearing of Jesus Christ" (1 Peter 1:7). In suffering, God was highlighting the precious, real faith in these believers. This great purpose of God is noted by William MacDonald when he wrote that, "Job probably sustained heavier losses in one day than any other man in the history of the world, yet he was able to say, "Though he slay me, yet will I trust in him" (Job 13:15)". Therefore, suffering for righteousness and for the name of Christ is never wasted and the time in trials is never lost. Instead, God's hand is working in our trials for the honour of His name and the good of His people.

Our Awareness

One of the great challenges in pressure situations is for believers to avoid turning on one another. For example, when a married couple is facing a financial challenge, they can either unite to address the crisis together or let the matter produce conflict between them. When the latter happens, there will be blaming, harsh and hurtful words, and great unhappiness. The same is true in an assembly. Peter's concern was that believers should unite in facing the opposition, rather than letting that problem cause conflict inside the assembly. Knowing that awful human tendency, Peter sprinkles reminders through his letter that they should have a "one another" mindset rather than a self-centred mindset. He tells them to "love one another" (1 Peter 1:22) and to "keep loving one another earnestly" (1 Peter 4:8). He adds that they should "Show hospitality to one another" (1 Peter 4:9), "serve one another" (1 Peter 4:10), and show "humility toward one another" (1 Peter 5:5). He even reminds them of the most basic action: "Greet one another" (1 Peter 5:14).

And in the middle of persecution and suffering, Peter exhorted them, "Finally, be ye all of one mind, having compassion one of another, love as brethren, be pitiful, be courteous: Not rendering evil for evil, or railing for railing: but contrariwise blessing; knowing that ye are thereunto called, that ye should inherit a blessing" (1 Peter 3:8-9). They were not to let stress in their individual lives lead them to bad attitudes and wrong treatment of one another. They were to pursue and maintain unity (one mind) which would be demonstrated in acts of kindness (having compassion), seeking the good of others (love as brethren), comprehending the challenges that others were facing (pitiful), and keeping humble rather than thinking that they could handle the trial better than their brothers (courteous). Each brother was to filter his words and not respond tit-for-tat, but rather "let him refrain his tongue from evil, and his lips that they speak no guile: Let him eschew evil, and do good; let him seek peace, and ensue it" (1 Peter 3:10-11). Instead of becoming defensive, reacting to hurtful words, or settling scores, they were to override emotions, and respond in a Christ-like manner: "Who, when he was reviled, reviled not again; when he suffered, he threatened not; but committed himself to him that judgeth righteously" (1 Peter 2:23).

Our Adoration

Trials are opportunities to turn pain and pressure into praise. Abraham understood this principle. When God called him to go to Moriah and offer up his son, Scripture says, "Now it came to pass after these things that God tested Abraham" (Gen 22:1, NKJV). What a trial! And yet, after three days of travel, "Abraham said unto his young men, 'Abide ye here with the ass; and I and the lad will go yonder and worship.'" (Gen 22.5). Peter had witnessed that principle in his Saviour too. Yes, "Christ also hath once suffered for sins" (1 Peter 3:18), but the cross was the greatest act of worship ever and it will never be eclipsed. Paul explained it this way: "Christ also hath loved us, and hath given himself for us an offering and a sacrifice to God for a sweetsmelling savour" (Eph 5:2).

Therefore, Peter appealed to these suffering saints reminding them, "if, when ye do well, and suffer *for it*, ye take it patiently, this *is* acceptable with God." (1 Peter 2:20). BDAG says that "acceptable with God" means that a suffering saint "wins a favourable response from God". His response, either now or in the future, will reflect divine appreciation for a believer passing through suffering. Peter added, "Yet if any man suffer as a Christian, let him not be ashamed; but let him glorify God on this behalf" (1 Peter 4:16). Therefore, suffering can either be viewed as opposition or opportunity. Admittedly, it is much more easily preached than practiced, but it is an outlook that all of us need to develop. Peter even said, "Forasmuch then as Christ hath suffered for us in the flesh, arm yourselves likewise with the same mind" (1 Peter 4:1). This Christ-like mindset is to view and act in every experience, whether suffering or service, so that in the end, "God in all things may be glorified through Jesus Christ, to whom be praise and dominion for ever and ever. Amen" (1 Peter 4:11).

CHAPTER 25

Peter the Martyr

Peter's Experiences with Death

Peter was no stranger to death. He knew people who died, he saw people die, and he met people who had died. Here are all the individuals in Scripture who died with whom Peter had some kind of connection:

- Jairus' daughter
- Lazarus of Bethany
- The widow of Nain's son
- Judas Iscariot
- James the Apostle
- Stephen
- Ananias and Sapphira
- Dorcas/Tabitha
- His Lord and Saviour Jesus Christ

Divine Sovereignty

The list above must have taught Peter a great lesson. In general, "it is appointed unto men once to die" (Heb 9:27), but death is far from predictable. Sometimes unsaved people do extremely wicked and cruel things and live long lives. Peter once watched as the Jewish leaders and temple guards treated the Lord Jesus in the most barbaric ways and yet there were no lightning bolts from heaven to instantly incinerate them for their sin against God's Son. And yet, Judas Iscariot, another unsaved friend of Peter, did something equally horrible and he died.

Similarly, sometimes Christians do hypocritical or hurtful things and seem to get away with it, while in other cases the Father moves in discipline upon His children. For example, Peter was present when two believers, a husband and wife, lied to him. Luke tells us that upon sinning, first, Ananias "fell down, and gave up the ghost" (Acts 5:5). Three hours later, Sapphira "fell...straightway at his feet, and yielded up the ghost: and the young men came in, and found her dead, and, carrying her forth, buried her by her husband" (Acts 5:10). As shocking and sad as cases like Judas and Ananias and Sapphira are, there is a part of us that feels that justice prevailed. At the same time, when people appear to get away with sin and wickedness, we wonder why God lets it happen.

Other confusing aspects of death include when innocent children die rather than older people as in the case of Jairus' daughter who was just "of the age of twelve years" (Mark 5:42). Sometimes, perverts, criminals and violent people carry on with life while genuinely kind and selfless people like Dorcas die. Luke tells us that "this woman was full of good works and almsdeeds which she did" (Acts 9:36). We all know cases of Christians whose lives hardly give evidence of salvation and yet they live up into old age. Meanwhile, there are spiritually committed and obedient believers with good testimonies whose lives, from our vantage point, are prematurely cut off. Who would have expected that the fruitful lives of the Apostle James and Stephen, "a man full of faith and of the Holy Ghost" (Acts 6:5), would suddenly come to an end in the middle of great usefulness for God? Despite our confusion and questions, the comforting lesson about death is that God is in control. While not easy, we should seek to reverence God and respect His sovereign decisions about human life. May we seek to have the attitude and mindset of Job who said, "the Lord gave, and the Lord hath taken away; blessed be the name of the Lord" (Job 1:21).

Divine Sympathy

The fact that Jesus could say, "I am the resurrection, and the life" (John 11:25), did not in any way numb His feelings for those who lost loved ones. When Mary of Bethany approached the Lord in all her sadness, "Jesus therefore [seeing] her weeping, and the Jews also weeping which came with her, he groaned in the spirit, and was troubled" (John 11:33). As He witnessed profound grief that day at the passing of the one He called "Our friend Lazarus" (John 11:11), "Jesus wept" (John 11:35). The Saviour showed similar emotion as He came across the funeral procession of the widow of Nain's son. Luke tells us that "when the Lord saw her, he had compassion on her" (Luke 7:13). Even when He was on the cross, He was concerned for His own mother, Mary, and His friend, John, who would experience grief when He died. And His sympathetic heart remains unchanged; He still has a special care for those who suffer the loss of one they love.

Divine Sensitivity

Death is a sombre process - every step of it. A person dies. Then, they are carried to a tomb and buried. There, the human remains slowly disintegrate. On the three occasions when Jesus raised people from the dead, He showed His power over each of these stages and Peter was privileged to witness it.

Jairus' daughter had died in their house and was still lying in her bed when Jesus arrived. On that occasion, the Saviour "suffered no man to follow him, save Peter, and James, and John the brother of James" (Mark 5:37). Peter, therefore, had a front row seat and must have watched in awe as Jesus "took her by the hand, and the maid arose" (Matt 9:25). The girl had just died, but the Lord raised her from the dead.

On another occasion, Jesus went to Nain and when "he came nigh to the gate of the city, behold, there was a dead man carried out" (Luke 7:12). The family and friends of this young man were in the process of transporting his remains to the cemetery. Although the widow of Nain's son had been dead longer than Jairus' daughter, this was no problem for the Prince of Life. The Saviour simply "touched the open coffin, and those who carried him stood still. And He said, 'Young man, I say to you, arise.' So, he who was dead sat up and began to speak" (Luke 7:14-15, NKJV).

When they arrived at the tomb of Lazarus in Bethany, Jesus did not come upon a person who had just died, or who was being buried. Instead, Martha even said about her brother, "Lord, by this time he stinketh: for he hath been dead four days". However, even the process of corruption in a human body was no obstacle to the power of the Son of God. Jesus simply "cried with a loud voice, 'Lazarus, Come forth' And he that was dead came forth" (John 11:43-44). At these three unforgettable events, Peter was present to see how the Lord responded successfully to every stage of death.

On each of these occasions, we are told of the family relations of the deceased. The Bible points out that to Mary and Martha, Lazarus was "their brother" (John 11:19). The young man in Nain was "the only son of his mother" (Luke 7:12). Likewise, we are told that Jairus "had one only daughter" (Luke 8:42) and he and his wife were "the father and the mother of the damsel" (Mark 5:40). These details underline that the Lord clearly understands that the loss of a loved one impacts the family most of all.

Also, Peter would have observed that the woman of Nain was a widow. In other words, her son dying was the second great loss in her life. If history is correct and Joseph, the husband of Mary, died, likewise Mary would have gone through the grief process twice when her oldest child died on a cross. So, Scripture recognises with great sensitivity the compounding effects of one loss after another. Often a current loss can reopen the emotional wound of a previous loss in our lives, mixing and magnifying the pain and sadness.

In addition, Peter would have noticed that two of the three that Jesus raised from the dead, died out of the normal chronological order. In Nain, the son died before his mother. Similarly, the daughter died before her parents, Jairus and his wife. Death is always difficult even for the families of Christians who have died. Yes, as Paul said, we "sorrow not, even as others which have no hope" (1 Thess 4:13), but we still sorrow. And when death comes unexpectedly and out of the general anticipated order in a family, the loss is felt even more profoundly. But regardless of the shock and sadness, the Saviour is present and sensitive to the grief of those who remain.

Divine Standpoint

Death seems so final from a human perspective. However, the Lord Jesus provided the divine perspective. When He arrived at Jairus's house that was full of mourners, Peter heard Him declare, "... the damsel is not dead, but sleepeth" (Mark 5:39. Even though Mary and Martha's brother would be dead and in the grave for four days, Jesus likewise announced, "Our friend Lazarus sleepeth; but I go, that I may awake him out of sleep" (John 11:11). He was not teaching the erroneous doctrine of "soul sleep". The body of every person who has died is only in the state of death for a short time compared to the eternal existence before them. Their bodies are still and perhaps out of sight, like someone taking a nap. Paul spoke of Christians who had died as being "asleep in Jesus" (1 Thess 4:14). At the resurrection for the rapture, the resurrection of the just, and the resurrection of the unjust, the Lord will transform and adapt human bodies for eternal existence in heaven or to endure unending punishment.

Peter's Expectation of Death

Peter never mentions the rapture. Why? He is the only believer in the New Testament who knew for sure that he would die before the rapture occurred. Therefore, he mainly focuses on the issue of resurrection after death. Jesus had told Peter directly, "Truly, truly, I say to you, when you were young, you used to dress yourself and walk wherever you wanted, but when you are old, you will stretch out your hands, and another will dress you and carry you where you do not want to go. (This he said to show by what kind of death he was to glorify God)" (John 21:18-19, ESV).

When the Lord Jesus spoke to him about "by what death he should glorify God" (John 21:19), Peter had heard that kind of discourse before. When the Saviour described His own death by being lifted up from the earth, "This he said, signifying what death he should die" (John 12:33). Therefore, just as He knew all the details of His own death, the Lord knew all the specifics of Peter's death as well. And beyond just knowing the details, the Lord would also look after the particulars. Peter could recall that when Lazarus passed away, no one had to run and inform the Lord Jesus. Instead, at the very moment, even though Jesus was a long journey from Bethany, the Saviour announced, "Lazarus is dead" (John 11:14). And when Stephen died, he prayed, "Lord Jesus, receive my spirit" (Acts 7:59). Luke tells us that at that point, "Jesus [was already] standing on the right hand of God" (Acts 7:55), ready to welcome His own. So, Peter could derive great comfort from the fact that the Lord knew the beginning from the end in the process of death. In one sentence, the Son of God told him the following details:

- When: "thou shalt be old"

- How: "thou shalt stretch forth thy hands, and another shall gird thee, and carry thee whither thou wouldest not"

- Why: "This spake He, signifying by what death he should glorify God."

So, as Peter lived and served his Lord, he would be especially conscious that as he aged, any day could be his last. In his final letter, he spoke of "Knowing that shortly I must put off this my tabernacle, even as our Lord Jesus Christ hath shewed me" (2 Peter 1:14). He did not know whether or not his death was immediate, but he did know it was imminent (it could happen at any time). The Lord didn't tell him a specific day, just as He has not given us a specific day for the Rapture. So, on each occasion when he was arrested and jailed in the book of the Acts, Peter may have thought, "This must be it!" And yet, he was not looking forward to death even when he was beaten or threatened.

Death was always, as the Lord described it, a place "where you do not want to go" (John 21:18). Peter was grateful for physical life and for his body in which the Holy Spirit of God was residing. And yet, he demonstrated how quickly he believed his life could end when he said, "...as long as I am in this tabernacle" (2 Peter 1:13). So, even if a Christian has a healthy and Biblical view of life and his body, the reality and uncertainty of death can produce anxiety. There is no question about where we are going, it is just that the experience is unknown to us. Thus, the New Testament considers the will to live and a desire to avoid death as normal and expected.

Peter learned, though, to look at death as an opportunity, not a duty. The Lord Jesus assured him that his eventual death by crucifixion would have a purpose: he was to glorify God. He could recall that when Lazarus died, Jesus told His disciples, "This sickness is not unto death, but for the glory of God, that the Son of God might be glorified thereby" (John 11:4). When the Lord Jesus raised the widow of Nain's son from the dead, "there came a fear on all: and they glorified God" (Luke 7:16). Thus, the how, when, and where of Peter's death, or the response of others to it, would ultimately result in glory for God. What a motivation to take that step! It would not so much be the means of release from difficult circumstances, pain, or suffering. Peter anticipated his death knowing it would be one final earthly opportunity to bring honour to his God.

Peter's Exposition about Death

Perhaps Peter's focus was the key to his living with the knowledge that he was going to die. In his writings, he does mention the death of unsaved people. Peter believed that those who speak falsely against believers and persecute them will not escape accountability for their actions through death. He plainly stated that they "shall give account to him that is ready to judge the quick and the dead" (1 Peter 4:5).

He also presented his view of the death of a Christian. In a verse difficult to interpret, Peter stated, that "For this cause was the gospel preached also to them that are dead, that they might be judged according to men in the flesh, but live according to God in the spirit" (1 Peter 4:6). It can be understood in simple terms as saying that believers who were dead when he wrote his epistle had previously had the gospel preached to them during their lives. The impact of that gospel was that even though they had been judged or punished by men (i.e., persecuted) in their bodies which led to their deaths, they were now alive enjoying their spiritual relationship with God and with His Son, Jesus Christ. Peter would remember Jesus's teaching about those "which kill the body, but are not able to kill the soul" (Matt 10:28). Death could be painful and violent, but his focus was beyond that to the thrilling, unimpeded, complete spiritual life with Christ that awaited him.

Primarily though, Peter kept his focus on the death and resurrection of Christ rather than worrying about his own demise. This is evident in that the resurrection of the Lord Jesus permeated every sermon Peter preached (Acts 2:24; 3:14-15; 4:10-11; 5:30-31; 10:39-40). And when he picked up his pen to write to believers who were facing suffering and potential death, he reminded them of how Christ was "put to death in the flesh but made alive in the spirit" (1 Peter 3:18, ESV). In fact, the first thing he mentions in the letter is, "Blessed be the God and Father of our Lord Jesus Christ, which according to his abundant mercy hath begotten us again unto a lively hope by the resurrection of Jesus Christ from the dead, To an inheritance incorruptible, and undefiled, and that fadeth not away, reserved in heaven for you" (1 Peter 1:3-4). In the same chapter he returns to the same great theme by speaking again of how "God...raised him [Jesus] up from the dead, and gave him glory; that your faith and hope might be in God" (1 Peter 1:21). Peter appreciated that the death of Christ, as violent a murder as it was, was never out of God's control. Instead, the Almighty was working out His purposes even in the suffering, death, and glorious resurrection of Christ.

The question hardly needs to be asked then, as the answer is obvious. But, dear believer, do you think the same Almighty God who controlled the timing and details of the death of His Son was any less in control of the death of His servant Peter? Likewise, do you think He will have any lesser control or less glorious plans in how you leave this world either by rapture or by death?

Peter's Entrance into Death

The Bible is completely silent on when, where, and how the Apostle Peter died. The long-held tradition is that his execution took place under the persecution of Nero in A.D. 64. Nero committed suicide in A.D. 68, so Peter most certainly died before that. Many scholars feel he wrote his second epistle at some point between A.D. 64 and A.D. 68, shortly before his exit from this world. To be fair, most of the men often called "the early church fathers" speak of Peter as having died in Rome. Clement of Rome provides the earliest reference to Peter's death in A.D. 90. However, the first suggestion of Peter's presence in Rome does not come until almost a century later.

The Roman Catholic tradition is that Peter not only visited the city, but that he also lived there, established the church in Rome, was the bishop of the church for more than a decade, and that he was martyred there. However, the gospels end with Peter in Jerusalem as does the book of Acts. The only time we know for sure that he was outside of Israel was when Paul confronted him in Asia Minor (Gal 2:9ff). Furthermore, Paul wrote the letter to the Roman church in about A.D. 57 and he makes no reference to Peter as having lived in Rome, having planted the church, or to "the bishop of the church". Later, Paul was imprisoned in Rome from A.D. 61 to A.D. 63. Again, in all four of the letters he wrote while under house arrest for that period (Ephesians, Philippians, Colossians, and Philemon), he never mentions Peter having been in Rome. Peter himself wrote his second epistle between A.D. 64 and A.D. 68 and he never mentions living in Rome in the past or being there before he died.

The International Standard Bible Encyclopaedia states, "It should be observed, however, that the tradition that he visited Rome IS only tradition and nothing more". As for his death and burial in Rome, there is no reliable evidence to support it. Even the secular Encyclopaedia Britannica, when addressing the burial of Peter and Paul in Rome, says. "None of the excavations, however, in all of the areas indicated at various times as the resting place of the apostolic relics, have produced any evidence whatsoever that the bodies of Peter and Paul were either buried there originally or brought there at a later time after earlier burials elsewhere". Foxe, in his Book of Martyrs, agrees as he says, "It is, however, very uncertain, whether Peter ever visited Rome at all, the evidence rather favouring the supposition that he ended his days in some other country".

Peter's Epitaph after Death

We don't know what was written above the tomb of Peter. As mentioned above, we don't even know if he had a tomb much less if his beloved friends, fellow-believers, fellow-apostles, and co-workers inscribed words above where he lay. They certainly could have summoned many glowing terms to describe him and with good reason. Had they done so, they may have had the final say about Peter's life. However, that did not happen.

It is interesting to consider Paul's view and commentary on Peter. When he wrote to the Galatian Christians in about A.D. 48-49, he noted with respect how "the gospel of the circumcision was unto Peter" and how God had "wrought effectually in Peter to the apostleship of the circumcision" (Gal 2:7-8). He also wrote with appreciation of "James, Cephas, and John, who seemed to be pillars" (Gal 2:9). Facing a shockingly different ministry of taking the gospel to the Gentiles, Paul seemed most grateful for the friendship and fellowship he enjoyed with Peter. He points out that "they gave to me and Barnabas the right hands of fellowship; that we should go unto the heathen" (Gal 2:9).

The last words of Paul written about Peter are found in 1 Corinthians. The believers in that city had great respect for Peter. Even as they were foolishly forming cliques and subgroups in the assembly, their appreciation for this great servant of God is evident in that some said, "I of Cephas" (1 Cor 1:12). Later in the same letter, Paul talked about his rights as an apostle and he said, "Have we not power to lead about a sister, a wife, as well as other apostles, and as the brethren of the Lord, and Cephas?" (1 Cor 9:5). What a commendation from Paul that Peter was a family man in God's service whose wife supported his ministry. The very final mention, though, is in Paul's great discourse on the resurrection. He is the last one to use his fellow-apostle's name when he recalls the post-resurrection appearances of Christ. After noting that Christ "rose again the third day according to the Scriptures", Paul adds, "And that he was seen of Cephas" (1 Cor 15:4-5). Peter, in Paul's eyes, was a privileged man who had completed his mission by giving "witness of the resurrection of the Lord Jesus" (Acts 4:33). However, as kind and true as Paul's utterances were, the final words in Scripture relative to Peter, come from Peter himself.

His Final Warning

Twice the Lord Jesus said specifically to Peter, "Follow me!" (Matt 4:19; John 21:19). At one point during the ministry of the Lord Jesus, Peter claimed, "Lo, we have left all, and have followed thee" (Mark 10:28). To his credit, after all 11 disciples had forsaken the Lord, Scripture implies that there was some reflection and a change of course as "Simon Peter followed Jesus" (John 18:15) to the high priest's palace.

And yet, Peter soon came to know what it was to make foolish spiritual detours in his Christian life as he followed his own flesh and fears when he denied the Lord Jesus. He also knew what it was to give in to pressure from other professing believers, so that when "certain came from James, he did eat with the Gentiles: but when they were come, he [Peter] withdrew and separated himself, fearing them which were of the circumcision" (Gal 2:12). Recognising the spiritual possibility of stepping out of God's will, Peter wrote, "Ye therefore, beloved, seeing ye know these things before, beware lest ye also, being led away with the error of the wicked, fall from your own stedfastness" (2 Peter 3:17). He exhorted believers to recognize their potential for failure and how very quickly they could find themselves following (being led away by) erring men and erroneous teachings rather than the Word of God. With great burden, Peter warned about men who "entice unsteady souls" (2 Peter 2:14, ESV), and those who are "unlearned and unstable" (2 Peter 3:16). Listening, learning, and living out their teachings would reproduce these men's instability in the lives of their followers. While they wouldn't be able to make believers lose their salvation, they could lead them to "fall from... [their] own stability" (2 Peter 3:17, HSCB). Simon had learned from his own spiritual failures, and, by God's grace, he had become a *petros*, a rock-like, steady saint. Thus, Peter the Pillar longed for fellow believers to learn from his experience.

His Final Wish

Peter clearly had a burden for the spiritual progress of others. He had come to appreciate how the Lord can transform us as he experienced the impact of divine power in his own life. Thus, in his first letter, he wrote, "As newborn babes, desire the sincere milk of the word, that ye may grow thereby: If so be ye have tasted that the Lord is gracious" (1 Peter 2:2-3). Likewise, his last recorded words reflect the same deep longing in his heart as he wrote, "But grow in grace, and in the knowledge of our Lord and Saviour Jesus Christ" (2 Peter 3:18). To Peter, the Christian life will have ups and downs and successes and failures. However, the Christian trajectory should be a steady progression towards spiritual strength and faithfulness.

Achieving spiritual growth is something Peter learned by experience as well. In his first letter, he exhorted believers to grow based on having "tasted that the Lord is gracious". In his second letter, they were to grow "in grace and in the knowledge of our Lord and Saviour Jesus Christ". His greatest desire was that believers would get to know the Lord Jesus Christ more and more which would have a practical impact on their lives. He believed that a greater appreciation of Christ would lead to increased faithfulness to the Lord.

His Final Words

If Peter could have pre-inscribed his own tombstone before his death, he likely would have left out all his accomplishments and even his own name. As a younger Christian, Peter had declared, "I will lay down my life for thy sake" (John 13:37). Now, the Lord would hold Peter to that commitment.

The tradition is that when he was informed that he was going to die by crucifixion, Peter stated that he was not worthy to die like his Lord and he asked to be crucified upside down instead. Supposedly, his request was granted. The reality is that there is no evidence or certainty that this transpired. And yet, if things did unfold that way, it would not surprise us. Peter would have not wanted anything to compete with or draw away from his beloved Saviour. This sentiment is certainly evident in the last words he penned about Christ, "To him be glory both now and forever. Amen." (2 Peter 3:18). Jesus had promised that Peter's death would "glorify God" (John 21:19). Remembering that great and comforting promise, Peter longed that his exit would bring that prayer to fruition.

So, may God help us to live with a Petrine Perspective. Remember, that he described his mindset when he said, "As long as I am in this tent..." (2 Peter 1:13, NKJV). His life was temporary, and he was honest enough to realize that at any moment, he would have to pull up the tent stakes of life, fold up the temporary house, and march over to glory. That is why he taught that every Christian, "no longer should live the rest of his time in the flesh to the lusts of men, but to the will of God" (1 Peter 4:2). What a change it would make in us if we truly viewed our lives with Peter's mentality.

And, if we are called to exit this world before the rapture, may we do it with the same grace and focus as Simon Peter. Without any doubt, there can be no higher aspiration than to enter death as a worshiper. Peter knew that the Saviour had lived and died with one great, eternal longing: "that God may be all in all" (1 Cor 15:28). Peter longed to imitate that noble goal in his own life and death. Thank God, he is now with his Lord and Saviour Jesus Christ which "is far better" (Phil 1:23). Thank God, we too will soon be there. In the meantime, may we also view our exit with the words of that old hymn, "To God be the glory!" Maranatha!

Other titles available in the Ritchie Character Study Series:

Samuel	A J Higgins	9781910513637
Abraham	J Hay	9781910513774
Solomon	A J Higgins	9781910513903
Elijah & Job	A J Higgins & D Petterson	9781912522309
Moses	T Wilson & A J Higgins	9781912522927
Jacob & Joseph	A J Higgins & M Cain	9781912522828
David	C Munro	9781914273216

www.ritchiechristianmedia.co.uk